KB042369

제3판

Standard Trade English

표준무역영어

조 영 정 지음

Robert Jalali 감수

박영사

제 3 판 머리말

미국에 장기체류하고 있는 지인으로부터 뜻밖의 감사편지를 받은 적이 있다. 그가 미국으로 갈 적에 본서를 선물로 주었는데 이 책이 미국에서 생활하는 데 크게 도움이 되었다는 것이었다. 물품과 서비스의 매매, 환불, 교환에서나 문제처리 등 일상의 여러 일들에서 유용한 표현들을 이 책에서 찾아 해결했다고 한다.

우리의 삶이라는 것이 사색과 명상을 하거나 예술과 인생을 논하는 시간이기보다는 필요한 재화와 서비스를 획득하면서 이런저런 일들을 하는 시간이 대부분이다. 언어의 사용에 있어서는 더욱 그렇고, 외국어로서의 언어사용에서는 더더욱 그렇다. 내가 법을 처음 공부하면서 새롭게 발견했던 것 중의 하나는 민법의 대부분이 경제적인 측면을 그 내용으로 하고 있다는 점이었다. 그리고 사람과 사람 간에 법이 있어야 할 가장 큰 부분이 경제적 측면에서의 이해관계라는 것을 알게 되었다. 사람은 재화와 서비스의 사용을 통하여 생존하므로 우리 삶의 많은 일들이 이와 관련되어 있고, 일상의 언어사용에 있어서도 이 영역이 큰 몫을 차지하는 것이다. 무역영어 또한 재화와 서비스의 거래에 대한 것으로서 그 범위가 세계일 뿐 기본에서는 일상생활에서의 영어와 큰 차이가 없다. 그래서 본서의 내용 중에는 외국에서 살아가는 데 일반 영어책 이상으로 도움될 만한 것들이 있었을 것이다.

이것이 본서의 장점이다. 많은 무역영어책들이 일상생활에서는 말할 것도 없고 실제 무역업무에서도 거의 사용되지 않는 후미진 곳의 지식을 담고 있는 경우가 많고, 무역영어 자격증 소지자도 무역영어 편지 한 줄 쓰기 어려워하는 현실을 생각하면 이 책이 부족하나마 나름대로 자신의 존재 이유에 맞게 그 소임을 다하고 있는 것 같아 다행으로 생각한다.

이 책만 있으면 영어에 자신이 없는 사람도 책 속의 이곳저곳 예문들을 보고

어떻게든 영어편지 한 장을 써낼 수 있다. 그리고 이 책을 통하여 일상의 영어나 회화 능력도 늘릴 수 있을 뿐만 아니라 반복적인 학습을 통하여 더 높은 수준의 실력을 쌓을 수 있다. 그것은 본서가 다양한 상황에서의 풍부한 예문들을 담고 있는 가운데 이들 예문 대부분이 정확하고 모범적인 것으로서의 선별된 문장들이기 때문이다.

　　최근의 세계 무역의 추세와 국제무역규칙의 변화를 반영하여 제3판을 내게 되었다. 새 판을 내는 김에 개선할 부분들을 손질하였다. 그동안 전국의 많은 교수님들께서 본서를 강의교재로 채택해 주셨고 많은 분들이 이 책을 읽어 주셨다. 이분들의 격려와 성원에 힘입어 판을 거듭하며 출간하고 있다. 이런 훌륭한 분들에게 교재를 제공하는 것이 저자로서는 더없는 영광이다. 앞으로도 계속 보완 발전시켜나가면서 성원에 보답하고자 하는 마음이다.

　　끝으로 본서의 출간을 위하여 지원해주시고 애써주신 안상준 대표님, 전채린 과장님, 오치웅 대리님을 비롯한 박영사 여러분께 감사드린다.

2020년 1월 30일

한강가에서

조영정 씀

제 2 판 머 리 말

한국인에 있어서 영어는 얼마나 큰 멍에인가? 아무리 열심히 해도 완성할 수 없는 영어공부에 우리는 소중한 시간을 끝없이 바쳐야 하고 헤아릴 수 없는 노력을 쏟아 부어야 한다. 영어라는 공부 아닌 공부를 두고 이렇게 힘들게 매달려야 하는 사람들에게 좀 더 나은 책이라도 있었으면 하는 생각에서 집필하게 된 본서가 다시 개정판을 내게 되었다.

완벽하고 싶은 욕심과 달리 초판에서 오탈자가 몇 군데 있어서 저자의 마음이 편치 아니 하였다. 이를 교정하는 김에 다른 내용도 함께 전면 재검토하여 미비한 점을 대폭 수정 보완하기로 하였다. 영어를 모국어로 하는 원어민에 의한 교정만으로 부족한 것 같아 국제무역 분야에 전문가이면서도 원어민인 Robert Jalali 교수의 도움을 받아 내용을 철저히 검토하여 교정하였다.

Robert Jalali 교수는 영국 캠브리지 대학 경영대학에서 강의하시는 분으로 국제무역업무에 경험도 많으셔서 무역영어 분야에 있어서 보기 드문 전문가이다. 본서의 영어에 관련내용은 Robert 교수가 일일이 내용을 점검하고 수정하였는데 그의 전문지식과 영어실력을 유감없이 발휘하여 각 상황마다 용례와 취지에 맞는 최적의 문장을 써 주었다. 바쁜 시간임에도 불구하고 자신이 하는 일에 어느 하나 소홀함이 없이 철저히 완벽을 기하고자 하는 모습이 인상적이었다. 이 자리를 빌려 본서의 수준을 한 단계 더 높여준 Robert Jalali 교수께 진심어린 감사의 뜻을 전하고 싶다.

본 개정작업을 통하여 더 많은 지식과 노력이 이 책에 보태졌다는 점에 저자는 이루 말할 수 없는 기쁨을 느낀다. 그럼에도 불구하고 저자의 부족한 능력으로 말미암아 아직도 미흡한 점이 많을 것으로 생각한다. 부족한 부분은 앞으로도 계속 수정 보완해 나갈 것을 약속드린다. 조언과 지도 그리고 질정을 기다리는 마음은 초판이나 지금이나 한결같다. 많은 석학 및 독자 제현의 기탄없는 질정을 기대한다.

　본서를 위하여 노고를 아끼지 않으신 안상준 상무님, 우석진 부장님을 비롯한 박영사의 출판담당자 여러분들께 감사드린다.

2014년 2월 20일
금문교가 보이는 언덕에서
조 영정 씀

머 리 말

대학에서 강의를 듣던 때부터 강의를 하는 오늘에 이르기까지 무역영어 책에 대하여 느껴온 두 가지가 있다. 하나는 책의 영어문장들이 진부하거나 오류가 많다는 점이고, 다른 하나는 내용이 복잡하고 체제가 산만하다는 점이다.

그래서 영어 문장의 표현이 모범적이어서 외워두면 그대로 사용할 수 있으며, 체제가 정돈되어 쉽게 읽히고 기억될 수 있는 책이 있으면 좋겠다는 생각을 항상 해왔다. 다행히 두 분의 미국인 교수님을 만나 이와 같은 책을 집필할 수 있게 되었다.

이 책이 가진 특징은 다음과 같다.

첫째, 정확하고 적절한 표현의 영어 문장이다. 모든 표현은 영어 원어민의 입장에서 가장 자연스러운 표현으로 하였다. 언어는 따라 하며 배운다. 오류와 어색한 표현이 많은 교재는 아무리 전문 영역의 영어라고 할지라도 학습효과를 바랄 수 없다. 그래서 본서에서는 두 분의 미국 원어민이 참여하여 모든 영문은 그대로 외워서 사용할 수 있는 모범예문이 되도록 하였다.

또, 생동감 있는 현대 미국식 영어를 표준으로 하였고 구식의 진부한 표현은 배제하였다. 오늘날 우리의 무역 상대방은 대부분 현대 미국식 영어를 하는 사람들이기 때문이다.

둘째, 공부하기 쉽도록 하였다. 가급적 쉬운 영어문장이 되도록 하였고, 자세한 설명을 덧붙였으며, 책의 형식이나 내용구성에서도 이 점을 염두에 두었다. 먼저 형식에 있어서 책의 체제를 요점 중심으로 간결하고 체계적으로 기술함으로써 산만하지 않도록 하였다. 또 내용에서는 몇 개의 회사를 주체로 하여 무역거래의 전체 과정에서 일어나는 통신을 일관성 있게 전개해 나감으로써 이해와 기억을 용이하게 하였다.

셋째, 오늘날의 무역에서 필요한 사항을 중심 내용으로 하였다. 과학기술의 발전에 따라 무역통신의 형태도 크게 변화하게 되었다. 과거에는 큰 역할을 했었으나 오늘날에는 의미를 거의 상실하게 된 텔렉스, 전보 등에 대한 내용 대신에 E-mail에 대한 내용을 포함시켰다.

넷째, 무역실무와 연계하여 공부할 수 있도록 하였다. 무역영어가 무역실무지식과 연관되어 있지만 무역영어 책에서 무역실무 내용까지 모두 다룰 수는 없다. 따라서 본서에서는 무역영어에서 꼭 알아야 할 기본적이고 중요한 무역실무지식은 빠짐없이 간추려 정리함으로써 무역실무 지식을 쉽게 익히고 더 깊은 실무지식이 필요한 경우에는 무역실무 관련 서적을 찾아보는 데 안내역할을 할 수 있도록 하였다.

본서를 완성하는 데에는 Susan N. Truitt 교수님과 Warner E. Bauer 교수님, 두 분의 헌신적인 기여가 있었다.

먼저 Bauer 교수님은 미국에서의 비즈니스 경험을 바탕으로 현장감 있고 생기 있는 문장을 만들어 주셨고 문제가 있을 때마다 저자와 활발히 토의하면서 해결책을 내어 주셨다. 또한 Truitt 교수님은 언어학자로서의 전문가답게 완벽에 가까운 정확성과 치밀성 그리고 열의로써 책의 모든 부분을 살펴봐 주셨다. Bauer 교수님은 낮에 토론하던 문제의 답을 드디어 찾았다고 기뻐하면서 한밤중에 전화를 주시기도 하였고, Truitt 교수님은 한글의 오류까지 지적해주실 정도였다. 이 분들의 열의와 진지한 태도는 저자를 항상 감동시켰다. 두 분께 다시 한 번 감사드린다.

그리고 책을 쓰는 동안에 항상 생각이 떠올랐던 어머니, 아버지, 형님, 누나, 선생님들을 비롯하여 저자로 하여금 배움의 길로 인도해주신 모든 분들께 고마움을 표한다.

본서는 저자의 2004년 무역영어 제2판을 수정 보완하여 만들어졌다. 출판사정으로 말미암아 박영사가 새로 출판을 맡게 되었고 이전의 미비점을 대거 보완하고 표준적인 내용과 모범적인 문장을 크게 보충하면서 이름도 표준무역영어로 출간하게 되었다.

보다 좋은 책을 내겠다는 저자의 욕심에도 불구하고 부족한 능력으로 말미암아 미흡한 점이 많을 것으로 생각한다. 현명한 독자 여러분들의 기탄없는 질정을 기다리며, 미흡한 점은 앞으로도 계속 착실히 수정·보완해 나갈 것을 약속드린다.

　끝으로 본서의 출간을 위해 애써주신 박영사의 안상준 팀장님, 우석진 부장님, 전채린 님을 비롯한 출판담당자 여러분께 깊은 감사를 드린다.

2011년 8월 8일
북한산 기슭에서
저자 씀

본서의 구성

본서는 모두 2개 Part, 16개 Chapter, 그리고 부록으로 구성되어 있다. Part 1에서는 무역영어와 영문서신에 대한 기초적인 지식을 다루고 있다. 그리고 무역거래절차에 대하여 간략하게 설명하고 있다. 무역의 실무적인 과정을 알아야만 각 단계에서의 무역영어를 이해할 수 있기 때문이다.

Part 2에서는 Part 1에서의 지식을 토대로 하여 무역의 각 단계에서 이루어지는 업무내용을 중심으로 무역영어를 다루고 있다.

부록에서는 영문지원서와 같은 취업관련 영문서면, 인사편지와 같은 업무관련 영문서신, 무역서신에 자주 등장하는 기초표현, 그리고 무역영어용어 등을 담고 있다.

무역영어가 가장 중점적으로 다루어지는 부분은 Part 2이다. Part 2는 단계별로 11개의 Chapter로 구성되는데 각 Chapter마다 먼저 무역업무의 주요내용을 설명하고, 여기에서 필요한 무역영문통신의 주요사항을 간략하게 설명한다. 그리고 다양한 상황에서의 무역영문 통신을 모범편지를 통하여 공부하게 되고 마지막으로 Useful Expressions를 통하여 중요한 영어표현들을 익히게 된다.

모든 모범편지는 책의 좌측 페이지에 영문을, 우측페이지에 해설을 담아 공부하기에 편리하도록 편집하였다. 체크포인트 표에 무역영어 관련지식을 요약하여 담음으로써 복잡하고 많은 지식을 쉽게 습득할 수 있도록 하였다. 그리고 해설과 Useful Expressions에서 대체가능한 여러 표현들을 제시하여 상황에 따라 다양하게 활용하고 응용할 수 있는 능력을 높이도록 하였다.

본서로 강의할 때 만약 한 학기의 교재로 사용하게 된다면 모두 16 Chapter 이므로 한 주에 한 Chapter를 기준하여 실제 강의가능 주수가 14주 전후가 된다면 Part 1의 5개장을 2−3주로 배정하게 되면 전체 내용을 다 다루기에 무난하다.

만약 두 학기 강의의 교재로 사용하게 된다면, 첫째 학기는 처음에서 Part 2의 Chapter 5까지 공부하고, 둘째 학기는 Part 2의 Chapter 6부터 끝까지 공부하면 될 것이다. 다른 방법으로는 첫째 학기는 Part 1과 Part 2의 모범편지를 공부하고,

둘째 학기는 Part 1의 필요내용과 Part 2의 Useful Expressions를 중심으로 공부할 수 있다. 그 외에도 교수님께서 학생들의 특성이나 강의사정에 맞추어 여러 가지의 다양한 방법으로 강의할 수 있으리라고 생각된다.

본서는 무역영어 자격시험 공부에서도 기본서로서 최적의 교재가 될 수 있도록 배려하였다. 모범편지와 Useful Expressions에서의 표현들을 익히고 각 Chapter의 무역업무의 주요내용과 체크포인트를 중심으로 실부지식을 섬검해나가면 최소의 시간으로 목표를 달성할 수 있을 것이다.

마지막으로 무역실무에 있어서 실무자들이 언제든지 업무과정에서 활용할 수 있도록 다양하고 풍부한 모범편지와 Useful Expressions를 담으려고 노력하였다. 본서에서 폭넓게 수록하고 있는 기본적인 무역실무지식과 무역영어에서의 상식과 지식들이 업무현장에서 큰 도움이 되었으면 한다.

차 례

✠ *C h e c k   P o i n t* ✠

P/A/R/T 1

무역영어의 기초

Standard
Trade
English

무역영어

① 무역영어의 정의

　　무역영어(International Trade English)는 국제무역에서 사용되는 영어이다. 무역영어는 국제무역에서 많이 사용되는 영어의 말과 글을 의미할 뿐 일반영어와 특별히 다른 것은 아니다. 다만 국제무역거래가 갖는 전문성으로 인하여 무역영어에는 이 분야의 전문적인 용어와 관용적인 어법이 많이 사용된다는 측면에서 일상의 영어와 다른 특성을 가지고 있다.

　　오늘날 국제무역거래가 많은 부분에서 영미의 상관습을 따르고 있고, 무역거래는 상거래의 한 부분이기 때문에 무역영어는 영미 국가의 상업영어(Business English, Commercial English)의 한 영역이 된다. 무역영어가 상업영어와 다른 점은 먼저, 국제 무역거래에서의 전문성으로 인하여 전문 용어가 많이 사용된다는 점, 다음으로, 비영어권국가의 사람에 의해서도 많이 사용되어진다는 점이다.

　　무역영어가 사용되는 형식은 매우 다양하다. 일반서신, E-mail, 무역서류, Fax, 텔렉스, 전보, 보고서, 광고문, 구두 및 전화상의 대화 등 그 수단과 형식에 관계없이 국제무역의 과정에서 사용되는 모든 매체를 포함하게 된다.

② 무역영어의 특성

　　무역영어는 전 세계 사람들이 자신의 모국어와 관계없이 무역을 하는 과정에서 사용되기 때문에 무역업무의 수행을 원활하게 돕는 수단으로서의 언어의 기능적인 측면이 중심이 된다. 이러한 가운데 무역영어는 다음과 같은 특성을 갖는다.

　　첫째, 무역영어에서는 경제적이고 효율적인 의사전달 측면에 중점이 주어지는 가운데 정확성, 명확성, 간결성 등이 두드러지게 된다.

　　둘째, 국제무역거래는 먼 거리의 당사자간에 이루어지기 때문에 국내거래처럼 직접 만나 행해지기보다는 주로 편지나 전화 같은 원거리 통신수단에 의존하게 되어 무역영어는 통신문이 중심이 된다.

　　셋째, 국제무역거래의 전문적인 성격 때문에 이 분야 고유의 전문적인 용어와 어법이 많은 것도 무역영어 특성 중의 하나이다.

③ 무역영어의 목적

무역영어는 크게 다음과 같은 세 가지의 목적을 갖는다.

첫째, 적정한 정보를 적시에 정확하게 상대방에게 전달하는 것이다. 무역거래의 과정에서 거래당사자는 수많은 정보와 의견을 서로 교환하지 않으면 안 된다. 국가와 언어를 달리하는 양당사자 간에 일단 거래를 가능하게 한다는 측면에서 이는 무역영어의 가장 기본적인 기능에 해당된다.

둘째, 상대방을 설득하는 것이다. 비즈니스과정에서 자신의 의도대로 상대방이 따라주도록 설득시켜야 하는 경우가 많다. 이 때 무역영어는 정보전달의 차원에서 한 걸음 더 나아가 상대방을 움직이게 하는 역할을 하게 된다.

셋째, 좋은 거래관계를 유지하는 것이다. 친구도 서로 연락하는 가운데 친밀감이 유지되듯이 거래관계도 서로 연락을 주고 받는 가운데 그 관계가 유지되고 발전될 수 있다.

이러한 목적을 달성하기 위해서 무역영어는 신속한 가운데 그 내용이 정확하고 명료해야 하고, 또한 필요한 경우에는 상대방을 움직이는 설득력을 지녀야 하며, 항상 정중한 가운데 친근감을 줌으로써 상대방으로부터 호의와 긍정적인 반응을 이끌어 낼 수 있는 것이어야 한다.

④ 무역영어연구의 필요성

세계무역의 대부분은 영어로 하기 때문에 무역을 하기 위해서는 영어가 필요하다. 국제거래에서 언어표현 능력이 부족하면 거래를 유리하게 이끄는 것은 말할 것도 없고 성사시키기도 어렵다. 뿐만 아니라 의사전달의 불비로 인하여 업무차질이나 분쟁가능성도 커지게 된다.

무역영어라고 해서 영어와 별개의 것은 아니기 때문에 이를 잘하기 위해서는 영어를 잘 해야 한다. 그러나 영어를 잘한다고 해서 무역영어를 잘 할 수 있는 것은 아니다. 영어 원어민이더라도 이에 대한 공부를 해야 할 정도로 전문성이 강하기 때문이다.

그러므로 무역영어에서의 전문적인 지식, 통상적으로 사용되는 표현의 형식과 방법, 전문 용어 등을 체계적으로 공부함과 동시에 무역에서 많이 사용되는 영어를 중심으로 학습함으로써 무역에서의 영어능력을 효과적으로 향상시킬 수 있고, 이를 통하여 무역에서의 업무 수행능력을 크게 증대시킬 수 있는 것이다.

5 무역영어 연구의 대상과 범위

무역영어를 잘하는 데에는 다음과 같은 다양한 지식과 능력을 필요로 한다.

첫째, 무역거래에 대한 전문적인 지식이다.

둘째, 영어의 구사능력이다.

셋째, 비즈니스에 대한 감각이다.

넷째, 국제적인 상식과 교양이다.

다섯째, 상대방과의 관계를 잘 이끌어 나가기 위한 커뮤니케이션에 대한 지식과 능력 등이다.

이러한 내용들이 무역영어 연구의 주요 대상이 되고, 따라서 무역영어의 연구 범위는 이러한 영역들을 포함하게 된다.

Standard
Trade
English

무역서신의 형식

① 편지용지

편지용지는 21.6cm×27.9cm(8 1/2″×11″) 규격이 표준이며, A4(21cm×29.7cm)규격도 사용된다.

업무상의 편지는 회사고유의 레터헤드가 미리 인쇄되어진 편지용지를 사용하게 된다. 편지는 될 수 있는 대로 한 페이지로 끝나는 것이 좋다. 그러나 내용이 많아 두 page 이상 되는 경우에는 둘째 page부터는 레터헤드가 인쇄되지 않은 후속용 용지(continuation sheet)를 사용하여야 한다.

후속용 용지는 크기나 지질에서 레터헤드 용지와 동일하여야 한다. 둘째 page 부터는 후속용 용지에 수신인 이름, page, 날짜를 상단에 기재한 후 본문을 이어 쓰게 된다. 전체와의 연결관계를 표시하기 위해서이다.

ArgoS

International Development & Pacific Region Operations
1220 Fifth Avenue, New York, NY 91401 U.S.A.
Tel: 1-429-891-2525 Fax: 1-429-891-2535 Email: apps@argos.com

두 page 이상 되는 경우, 마지막 page에 서명부분만 들어가게 하거나, 본문의 마지막 줄만 남게 해서는 안 되며 적어도 본문이 2행 이상 되어야 한다. 2행 미만이 되는 경우에는 앞 page의 줄간격을 조정해서 편지를 앞 page에서 끝맺든지 아니면 마지막 page의 본문이 2행 이상 되도록 해야 한다.

| Asia System Co., Ltd. | -2- | May 21, 2021 |

2 서신의 구성

편지는 편지용지 안에 그 내용을 정연하고 조화롭게 배치하여 전체적으로 품위와 깨끗한 느낌이 들도록 하여야 한다. 대략 편지용지의 상단 3cm, 하단 2cm, 왼편 2.5cm, 오른편 2~2.5cm 정도의 여백을 두고 내용이 들어가게 된다. 그리고 내용의 분량에 따라 각 구성요소 상호간에 띄우는 간격과 줄간격을 조정하여 아래 또는 위로 치우침 없이 전체가 균형되도록 하여야 한다.

무역서신에는 일반적으로 반드시 포함되어지는 기본적 요소(basic parts)와 필요에 따라서 포함되는 부가적 요소(supplementary parts)가 있다.

1) 기본적 요소와 부가적 요소

(1) 기본적 요소
① 편지머리(레터헤드 Letter Head)
② 일자(Date)
③ 수신인 주소(Inside Address)
④ 인사호칭(Salutation)
⑤ 본문(Body of Letter)
⑥ 인사결문(Complimentary Close)
⑦ 서명(Signature)

(2) 부가적 요소
① 참조번호(Reference Number)
② 참조인(Attention)
③ 제목(Subject)
④ 관계자 기호(Identification Marks)
⑤ 동봉물 표시(Enclosure Notation)
⑥ 사본배부처 표시(Carbon Copy Notation)
⑦ 추신(Postscript)

[그림 2-1] 무역서신의 구성

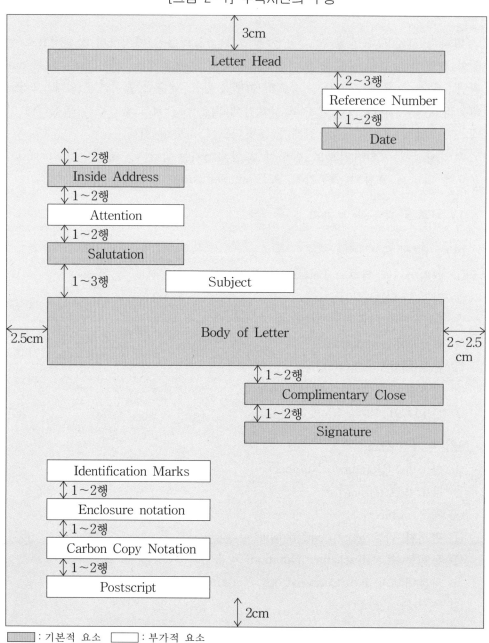

3 무역서신의 양식

영문서신은 각 구성요소의 배치 형태나 구두점의 표시 형태에 따라 그 양식 (style/form/format)이 나누어진다.

1) 구성요소의 배치와 편지 Style

오늘날 무역통신에서는 완전 수직식, 수직식, 반수직식, 간이식의 네 가지의 유형이 주로 사용된다.

(1) 완전수직식(Full Block Style)

모든 구성요소가 왼쪽 끝에서 시작되어 서면의 왼편 첫 글자가 수직 아래로 일직선이 되는 형식이다. 본문의 문단은 들여쓰기를 하지 않는다. 레터헤드가 인쇄되어 있지 않은 용지를 사용할 때에는 레터헤드도 왼편에 같이 맞추어 작성한다.

시각적으로 왼쪽에 치우치는 단점이 있지만 작성하기 용이한 실용적인 장점 때문에 오늘날 많이 사용되고 있다(그림 2-2의 (1)).

(2) 수직식(Block Style)

다른 부분은 완전수직식과 동일하나 날짜, 인사결문, 서명이 서신의 중간 또는 오른쪽에 위치한다(그림 (2)).

(3) 반수직식(Semi-block Style)

수직식에서와 같이 날짜, 인사결문, 서명이 서신의 중간 또는 오른쪽에 위치하며, 이에 더하여 본문에서 각 문단에 들여쓰기를 한다. 보통 5 space 정도 들여쓰기를 한다(그림 (3)).

(4) 간이식(Simplified Style)

간이식은 간편하게 사용되는 형식으로서 공식적인 편지에 많이 사용된다. 다른 부분은 완전수직식과 동일하나 ① 인사호칭과 인사결문이 생략되며, ② 제목을 두는데 대문자로 표기하며, ③ 서명인의 직위 및 성명을 대문자로 표기하는 점에서 다르다(그림 (4)).

[그림 2-2] 서신의 양식(style)

(1) Full Block Style

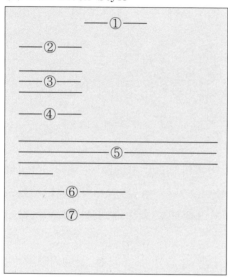

(2) Block Style

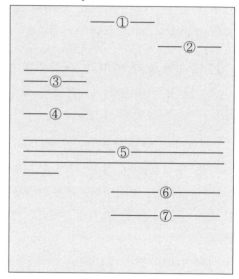

(3) Semi-block Style

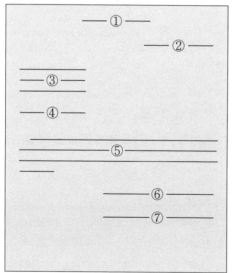

(4) Simplified Style

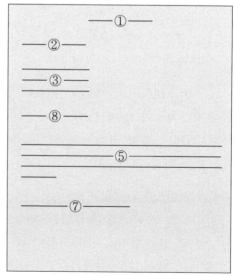

① Letter Head   ② Date   ③ Inside Address   ④ Salutation   ⑤ Body of Letter
⑥ Complimentary Close   ⑦ Signature   ⑧ Subject

이상의 여러 양식 중에서 어느 것을 사용해도 무방하다. 그러나 두 개 이상의 양식을 혼합해서 사용하거나 임의대로 변형시켜 사용해서는 안 된다(예 : 완전수직식 양식에서 들여쓰기 문단 사용).

이상의 방식 이외에도 사선식(Indented Style)이 있으나 지금은 잘 사용되지 않는다.

2) 구두점

구두점의 사용 범위에 따라서 Punctuation Style이 있는데 개방식과 혼합식 두 가지 양식이 일반적으로 사용된다.

(1) 개방식 구두점(Open Punctuation)

본문 이외에는 구성요소의 행의 끝에 구두점을 사용하지 않는 형태이다. 본문은 일반 문장에서의 구두점 사용방식대로 한다(그림 2-3의 (1)).

(2) 혼합식 구두점(Mixed Punctuation)

본문뿐만 아니라 인사호칭과 인사결문에도 구두점을 사용하는 것이다. 인사

[그림 2-3] Punctuation Style

(1) Open Punctuation

(2) Mixed Punctuation

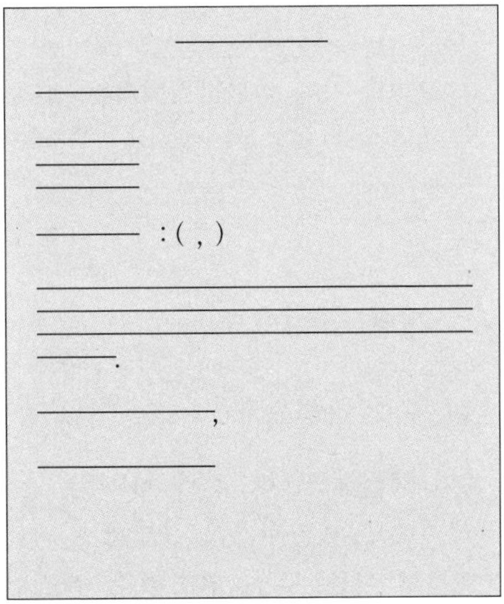

호칭에는 colon(:)이나 comma(,)가 사용되고 인사 결문에는 comma(,)가 사용된다. 인사호칭과 인사결문의 어느 하나에만 구두점을 사용해서는 안 된다(그림 (2)).

구두점 사용은 구성요소의 배치에 따른 양식과는 상관없다. 오늘날 일반적으로 혼합식 구두점이 많이 사용되고 있으며, 이 두 가지 외에 모든 구성요소에 구두점을 사용하는 폐쇄식 구두점(Closed Punctuation)이 있으나 잘 사용되지 않는다.

✓ **Handwriting과 Typewriting**

종전에는 공적이고 업무에 관한 편지는 타자를 사용하고 사적이고 사교적인 편지는 손으로 쓰는 것이 좋다고 생각되어 왔다.

그러나 최근 컴퓨터의 발달로 누구나 타자를 쉽게 이용할 수 있게 되었고, 또 매우 편리하게 작성할 수 있게 되었기 때문에 사적이고 사교적인 편지에도 타자의 사용이 일반화되고 있다.

손으로 쓰는 편지는 불편하고 수고스럽지만 작성자가 직접 썼다는 사실, 같은 편지가 다른 여러 사람에게도 가지 않았다는 사실, 그리고 무엇보다 작성자의 정성을 나타내 보인다는 점에서 타자가 갖지 못하는 장점을 가지고 있다. 그래서 매우 친밀한 관계에서의 편지, 중요한 사교편지, 정치인의 지지 호소편지 등에서는 아직도 손으로 쓰기도 한다.

그러나 국제 비즈니스에서는 대부분 타자를 사용하게 된다. 지구의 오지에서 오는 편지와 같이 특수한 상황에서는 물론 예외이다.

---

4 **개별 구성요소**

1) 주요 구성요소

(1) 레터헤드(Letter Head)

레터헤드는 편지용지 상단에 인쇄해 두는 편지의 머리부분이다. 여기에는 발신회사의 이름, 주소, 전화번호, 팩스번호, 영업품목, 영업지역 등에 관한 사항이 들어가게 된다.

　레터헤드는 발신자에 대한 정보를 제공할 뿐만 아니라 발신자 자신을 홍보하는 역할도 하기 때문에 회사의 로고를 넣어서 시각적으로 보기 좋게 디자인하게 된다. 너무 많은 내용을 포함하게 되면 지저분하게 보일 수 있으므로 꼭 필요한 사항만을 넣는 것이 일반적이다.

　인쇄된 편지용지를 사용하지 않고 일반백지를 사용하는 경우 용지상단에 이에 해당하는 부분을 타자하여 넣으면 된다.

EUROMONEY

Euromoney Publications PLC, NesterHouse, Playhouse Yard, London, EC4V 5EX, UK.
Telephone : +44 207 779 8610. Fax:+44 207 779 8602. Email: svcs@euromoney.com

---

(2) 일자(Date)

　발신일자는 letterhead의 3행 정도 아래에 둔다. 일자 표시 방법은 미국식과 영국식이 있다.

　미국식 : 월-일-년 순으로 쓰고, 일자는 기수로 쓰며, 연도 앞에 comma를 붙인다.

　예 April 5, 2021

　영국식 : 일-월-년 순으로 쓰고, 일자는 서수로 한다.

　예 5th April, 2021

　정확성을 기하기 위하여 일자는 4-5-2021나 4/5/2021과 같이 표기하지 않는 것이 좋으며, 월이나 연도를 Jan., '12와 같이 약자로 표기하지 말고 January, 2021과 같이 전체를 쓰는 것이 좋다.

(3) 수신인 주소(Inside Address)

　편지 안에 수신인 주소를 기재함으로써 봉투가 없더라도 수신인을 확인할 수 있는 역할을 하는 것으로 Date란 아래 2행 정도 띄우고 쓴다. 수신인 주소에는 맨 위의 행에 수신인의 성명을 쓰고 다음 행에 회사명, 그리고 아래에 회사주소를 2~3행 정도로 나누어 쓴다.

예

① Mr. John A. Baker, President   ② British Technology Co., Ltd.
   INS Software Corporation   389 Chiswick High Road
   2 Park Avenue   London W4 4AE
   New York, NY 10016   United Kingdom
   U.S.A.

성명 앞에는 반드시 존칭을 붙이는데 일반인에게는 Mr., Miss., Mrs., 등의 존칭을, 특수한 존칭 대상인 경우에는 Dr., Professor, Honorable, Reverend 등의 그에 맞는 존칭을 사용하여야 한다. Mr. 대신에 Esq.(Esquire)를 사용하는 경우에는 성명 뒤에 comma(,)를 찍고 Esq.를 붙인다.

Chairman, President, Manager 등과 같이 직함을 사용하는 경우에는 존칭과 이름 뒤에 comma를 찍고 직함을 쓴다(예 : Mr. John A. Baker, President).

<표 2-1> 일반존칭

성별 수		단수	복수
남자		Mr.	Messrs.
여자	미혼	Miss / Ms.	Misses / Mses.
	기혼	Mrs. / Madam / Ms.	Mmes. / Mses.

(4) 인사호칭(Salutation)

인사호칭은 본문이 시작되기 전에 상대방을 부르는 인사말로서 보통 Inside Address 아래 2행 정도 띄우고 쓴다. Salutation은 그 끝에 미국식은 colon(:)을 찍고 영국식은 comma(,)를 찍는다. 회사의 경우 미국식은 Gentlemen: 으로, 영국식은 Dear Sirs, 로 쓴다. 모르는 상대에 대해서는 To Whom It May Concern:을 쓰기도 한다.

<표 2-2> 인사호칭(Salutation)

관계 \ 성별		남 자	여 자	비 고
회사		Gentlemen:(미) Dear Sirs,(영)	Ladies:(미) Dear Madam,(영)	
개인	이름을 모르는 경우	Sir(s)	Madam	Formal ↑ ↓ Informal
		Dear Sir(s) My Dear Sir(s)	Dear Madam My Dear Madam	
	이름을 아는 경우	Dear Mr. Brown	Dear Mrs. Brown	
		My Dear Mr. Brown Dear Tom	My Dear Mrs. Brown Dear Judy	

미국에서도 informal한 서신의 경우에는 comma(,)를 많이 사용한다. 이름을 아는 경우는 이름을 사용한 Salutation을 사용하여야 한다. 이와 같이 Salutation 은 위의 Inside Address에서 수신인이 회사명인가 인명인가, 남성인가 여성인가, 단수인가 복수인가에 따라 이에 맞추어 써야 한다.

(5) 본문(Body of Letter)

Inside Address에서 본문은 Salutation에서 2행 정도 띄우고 시작한다. 두 절 (paragraph) 이상 되는 경우 절과 절 사이에는 줄 사이 간격을 넓게 하거나 한 줄 띄우는 것을 원칙으로 하며, 될 수 있는 대로 하나의 서신에서는 하나의 절 (paragraph)로 끝나게 하는 것이 좋다.

본문의 분량이 작으면 줄 사이의 간격을 넓히고 분량이 많으면 줄 사이의 간 격을 좁혀 본문의 시각적인 크기를 조정한다. 분량이 많아 두 장 이상이 될 경우 에는 후속편지지(continuation sheet)를 사용하며 분철할 때는 분철법을 따른다.

분 철

문장을 쓰는데 영어에는 한글과 달리 분철법(syllabication)이 있다. 분철법은 줄이 바뀔 때 줄의 끝에서 한 단어의 중간이 잘려질 때 지켜야 할 규칙이다. 자 간을 조정하여 단어가 중간에 잘려지지 않도록 하는 것이 좋지만 끝에 긴 단어 가 올 때는 단어를 중간에서 나누는 분철을 해야 한다. 그런데 분철은 아무 곳에서나 단어를 나누어서는 안 되고 규칙에 따라야 하며, 단어의 나누어진 앞쪽 부분 끝에 hyphen(-)을 찍어야 한다.

예 You will be pleased to know that most of our customers were very impressed by your presentation.

분철은 기본적으로 영어 사전에 나오는 분철표시를 참조하면 되고, 그 기초적인 규칙으로 다음 몇 가지를 들 수 있다.

① 1음절어는 자르지 못하고

② 접두사, 접미사는 자를 수 있고

③ 이중자음은 그 사이에 자를 수 있다.

(6) 인사결문(Complimentary Close)

인사결문은 편지를 끝맺으면서 하는 인사로서 본문에서 2행 정도 띄우고 쓴다. 결문인사의 마지막은 comma(,)를 찍는다. 그러나 Open Punctuation Style의 경우에는 Salutation과 함께 아무런 구두점이 없는 상태로 둔다. Yours very truly와 Very truly yours와 같이 yours를 앞에 둘 수도 있고 뒤에 둘 수도 있다.

<표 2-3> 인사결문(Complimentary Close)

Tone	Complimentary Close	비고
Formal	Respectfully yours, / Respectfully,	성직자나 손위사람
	Very truly yours,	미국에서 가장 보편적
	Yours faithfully,	영국에서만 사용
	Yours truly, Very sincerely yours, Very cordially yours,	formal ↑
Informal	Sincerely yours, Cordially yours, Sincerely, Cordially, Best regards,	↓ informal

인사결문은 앞의 인사호칭과 관련되어 있다. 예를 들어 인사호칭에서는 어려운 사이에서 사용되는 "Sir,"를 사용하고 인사결문에서는 가까운 사이에서 사용되는 "Cordially,"로 쓰게 되면 앞뒤가 맞지 않는다. 따라서 인사호칭과 인사결문은 그 친밀도에서 같은 수준을 나타내는 표현을 사용하는 것이 중요하다.

(7) 서명(Signature)

서명은 본인의 확인과 편지의 책임소재를 명시하는 역할을 하는 것으로, 회사명, 친필서명, 서명자이름, 서명자직책으로 구성된다. 맨 위의 회사명은 Complimentary close 아래로 2행 정도 띄운 곳에 대문자로 타자한다. 아래로 4행 정도 비워 친필서명의 공간으로 사용하고 그 아래로 서명자의 이름을 타이핑하고 그 옆이나 아래에 직책을 타이핑한다. 레터헤더에 회사명이 있으므로 회사명은 생략하기도 한다. 성명 앞에는 Mr.와 같은 존칭을 붙이지 않는다.

예

AMS Corporation
Bruce C. Lee
Bruce C. Lee
Director of Marketing

AMS Corporation
Bruce C. Lee
Bruce C. Lee, Director

Bruce C. Lee
Bruce C. Lee
Director of Marketing

대리서명

위임 등으로 대리서명의 권한을 가진 대리서명권자가 서명권자를 대리하여 서명하는 경우에는 회사명 앞에 "P.P." 또는 "per pro."[1]를 붙인다.

또, 대리서명의 권한이 없는 자가 서명권자를 대리하여 서명하는 경우에는 회사명 앞에 "for"를 붙이거나 서명 앞에 "by"를 붙인다.

2) 부가적 요소

(1) 참조번호(Reference Number)

서신의 분류 및 관리를 위하여 필요한 경우 Date 위나 아래에 참조번호를 명시

---

1) 라틴어 per procurationem의 약자 「대리로」(by proxy, as agent for)의 의미.

한다.

예 Ref : A0914   Our Ref : HB-12-123
                                                         Your Ref : 01/391

(2) 참조인(Attention)

회사 내의 특정인이나 특정부서가 수신하도록 기재한다. Particular Address 라고도 하며 Inside Address와 Salutation 사이에 다음과 같은 형태로 표시된다.

예 Attention : Mr. Minsoo Kim
   Attention of Mr. Minsoo Kim
   Attention : Sales Dept.

(3) 제목(Subject)

제목은 Salutation과 본문 사이에 표기하는데 Salutation과 같은 행이나 아래 행에 용지의 중앙부에 둔다. 제목을 둠으로써 본문의 내용을 빠르고 쉽게 이해할 수 있기 때문에 필요한 경우 제목을 달게 된다.

대문자로 표기하거나 밑줄을 긋기도 하고 앞에 "Re:" 또는 "Subject:"를 두기도 한다.

예 Gentlemen :   Your Order of May 21
                    COMPUTER ORDER
                    Re : Your Order of May 21

(4) 관계자 표시(Identification Marks)

관계자 표시는 발신자쪽을 위해서 두는 것이다. 편지 작성에 관계한 기안자, 번역자, 타이피스트 등의 이니셜을 식별기호로서 명시해 두는 것이다. 예를 들어 기안자의 이니셜이 JK이고 타자수가 ns라면 다음과 같이 표시한다.

예 JK/ns 또는, JK : ns 또는, JK-ns

(5) 동봉물 표시(Enclosure Notation)

편지와 함께 수인자에게 보내는 동봉물이 있는 경우에는 "Enclosure" 또는

"Encl."을 표시하고 그 이름과 부수를 기재한다.

> **예** Enclosures : 1. Commercial Invoice   Three Copies
>   2. Packing List   Two Copies

(6) 사본배부처 표시(Carbon Copy Notation)

이 편지의 사본을 수신자 이외의 제3자에게 보내는 경우에 명시하는 것으로 "C.C. : " 또는 "Copy to : "를 표시하고 사본배부처를 기재한다.

> **예** C.C. : Korea Trading Co., Ltd.
>   Copies to : Mr. Dongsoo Kim
>   Mr. James J. Baker

Blind Copy Notation(BC)

수신자에게는 사본배부사실을 알리지 않고 사본을 보내는 경우에 사용된다. 편지원본에는 표시되지 않으며 편지 작성자의 편지철의 사본에만 명시되는 사본배부처이다. E-mail에서 많이 사용된다.

(7) 추신(Postscript)

본문을 다 쓴 이후에 추가할 사항이 있는 경우에 기재하는 것으로, 어떤 사항을 강조하거나 주위를 환기시키기 위한 한 방법으로도 사용된다. 앞에 P.S.를 표시하고 내용을 기재한다.

> **예** P.S. Your letter of May 10 reached us today. It will be given our fullest attention.

5 봉 투

봉투는 16.3cm×9.2cm(6 1/2″×3 1/2″) 규격과 24cm×10.5cm(9 1/2″×4″) 규격이 많이 사용된다. 봉투의 중앙에 가까운 우측하단에 수신인의 주소(mailing address)를 기재하고, 좌측상단에 반송주소(return address)를 기재하며, 그리고 우측상단에 우표를 붙이게 된다. 주소의 기재요령은 Inside Address와 동일하다.

PRIVATE(친전)과 같은 우송안내의 표시를 하는 경우에는 발신인 주소 아래의 좌측하단의 여백에 기재하고, REGISTERED MAIL(등기) 등과 같은 우편발송에 대한 지시사항은 우표 붙일 곳 아래에 기재한다.

[그림 2-4] 편지 봉투 양식

Asia Technology Co., Ltd.
159-1, Myung-Dong, Jung-Ku
Seoul Korea 135-729

STAMP

EXPRESS DELIVERY

CONFIDENTIAL

Mr. John M. Baker
12/Floor, St. John's Building
33 Garden Road
Central, Hong Kong

<표 2-4> 봉투 특별기재사항의 예

우송안내		발송지시	
PRIVATE / PERSONAL	친전	REGISTERED MAIL	등기
CONFIDENTIAL	대외비	EXPRESS DELIVERY	속달
PRINTED MATTER	인쇄물재중	SPECIAL DELIVERY	특별배달
PHOTO	사진재중	FIRST CLASS MAIL	1종우편
SAMPLE	샘플재중	VIA AIRMAIL	항공우편
ATTENTION OF MR. KIM	김씨 앞	VIA DHL	DHL로

편지지 접어 넣기

　편지를 가로로 두 번 접어 3등분하되 맨 위의 부분은 좀 크게 접어 편지전면의 윗부분이 1.5cm 정도 보이도록 한다. 편지전면이 보이도록 한 윗부분이 편지봉투의 풀로 붙이는 쪽에 들어가도록 넣는다.

　소형 봉투의 경우는 편지를 가로로 한 번 접어 2등분하되 윗 부분을 좀 크게 접어 편지의 레터헤더 부분이 보이도록 하거나 윗부분이 1.5cm 정도 보이도록 한 후 다시 좌우로 2번 접어 삼등분으로 접은 후 넣는다.

　이런 방식으로 편지를 접어 넣는 것은 최대한 상대방이 열어 보기에 좋도록 하기 위함이다.

[그림 2-5] 편지 접는 방법

(1) 대형봉투 사용시

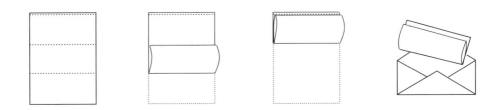

(2) 소형봉투 사용시

Standard
Trade
English

무역통신의 내용전개

① 무역 영문 통신의 종류

무역통신은 어떤 사실을 알리기만 하면 되는 단순한 것에서부터 상대방의 마음을 움직이고 설득시켜야 하는 고도의 기술적인 것에 이르기까지 매우 다양하다. 무역의 과정에서 사용되는 이러한 서신들을 그 성격에 따라 다음 몇 가지로 나누어 볼 수 있다.

1) 정보 전달 편지

무역통신에서 가장 일반적인 편지이다. 거래과정에서 발생하는 사실내용을 상대방에게 알리거나 서로의 의사를 주고 받는 편지이다. 상대방에게 도움되는 정보를 줌으로써 좋은 관계를 유지할 수 있을 뿐 아니라, 거래 당사자는 상대방에게 필요한 정보를 적시에 알려야 할 의무가 있기 때문에 필요한 경우에는 반드시 편지를 해야만 한다.

일반적인 정보 요청과 정보 제공, 오퍼, 주문, 신용장 개설 및 조건변경, 선적통지, 적하보험부보, 물품수령통지, 대금요청 및 지급통지 등이 이에 해당한다.

이러한 편지는 그 내용이 대개 다음과 같은 순서로 구성된다.

1. 편지 목적
2. 구체적인 사실
3. 끝맺음을 위한 인사

2) 설득 편지

설득 편지는 상대방의 마음을 움직여야 하기 때문에 고도의 기술을 필요로 하는 편지이다. 상대방의 마음을 움직이게 하는 수단은 편지내용의 전개나 문장의 표현이므로 사람의 심리 파악과 언어 구사 능력이 중요한 역할을 한다. 제품의 판촉편지(Sales Letter), 유리한 거래조건을 위한 설득 편지, 클레임에서의 설득 편지 등이 이에 해당된다.

이러한 편지의 내용구성과 그 전개방식은 대개 다음과 같다.

1. 편지를 계속 읽도록 상대방의 주의를 끄는 내용
2. 상대방에게 흥미를 주거나 욕구를 자극하는 내용

3. 자신이 권유하는 것이 상대방에게 유익하다는 내용

4. 상대방의 받아들이는 행동을 자극하는 내용

이와 같은 설득을 위한 내용전개의 방법으로서 AIDA 원칙 또는 ABCD 원칙 등이 있다.

AIDA	ABCD
A : Attention ↓ (주의를 끔)	A : Attracting attention ↓ (주의를 끔)
I : Interest ↓ (흥미의 유발)	B : Building interest and desire ↓ (흥미와 욕구를 갖게 함)
D : Desire ↓ (욕구창출)	C : Convincing the reader ↓ (상대방을 확신시킴)
A : Action (행동의 자극)	D : Directing action (행동을 하도록 함)

3) 수락 편지

상대방의 제의에 대하여 수락하는 편지이다. 상대방의 입장에서 좋은 소식이 되므로 사실내용 외에 기쁨을 나누는 감정적인 표현도 들어가게 된다. 청약에 대한 승낙, 주문의 수락, 신용의 제공, 낙찰의 통지, 클레임의 해결, 기타 어려운 문제의 해결 등에 대한 편지가 이에 해당한다.

이러한 편지는 그 내용이 대개 다음과 같이 구성된다.

1. 상대방의 제의 건에 대한 명시

2. 제의에 대한 수락의사의 표시

3. 구체적인 내용이나 앞으로의 진행사항

4. 끝맺음을 위한 인사

4) 거절 편지

상대방의 제의에 대하여 거절을 하는 상대방의 입장에서 나쁜 소식의 편지이다. 나쁜 소식이 자신에 대한 나쁜 감정으로 연결되지 않도록 하기 위해서 거절 내용 외에 자기입장에 대한 해명, 위로와 희망의 표시 등 감정적·심리적인 요소를 많이 감안해야 하기 때문에 쓰기에 쉽지 않다. 협조 요청의 거절, 청약의 거절, 주문의 거절, 입찰의 탈락, 클레임에서의 요구거절 등의 편지가 이에 해당한다.

이러한 편지는 그 내용이 대개 다음과 같이 구성된다.

1. 상대방의 제의 건에 대한 명시
2. 상대방과 자신 모두가 인정하는 객관적 사실 내용
3. 앞의 객관적 사실에 기초한 거절이유와 함께 거절함을 정중하게 표현
4. 가능한 경우 대안의 권유
5. 선린관계유지에 대한 말과 끝맺음 인사

✓ 설득편지의 예

Dear Sir:

We are certain that if you spend a few minutes reading these materials, it will be time well spent.

In the enclosed catalog, you will find our new Learner's Dictionary for English language learning. It contains 150,000 clear definitions in simple English, including both British and American English.

The Dictionary comes with an audio file, which has sound recordings of the pronunciation of each word, and interactive exercises to practice using the words in context. These features make the Dictionary an invaluable tool for English learners who wish to speak English properly.

Any of the books may be obtained through a bookseller, our website, or directly from this office. Please give us a call, and we will be glad to assist you.

✓	좋은 편지를 쓰기 위한 하나의 방법

1. 작성 전의 생각정리
   ① 편지를 쓰는 목적이 무엇인가?
   ② 목표로 하는 수신인의 반응은 무엇인가?
   ③ 무엇을 쓸 것인가?
   ④ 어떻게 쓸 것인가?

2. 편지의 작성
   ① 내용에 포함시킬 것을 열거한다.
   ② 열거된 사항의 순서를 정한다.
   ③ 순서대로 연결하여 작성한다.

3. 작성 후의 검토
   ① 수신인의 입장에서 읽어 본다.
   ② 빠진 내용이나 오자, 탈자를 점검한다.

② 무역 서신의 작성원칙 : 5C's

무역서신은 업무활동에서의 편지이기 때문에 일반 편지와 다른 특성을 가지고 있다. 무역서신이 소기의 목적을 효과적으로 달성하기 위해서는 명료하고, 정확하면서도, 간결해야 하고, 상대방의 관심을 끌고, 호감을 줄 수 있어야 한다. 이와 같이 좋은 무역서신이 되기 위한 중요한 요소들을 학자에 따라서 다양하게 언급하고 있으나, 여기서는 가장 일반적으로 알려져 있는 다섯 가지의 5C's를 중심으로 살펴보기로 한다.

1) Clearness(명확)

쓰는 사람의 의도를 명료하게 표현하여 읽는 사람이 쉽고 명확하게 이해할 수 있도록 해야 한다. 편지 쓰는 사람의 의도를 이해하지 못하거나 잘못 이해하는 경우 편지 본래의 목적을 달성할 수 없을 뿐만 아니라 손실이나 분쟁이 발생할 수도 있으므로 무역서신에서의 명료성은 매우 중요하다. 편지를 보다 명료하게 쓰는 데는 다음 사항에 대한 고려가 도움이 된다.

(1) 모호하고 암시적인 표현보다 구체적인 표현으로

Obscure : We have received your letter recently.

Clear : We have received your letter dated September 15.

Obscure : I plan to meet somebody there soon.

Clear : I plan to meet Mr. Kim in Seoul by May 10.

Obscure : A girl takes a walk in the park with a dog.

Clear : Younghee takes a walk in Namsan park with Badukee.

(2) 가능한 한 구문상 오해의 소지 제거

Obscure : I was advised frequently to send promotional mail.

Clear : I was frequently advised to send promotional mail.

Obscure : Jack wrote to Tom that he had accepted his proposal.

Clear : Jack wrote to Tom and stated that he had accepted Tom's proposal.

Obscure : Before you order their stock records should be checked.

Clear : Before you order, their stock records should be checked.

Clear : Before you order their stock, records should be checked.

(3) 수동태보다는 능동태가 이해하기 쉽다.

Obscure : Consideration will be given to all aspects of this matter by us.

Clear : We will consider all aspects of this matter.

(4) 사물보다는 사람을 주어로

Obscure : Your check will be sent upon receipt of the enclosed form.

Clear : We will send your check when we receive the enclosed form.

(5) 어렵고 생소한 용어보다는 쉽고 익숙한 용어사용

interrogate → ask   equitable → fair

exacerbate → make worse   cognizant → aware

terminate → end   aggregate → total

✓   **효율적인 의사전달**

Inho : "I bought a dog."

Judy　: "Oh yeah! What kind?"

Inho : "A bulldog"

Judy　: "When?"

Inho : "Yesterday"

Judy　: "Puppy or full grown?"

Inho : "Puppy."

Judy　: "Male or female?"

Inho : "Male"

Judy　: "What color?"

Inho : "Black"

Judy　: "Why didn't you say in the first place that you bought a black male bulldog puppy yesterday?

－대화를 즐기기 위한 대화라면 문제가 없다. 그러나 한국과 미국간에 편지로서 이와 같이 의사전달을 한다면 시간이 얼마나 걸리게 될까? 아마도 중간에 그만두게 될 것이다.－

---

2) Conciseness(간결)

무역서신은 될 수 있는 대로 간결하여야 한다. 바쁜 업무과정에서 읽는 것이기 때문에 의미가 없는 말, 반복되는 말, 상투적인 표현 등은 배제하고 용건만 간략하게 쓰는 것이 읽는 사람에게 불편을 들어주는 것이 되며, 또한 이해를 쉽게 해준다.

(1) 표현을 간결하게

wordy : Permit us to take the liberty of thanking you for your letter which we have just received. In reply, we wish to state that we shall be very glad to send you our catalog in accordance with your request.

concise : We are glad to send you our catalog per your request.

wordy : For your information we are more than glad to make available to you the data requested, which we are enclosing herewith.

concise : Enclosed, please find the requested information.

(2) 절보다는 구, 구보다는 단어로

wordy : I like the man who has courage.

concise : I like a man of courage.

concise : I like a courageous man.

wordy : Mr. Kang had the kindness of introducing me to Mr. Baker.

concise : Mr. Kang kindly introduced me to Mr. Baker.

(3) 짧은 어구의 사용

in the event that → if

a large number of → many

at the present time → now

for the reason that → because

take into consideration → consider

at your earliest convenience → soon

(4) 긴 전치사적 구문은 짧은 전치사로

check in the amount of US$ 500 → check for US$ 500

letter under the date of May 20 → letter of May 20

the month of May → May

during the course of → during

at a price of US$ 100 → at US$ 100

(5) 불필요한 형용사, 부사의 생략

the color white → white

enclosed herewith → enclosed

new innovation → innovation

basic fundamentals → fundamentals

(6) 불필요한 어구의 생략

needless to say   it goes without saying

what I want to say   as a matter of fact

3) Correctness(정확)

무역서신은 틀림이 없어야 한다. 내용에서는 물론이고 철자, 구두점, 문법, 문장구조, 편지외양에서도 정확해야 한다. 틀리게 쓰게 되면 상대방이 이해를 못하거나 잘못 이해하게 되는 원인이 된다. 또, 서신에 틀린 곳이 많으면 편지에 대한 믿음성이 줄고 좋지 않은 인상을 주게 되며, 이에 더 나아가 편지 보내는 사람이나 회사에 대해서도 이미지의 손상을 가져오게 된다.

그런데 이것은 한국인에 있어서 상당히 난감한 부분이다. 비모국어 사용자로서 아무리 주의를 기울여도 틀리는 경우를 피하기 어려운데 이것이 두려워서 편지를 보내지 않거나 적시에 보내지 못하는 일이 있어서는 안 된다. 상대방도 자신이 영어 원어민이 아님을 알기 때문에 이러한 사정을 어느 정도 이해하기 마련이므로 언어 사용상의 잘못을 너무 크게 의식하지 않는 것이 좋다.

잘못을 범하는 형태는 수 없이 다양하지만 몇 가지의 예를 들어 보면 다음과 같다.

Incorrect : May 21th, 2021
Correct : May 21, 2021 / the 21st of May, 2021

Incorrect : US$ 1.234.50
Correct : US$ 1,234.50

Incorrect : Respectably yours.
Correct : Respectfully yours,

Incorrect : The newborn baby looks after his mother.
Correct : The newborn baby takes after his mother.

Incorrect : Our rates are lower than other hotels offering similar services.
Correct : Our rates are lower than those of other hotels offering similar

services.

Incorrect : He caught the sight of the train passing through the window.

Correct : Through the window, he caught sight of the train.

4) Courtesy(예의)

무역서신은 예의 바르고 정중해야 한다. 편지에서도 상대방을 존중하고 우호적으로 대함으로써 상대방으로부터 호감을 얻을 수 있다. 그러나 지나친 겸손과 존중은 자칫 진실성을 의심받거나 비굴한 인상을 주는 역효과를 가져올 수 있다. 따라서 적절한 자신감과 적절한 존중 속에 품격이 우러나오도록 하는 것이 필요하다.

(1) would, should, may, have to, ought to와 같은 조동사의 적절한 사용

Poor : We appreciate it if you send us the sample.

Better : We would appreciate it if you would send us the sample.

Poor : Don't forget your overdue account.

Better : May I remind you of your overdue account?

Poor : We inform you that the quality is not satisfactory.

Better : We have to inform you that the quality is not satisfactory.

(2) please, appreciate, grateful, happy, kind, value, esteemed와 같은 용어의 적절한 사용.

Poor : Contact us if you need assistance.

Better : Please contact us if you need assistance.

Poor : We request you to answer immediately.

Better : Your prompt answer would be greatly appreciated.

(3) 단정적인 표현의 완화

Poor : I will go now.

Better : I'm afraid I must be going now.

Poor : It was unwise of you to have sold them.

Better : May say that it was unwise to have sold them.

(4) 거절의 경우 단호한 표현보다 완곡한 표현

Poor : We must refuse your proposal.

Better : Regretfully, we are unable to accept your proposal.

Poor : We cannot accept your offer.

Better : We are not in a position to accept the offer.

(5) 상대방을 질책, 의심, 강요, 무시하는 표현의 회피

Poor : You failed to enclose the packing list.

Better : The packing list was not enclosed.

Poor : You must know that we cannot comply with your request.

Better : In view of these facts, we are unable to comply with the request.

(6) 기쁨, 슬픔 등의 감정을 함께 나누는 표현

We are glad to, We are pleased to, We are happy to, We congratulate, We are sorry to, We regret to, I am afraid that, I hope, This must be hard for you, unfortunately, regretfully, thank you for, appreciate, grateful .... 등의 문구 를 사용하여 상대방에 기쁜 소식인 경우에는 축하를, 나쁜 소식인 경우 위로를 가미하는 표현을 하며, 보통의 경우에도 상대방에 감사하며 희망과 축원을 보내 는 표현을 한다.

Poor : I heard that you had been elected to the board.

Better : I was very glad to hear about your election to the board.

Poor : We learnt from your letter that the machine you purchased from us didn't function properly.

Better : We are sorry to learn from your letter that the machine you purchased from us does not function properly.

(7) "You" attitude

Poor : We credited your account with the amount.

Better : Your account has been credited with the amount.

Poor : As to our financial status, we refer you to the Asia Bank.

Better : As to our financial status, please refer to the Asia Bank.

Poor : We are pleased to inform you that the new model is selling very well.

Better : You will be pleased to know that the new model is selling very well.

✓ **"You" Attitude**

　　"You" Attitude란 상대방의 입장에서 생각하고 상대방을 우선하며 존중하는 태도를 말한다. 이는 편지작성자가 지켜야 할 기본 태도이다. 내용이 이해가 잘 될 것인지, 문체와 분위기가 적절한지, 편지를 읽고 어떤 느낌을 가지게 될 것인지 등의 제반 사항을 상대방 입장에서 판단할 때 의사를 잘 전달할 수 있게 된다. 그리고 상대방을 우선하고 존중하는 이러한 배려는 결국 편지에서 자신이 목적하는 바를 이루기 쉽게 한다.

　　형식적인 면에서는 될 수 있는 대로 "I"나 "We"보다는 "You"가 들어가는 표현을 더 많이 쓴다. 그러나 무조건 "You"를 많이 쓰는 것을 의미하는 것이 아니고 상대방 입장에서 배려하고 상대방을 존중한다는 의미이니만큼 좋지 않는 내용에서는 오히려 You를 쓰지 않는 것이 "You" Attitude이다.

예

"We" Attitude : We are going to dispatch some samples soon.

"You" Attitude : Within two weeks, you will receive three kinds of samples
　　　　　　　by airmail.

"We" Attitude : You failed to include last year's financial statement.

"You" Attitude : May we have last year's financial statement?

5) Character(개성)

무역서신은 인간적인 친밀감과 생동감을 줄 수 있도록 하는 것이 중요하다. 업무상에서의 편지이기 때문에 자칫 딱딱하고 사무적으로 흐르기 쉬운데 이래서는 상대방에게 좋은 느낌을 줄 수가 없다. 상대에게 호감을 주기 위해서는 참신하고 솔직하게 표현하며 긍정적이고 적극적인 표현으로 인간적인 면모의 개성이 나타날 수 있도록 하여야 한다.

(1) 부정적인 표현보다 긍정적인 표현

No, not, impossible, unfortunately, misfortune, bad, difficult, problem, inferior, refuse, apologize, complaint 등과 같은 부정적인 느낌이 강한 말은 가급적 피한다.

Negative : Shipment can't be made until May 1.

Positive : Shipment can be made on May 1.

Negative : We have received your complaint about poor packing.

Positive : Thank you very much for writing us about the poor packing.

Negative : We have only one brochure, but will mail it to you today.

Positive : We still have one brochure which we can gladly to send to you today.

(2) 소극적인 표현보다 적극적이고 자신감 있는 표현

Poor : Unfortunately, we cannot fill your order because you failed to send your check.

Better : We will gladly fill your order as soon as we receive your check.

Poor : Don't hesitate to tell us if we have not answered all your questions.

Better : Is there any more information that you require?

(3) There is..., It is... 와 같은 표현을 피함

There is..., It is... 로 시작되는 문장보다 실질적 주어와 구체적 행동을 나타내는 동사의 문장이 짧으면서도 생동감 있다.

Poor : In my college, there are seven departments.

Better : My college has seven departments.

Poor : There are some problems that confront the panel.

Better : Some problems confront the panel.

Poor : Some reduction of costs was effected by this factory this month.

Better : This factory reduced costs this month.

(4) 상투적이고 진부한 표현의 회피

Poor : We have to acknowledge receipt of your esteemed favor dated the 5th ult.

Better : Thank you for your letter of May 5.

Poor : We take the liberty of requesting you to be good enough to inform us whether you can send us samples.

Better : We would like to know whether you can send us samples.

Poor : We wish to acknowledge receipt of your order.

Better : Thank you very much for your order.

Poor : We enclose herewith the catalog for our products.

Better : Enclosed is the catalog for our products.

(5) 비일상적인 표현보다 대화체 사용

Poor : I have the pleasure of informing you.

Better : I am pleased to tell you.

Poor : Please favor us with an early expression of your views.

Better : Please let us have your opinion.

Poor : Assuring you of our cooperation at all times, we remain.

Better : We assure you of our cooperation at all times.

Poor : Regretting our inability to serve you at this time, we are.

Better : Perhaps the next time we can serve you better.

(6) 인간적인 표현

Poor : This is in reply to your letter dated May 15.
Better : We are replying to your letter dated May 15.

Poor : If there is any additional information needed, please let us know.
Better : If you need additional information, please let us know.

Poor : Please be informed that your order is expected to leave our factory on May 7.
Better : We are glad to inform you that your order will leave our factory on May 7.

(7) 수동적 문장보다는 능동적인 문장

Poor : The document has just been received by us.
Better : We have just received the document.

Poor : It is suggested by Mr. Kim that your consideration be given to the findings in the report.
Better : Mr. Kim suggests that you consider the findings in the report.

(8) 딱딱하고 법률적인 단어의 회피

notwithstanding → in spite of   hereafter → in the future
demonstrate → show   de facto → actual
prior to → before   subsequent to → after
in regard to → about   heretofore → until now

사람에 따라서는 5C's로 Character(개성) 대신에 Completeness(완전성)를 들기도 한다. Completeness(완전성)는 무역서신은 전달하고자 하는 정보를 빠짐없이 포함하여야 한다는 것이다. 전달하고자 하는 정보를 충분하게 전달하지 못하는 서신은 제 기능을 다할 수 없다. 서신 발송 전 자신이 전달하고자 하는 사항이 모두 표현되었는지, 상대방이 이를 읽고 의문을 가질 수 있는 사항은 없는지를 점검해 보아야 한다.

Standard
Trade
English

E-mail

1 E-mail의 의의

1) E-mail의 정의

E-mail은 전기적 신호 통신망을 이용하여 주고 받는 편지이다. 일반편지와 유사하지만 ① 전기적 통신망을 통하여 전달된다는 점, ② 시간이 걸리지 않는다는 점, ③ 상대방이 부재중이라도 편지나 자료를 전달할 수 있다는 점 등에서 다르다. 즉, 전자우편은 편지의 기록성과 전화의 즉시성의 장점을 동시에 가지는 통신방법이다.

2) 사용상의 장단점

(1) 장 점

① 시간과 거리에 관계없이 신속하게 보낼 수 있다
② 간편하게 우편기관과 관련된 절차 없이 보낼 수 있다.
③ 비용이 저렴하다.
④ 동시에 여러 명에게 발송 가능하다.
⑤ 받은 우편물의 편집이 용이하여 정보의 재가공 사용에 유리하다.
⑥ 즉시 답신이 가능하여 쌍방향 대화형태의 통신이 가능하며 송수신 여부 확인이 가능하다.
⑦ 종래의 편지 형식을 넘어 음악, 그림 등을 첨가하여 다양한 메시지를 전달할 수 있다.

(2) 단 점

① 비밀의 보안 측면에서 불완전하다.
② 스팸성 메일의 수신에 노출되어 있다.
③ 매우 복잡한 내용, 정중한 사교편지 등에서는 적합하지 않다.
④ 수신인 주소가 정확하지 못하면 송달이 불가능하다.

3) E-mail과 국제비지니스

최근 통신기술이 혁명적으로 발전하면서 국제비지니스의 통신 형태도 크게 바뀌고 있다. 텔렉스, 전보와 같은 통신수단이 거의 사라져가고 있고 컴퓨터와 전자통신망을 근간으로 하는 E-mail, Fax, 전화 등이 통신수단에서 중요한 자리를 잡아가고 있다.

2 E-mail의 편지 형식

E-mail은 누구나 쉽게 이용할 수 있도록 형식이 단순하며 주요사항은 빈 칸속에 해당사항을 넣도록 되어 있다.

E-mail은 상단의 헤드(head)와 하단의 텍스트영역(text area)으로 구성된다. 헤더에는 받는 사람 메일주소, 참조 메일주소, 숨은 참조 메일주소, 제목을 입력하게 되는데, 이 중 받는 사람 주소는 반드시 입력해야 하고 나머지는 필요에 따라 사용하게 된다. 하단 텍스터영역에는 인사호칭, 본문, 인사결문, 서명 등을 입력하게 된다. 받는 사람의 주소 성명과 발신일자는 입력하지 않아도 자동으로 전달된다.

[그림 4-1] E-mail 형식

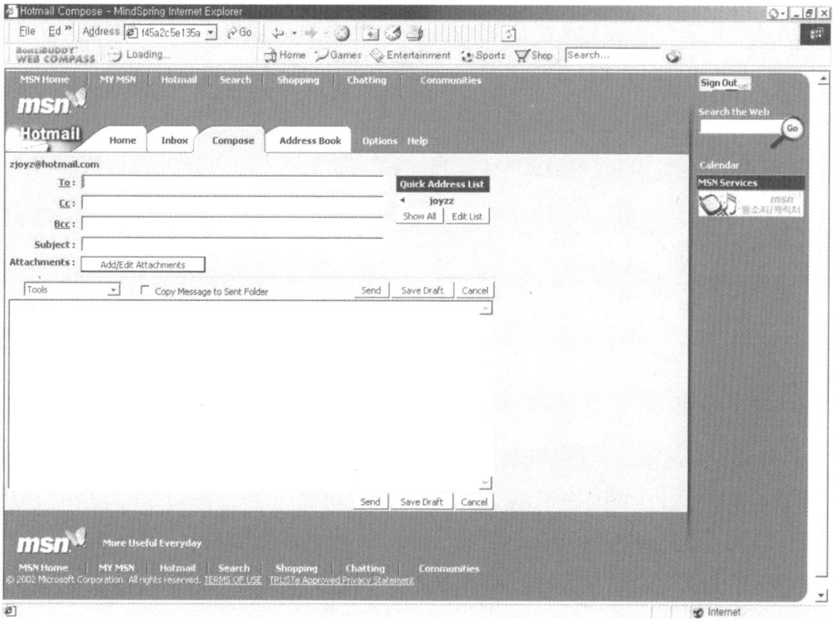

1) 받는 사람(To)

E-mail의 주소는 크게 세 부분으로 나누어지는데 사용자 계정(User ID), @(at) 표시, 그리고 사용기관의 도메인이름(Domain Name)으로 구성되어 있다. 만약 ID가 nskim이고 회사의 도메인명이 sgs.co.kr이라면 주소의 형식은 다음과 같다.

> nskim@sgs.co.kr

같은 메일을 여러 사람에게 보내는 경우는 이메일 주소를 세미콜론(;)이나 쉼표(,)로 분리하여 입력하면 동시에 여러 사람에게 보낼 수 있다.

> nskim@sgs.co.kr, jjlee@kyk.co.kr, jypark@skbs.co.kr

2) 참조(Cc) 및 숨은 참조(Bcc)

참조(Cc : Carbon copy)의 경우는 메일을 수신인 외에 메일내용을 알 필요가 있는 사람에게 보내게 된다. 숨은 참조(Bcc : Blind carbon copy)도 마찬가지이나 참조는 누가 참조자로 메일을 받았는지 수신인이 알 수 있지만, 숨은 참조는 누가 또 메일을 받았는지 수신인이 알 수 없다. 그러나 Bcc로 보내졌다는 사실은 알 수 있다.

작성요령은 받는 사람(To)의 경우와 동일하다.

3) 제목(Subject)

그 편지에 대한 적절한 제목(title)을 달아주는 것으로 일반편지의 경우와 동일하다.

4) 텍스트 영역

일반편지의 경우와 동일하다. 다만 E-mail에서는 일반편지에서의 레터헤더가 없고 서명부분이 다르다. 레터헤더가 없기 때문에 마지막 서명부분이 일반편지에서의 서명과 레터헤더의 기능을 동시에 한다. 이름, 직책 외에 일반 편지에서의 헤더에 포함될 사항, 즉 회사명, 주소, 전화번호, 팩스번호 등을 함께 기재하

게 된다. 서명은 일반편지에서와 같은 자필의 서명(signature) 없이 이름만 기재
하게 된다.

> Namsoo Kim<nskim@sgs.co.kr>
> Manager, Export Department, SGS Co.,Ltd.
> 125 Sogong-dong, Jung-gu, Korea 110-201
> Phone:+82-2-736-1025 Fax:+82-2-736-1026[1]

3 E-mail의 작성방법

무역영어에서 E-mail은 일반 편지와 그 작성요령이 대체적으로 동일하다. 그
러나 일반 편지에 비하여 E-mail은 특히 신속성을 중시하기 때문에 쉽게 읽고
쉽게 쓸 수 있는 문장구성이 된다.

비즈니스영어에서 간단하고 명료한 가운데 쉽게 쓰고 쉽게 읽힐 수 있는 문
장이 강조되는데, 이러한 것들은 E-mail 작성에서 또한 강조되는 중요한 요소
이다. 따라서 E-mail에 의한 비즈니스 서신에서는 이러한 요인들의 중요성이
한층 더 커진다고 할 수 있기 때문에 다음과 같은 사항에 더욱 유의할 필요가
있다.

① 명료하게 표현한다.
② 짧고 간단한 문장 구조가 되도록 한다.
③ 쉬운 용어를 선택한다.
④ 가급적 구어체의 글이 되도록 한다.
⑤ 이해가 용이한 내용전개가 되도록 한다.

4 E-mail의 관리방법

이상과 같이 비즈니스 영어에서도 기본원칙으로 되어 있는 사항 이외에

---

1) 전화번호의 맨 앞은 +를 기재한다.

E-mail 특성과 관련해서 다음과 같은 점을 특히 염두에 둘 필요가 있다.

1) 신속한 관리

E-mail의 최대의 장점은 신속성이다. 가급적 48시간 이내에 회신하는 것이 좋다. 빠른 답신을 요청한다고 했을 때 일반편지에서는 몇 일 내를 의미하지만 E-mail에서는 몇 시간 내를 의미하게 된다. 짧은 시간 내에 회신하기 어려운 상황이면 메일도착 확인과 언제 회신하겠다는 내용만이라도 간단히 보내는 것이 좋다.

2) 간결한 내용구성

E-mail은 신속함을 특성으로 하기 때문에 간결하게 쓰는 것이 좋다. E-mail에서는 가급적 하나의 편지는 하나의 주제에 대한 것으로 하고 분량도 한 화면을 넘지 않도록 유의할 필요가 있다.

E-mail에서는 격식에 얽매임 없이 시작과 끝에 간단한 인사를 덧붙이거나 시작과 끝 인사를 생략할 수도 있다. 그러나 이러한 점은 전반적인 상황 속에서 고려되어야 할 것이다. 너무 간결한 면만 감안하여 용건만 쓰게 되면 무미건조하고 예의를 잃을 수 있기 때문에 간결한 가운데서도 정중함과 친밀감을 잃지 않도록 유의할 필요가 있다.

3) 남의 글의 신중한 취급

전자문서의 글들은 쉽게 복사할 수 있고 전송할 수 있기 때문에 남의 글을 취급하게 되는 경우가 많다. 따라서 이로 인한 문제가 발생하기도 쉽다. 받은 메일은 마음대로 제3자에게 보내서는 안 된다. 또 남의 글을 가져올 때는 자신의 글과 남의 글이 쉽게 구분하여 이해할 수 있도록 하고, 인용하는 경우는 그 출처를 반드시 명시하여야 한다.

4) 발송 전의 충실한 검토

E-mail은 전자문서이고 신속성을 중시하기 때문에 내용 작성상의 잘못이나 오류 또는 오타 등이 발생하기 쉽다. 따라서 발송 전에 이러한 점에 대한 충실한 검토가 필요하다.

Standard
Trade
English

무역거래의 절차

무역의 절차를 일반적인 무역방식에서의 수출 업무와 수입 업무를 중심으로 간략하게 살펴보기로 한다.

[그림 5-1]은 수출절차와 수입절차를 보여 주고 있는데 시장조사에서부터 무역계약에 이르기까지는 수출과 수입 공통의 절차과정이 되며 그 이후에는 수입과 수출의 절차가 각기 달라지게 된다.[1) 또한 뒤의 [그림 5-2]는 이러한 무역절차와 관련하여 관련당사자들간의 업무연관구도를 보여주고 있다.

① 해외시장조사

무역은 먼저 수출 또는 수입을 할 지역을 정해야만 하므로 이를 위해서는 해외시장조사를 하게 된다.

② 거래선의 물색

거래하고자 하는 시장이 선정된 다음에는 그 시장에서 해당 상품을 취급할 수 있는 거래선을 찾아야만 한다.

③ 신용조회

국제거래에서는 거래과정에서 손해를 입을 경우 법적인 보호를 받기 어렵기 때문에 상대방의 신용에 대한 조사를 하게 된다.

④ 거래의 권유 및 조회

해당시장에서 유망한 거래선을 찾은 다음에는 이들에 대해서 거래관계나 물품거래를 권유하거나 상품이나 거래조건에 대하여 조회하게 된다.

⑤ 청 약

이러한 권유와 조회의 단계를 거쳐 어느 일방이 구체적인 거래안으로 오퍼를 하게 된다.

---

1) 여기서 수출과정은 반드시 수출자가 하고 수입과정은 반드시 수입자가 하게 되는 것은 아니다. 일반적인 경우는 물론 그렇게 하지만 특수한 경우는 그렇지 않은 것이다. 예를 들어 현장인도조건(EXW)의 경우에는 수입자가 수출을 위한 운송계약, 수출통관 등을 하게 되며, 관세지급인도조건(DDP)의 경우는 수출자가 수입을 위한 물품양륙, 수입통관 등을 하게 된다. 즉 계약조건에 따라 수출자와 수입자의 업무분담은 다양하게 달라질 수 있는 것이다.

[그림 5-1] 무역의 절차

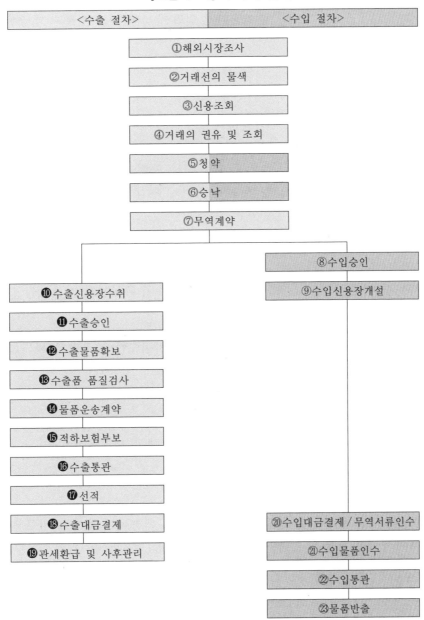

⑥ 승 낙

오퍼를 받은 상대방이 이를 받아들이게 되면 승낙이 되고 이로써 계약이 성립하게 된다.

⑦ 무역계약

승낙으로서 사실상 무역계약이 성립되었지만 오해나 후일의 분쟁소지를 사전에 없애기 위하여 무역계약서를 작성하기도 한다.

⑧ 수입승인

해당상품의 수입이 국가의 승인을 요하는 경우에는 수입상은 신용장을 개설하기 전에 승인절차를 거치게 된다. 이는 국가가 수입승인절차를 거치도록 한 일부품목에 해당된다.

⑨ 신용장개설

수입상이 자신이 거래하는 은행에 신용장 개설을 신청하게 되면 개설은행은 수출상의 지역에 있는 자신의 거래은행을 통하여 수출상에게 신용장을 보낸다.

❿ 신용장수취

수출상은 신용장을 받게 되면 수출과 수출대금회수를 보장받게 되므로 확신을 갖고 수출업무를 하게 된다.

⓫ 수출승인

만약 해당상품에 대한 수출이 국가의 승인을 요하는 경우에는 수출상은 신용장을 받은 이후에 승인절차를 거치게 된다. 이는 국가가 수출승인절차를 거치도록 한 일부품목에 해당된다.

⓬ 수출물품 확보

신용장을 받은 수출상은 물품을 생산하거나 구매하여 수출을 준비하게 된다. 이 과정에서 원자재를 수입하거나 무역금융지원을 받기도 한다.

⓭ 수출품 품질검사

해당상품이 수출품 품질검사 대상인 경우에는 검사과정을 거치게 된다. 수출품 품질검사는 수출국 상품의 대외 신인도와 평판 유지를 위한 제도이다.

⓮ 물품운송계약

상품을 수입국으로 운송하기 위해서 선박을 수배하여 운송업자와 운송계약을 체결하게 된다.

⓯ 적하보험부보

운송일정이 정해지면 운송과정에서 발생할 수 있는 상품의 경제적 가치의 상실 및 감소 위험에 대비하여 적하보험에 들게 된다.

⓰ 수출통관

수출선적하기 위해서 보세구역에 물품을 반입하고 수출신고를 하면 세관장은 수출결격유무를 조사한 후 수출면장을 교부한다.

⓱ 선 적

물품이 보세구역에 반입되어 검량과 수출면허의 과정이 끝나면 선박회사의 선적지시서에 의하여 선적되고 선하증권이 발급된다.

⓲ 수출대금결제

상품을 선적한 수출상은 선하증권과 상업송장을 비롯한 신용장상에서 요구하는 무역서류를 정비하여 자신의 거래은행에 매입을 의뢰하여 수출대금을 받는다. 이후 매입은행은 개설은행에 무역서류를 송부하고 대금을 상환받게 된다.

⓳ 관세환급 및 사후관리

수출상은 수출절차를 끝내면 세관 및 외국환은행에서 수출용원자재 수입 시 납부한 관세 및 내국세를 돌려 받고 그 외 필요한 사후관리를 하게 된다.

⑳ 수입대금결제 및 무역서류인수

개설은행은 매입은행으로부터 무역서류를 받으면 그 내용이 신용장 조건과 일치하는지 조사한 후 대금을 결제하고 수입상에 수입대금을 받고 무역서류를 인계한다.

㉑ 수입물품인수

무역서류를 인수한 수입상은 물품이 도착하게 되면 운송인에게 선하증권을 제시하고 물품을 인수하게 된다.

㉒ 수입통관

수입상은 수입물품을 보세구역이나 타소장치에 반입한 후 수입신고를 하고 관세 및 제세공과금을 납부하면 수입면장이 발부된다.

㉓ 물품반출

수입통관절차를 끝낸 수입상은 물품을 보세구역에서 반출하여 처분 또는 사용하게 된다.

[그림 5-2] 무역거래 연관도

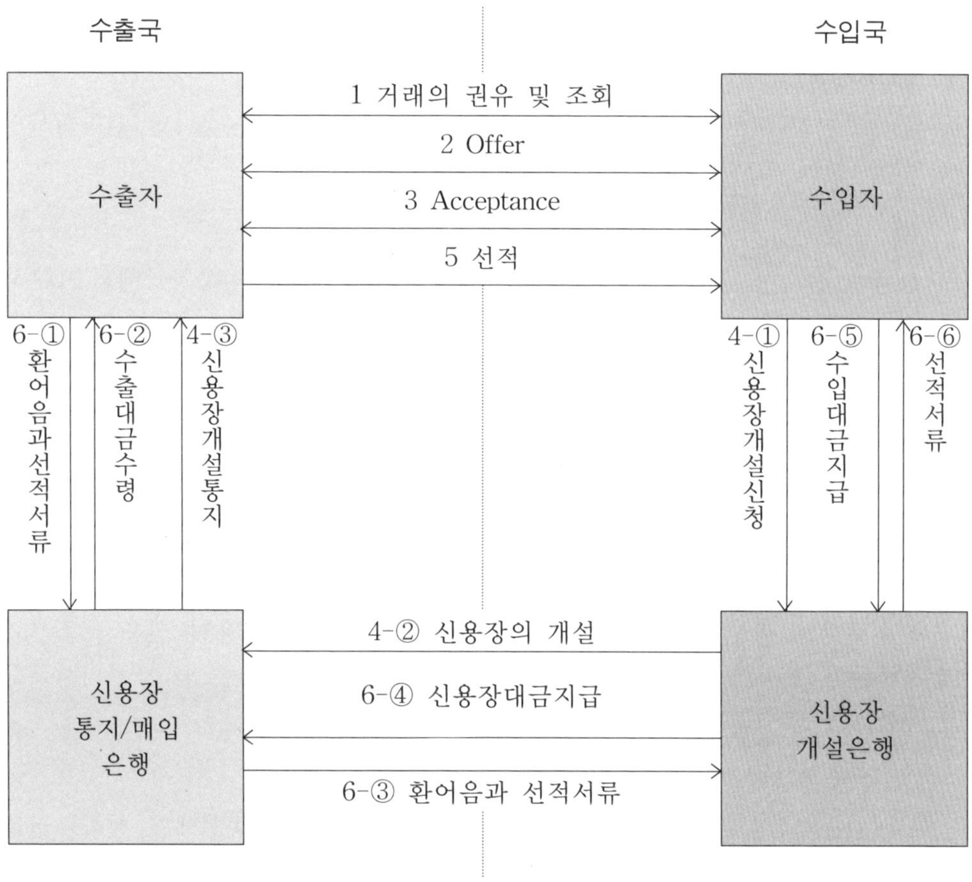

P/A/R/T 2

무역단계별 무역통신

Standard
Trade
English

거래선 소개의뢰

무역업무의 주요 내용

무역절차는 거래선의 선정으로부터 시작된다. 거래선을 선정하기 위해서는 먼저 해외시장조사로 목표시장을 선정하고 이 목표시장에서 거래 상대방을 찾게 된다.

1 해외시장조사

해외시장조사는 수출자의 입장에서는 수출희망상품을 수요하는 최적 지역을 찾는 것이며, 수입자의 입장에서는 수입희망상품을 공급하는 최적 지역을 찾는 것이다. 해외시장조사는 해당상품의 가격, 수요와 공급, 시장구조 등에 관한 사항뿐만 아니라 취급상품과 관련하여 해당국가의 정치, 경제, 사회, 문화, 지리, 무역관리제도, 거래방식, 고객 등의 모든 여건을 종합적으로 조사·분석하게 된다.

2 거래선의 물색

거래하고자 하는 목적시장이 결정된 다음에는 그 지역에서 상품을 취급할 업자를 선정해야 한다. 해외시장에서 해당상품의 취급업자를 찾는 방법은 ① 인터넷 검색, ② 대한무역투자진흥공사, 상공회의소, 재외공관, 상대국의 국내주재 공관 등의 공공기관에 의뢰, ③ 외국환은행에 의뢰, ④ 기존의 해외 지점, 대리점, 거래처의 이용, ⑤ 상공인명록의 이용, ⑥ 정기간행물 광고의 이용, ⑦ 무역박람회나 전시회 등의 행사에 참가, ⑧ 현지출장 등의 방법이 있다.

✓ **상공인명록(directory)**

상공인명록은 그 종류에 따라 전 세계, 대륙별, 국가별로 회사들에 대한 정보를 수록하고 있다. 많은 종류가 있는데 간단히 몇 개의 예를 들면 다음과 같다.
Kelly's Directory of Merchants, Manufacturers, and Shippers of the World.
World Marketing Guide.(이상 전 세계)
Directory of United States Importers.(미국)
Korea Trade Directory.(한국)

무역영문통신의 주요 사항

1 거래선 소개의뢰 서신

거래선을 찾기 위해서 서한을 내게 된다. 상공인명록이나 인터넷, 무역간행물 등을 통하여 알게 된 업자에 대하여 직접 거래 제의장을 내는 경우가 많지만, 다른 사람이나 기관에게 서한을 내서 거래할 만한 업자를 소개해 줄 것을 부탁하는 경우도 있다.

각국의 상업회의소, 무역투자진흥공사, 무역협회, 외교공관, 기타 무역업무를 도와주는 공공기관이나 외국환은행, 현지의 업자 등이 이러한 소개의뢰의 서한을 보내게 되는 주요 대상이다.

소개의뢰를 요청하는 서한은 대개 다음과 같은 내용으로 구성된다.

1. 소개의뢰 취지와 희망사항
2. 자사의 소개 : 업종, 취급상품, 규모 등 주요 내용
3. 자사의 신용조회처
4. 도움의 요청 및 감사 표시

2 거래선 소개의뢰에 대한 답신

소개를 요청받은 상대방은 적합한 업자를 물색하여 그 업자에게 소개의뢰인을 소개하거나, 소개의뢰인이 직접 그 업자와 접촉할 수 있도록 주소나 연락처 등을 제공하게 된다.

이러한 소개 의뢰에 대한 답신에서는 대개 다음과 같은 사항들을 포함하게 된다.

1. 회사의 소개, 또는 업자들에 대한 자료나 접촉할 수 있는 방법
2. 소개되는 회사에 대한 평가나 조언
3. 소개된 업자의 신용 등에 대해서는 자신이 책임지지는 않는다는 표시
4. 계속적인 협조의사 표시

A1 거래선 소개의뢰

SM Company, Inc.

4501, 45th Floor, Trade Tower
511 Yeongdong-daero, Kangnam-gu, Seoul, Korea 06164

January 5, 2021

International Trade Dept.
New York Chamber of Commerce
1555 Third Avenue
New York, NY 10128 U.S.A.

Gentlemen:

We are a well-established firm which produces multimedia speakers for the consumer electronics market. We have about 20 years experience in this line of business and enjoy an excellent reputation in Korea for providing high-quality products.

We are interested in expanding our business to overseas markets and wish to establish business relations with qualified firms in your country. We would appreciate it if you would introduce us to reliable distributors or agents who are interested in marketing our products in your area.

Should you require any references regarding our standing and reputation we suggest that you contact the following bank:

Korea Best Bank, Kangnam Branch
515 Yeongdong-daero, Kangnam-gu
Seoul, Korea 06161

We look forward to your kind cooperation.

Very truly yours,

내용 한국의 SM사가 미국 New York 지역에 수출 대리상을 찾기 위해서 뉴욕 상업회의소에 소개를 의뢰하는 서한이다.

• 주요 용어 및 표현 •

- firm : 회사, 기업
- which produces : which has been producing으로 해도 된다.
- in this line of business : 여기서 line은 특정상품군이나 특정업계를 말한다.
- enjoy : 받고 있다. 누리고 있다.
- excellent reputation : 좋은 평판(=good reputation, high reputation)
- We are now interested in expanding our business to ~는

  We now endeavor to expand our operations to ~

  We now wish to expand to ~

  We are now prepared to expand to ~

  등으로 표현할 수도 있다.
- distributor : 판매점, 보급소
- agent : 대리점, 대리인, 특약점, 중개상
- your area : 당신의 지역(=your market, your country)
- We would appreciate it if ~ : ~ 해주시면 감사하겠습니다. would 대신 should를 사용하는 것은 영국식이다.
- Should you require ~ : 만약 ~이 필요하다면(=If you require ~)
- standing and reputation : 지위와 평판. 일반적으로 standing은 재무적인 신용상태(credit status)를 말하고 reputation은 영업 및 사회적인 평판(business reputation)을 말한다.
- We look forward to ~ : ~를 기대합니다. We are looking forward to ~와 같이 진행형으로 사용해도 된다. 같은 의미로 We expect ~, We wait for ~, we await ~ 등이 사용되며 마찬가지로 진행형을 사용해도 된다.
- your kind cooperation : 당신의 협력. 당신의 답신이라면 your kind reply로 한다.

A2 거래선 소개의뢰에 대한 답신

New York
Chamber of Commerce
1555 Third Avenue
New York, NY 10128 U.S.A.

January 27, 2021

SM Company, Inc.
4501, 45th Floor, Trade Tower
511 Yeongdong-daero, Kangnam-gu
Seoul, Korea 06164

Gentlemen:

Thank you very much for your letter of January 5, 2021 expressing your desire to establish trade relations with firms in our country.

You will be pleased to know that we mentioned your letter in the January 21st issue of "Trader News", our daily newsletter, which reaches thousands of merchants within the state of New York and surrounding areas. You should henceforth expect to hear directly from interested firms.

If we can be of any further assistance, please do not hesitate to ask.

Very truly yours,

내용 New York 상업회의소가 한국 SM사의 거래선 소개요청에 대하여 이에 대한 내용을 무역회보에 게재하였음을 통지하는 서한이다.

• 주 요 용 어 및 표 현 •

- your letter of January 5, 2021 : 당신의 2021년 1월 5일자 편지
  =your letter dated January 5, 2021
- expressing your desire to establish ~ : 당신의 ~의 개설의사를 표현한
- letter of January 5, 2021 expressing your desire to establish ~
  =letter of January 5, 2021 expressing your desire of establishing ~
  =letter of January 5, 2021, in which you express the desire to establish ~
- establish trade relations with ~ : ~와 거래관계를 설립하다.
  =establish a business relationship with ~
  =open an account with ~
  =open a business connection with ~
- 21st issue of "Trader News" : 21일자 무역뉴스
  아라비아 숫자를 사용한 서수표현은 1st, 2nd, 3rd, 4th, 5th, ---, 11th, 12th, 13th, ---, 21st, 22nd, 23rd, 24th, --- 등으로 된다.
- surrounding areas : 주변지역
- henceforth : 지금부터, 앞으로(=from now on)
- be of any further assistance : 도움이 더 필요한(=be of any further service).
- Please do not hesitate to ~ : 주저말고 ~하십시오. ~에 부담갖지 마십시오.

✓	날짜표시

1. 날짜표시는 다음 세 가지 방법이 사용된다. 연도 앞에 항상 쉼표(,)가 붙는다.
① the 5th of January, 2021
② January 5th, 2021
③ January 5, 2021

2. 달에 관한 옛날식의 표현으로 inst.(=instant : 이 달), ult.(=ultimo : 지난 달), prox.(=proximo : 다음달) 등이 있다는데 지금은 거의 쓰지 않는다.
  the 10th inst. : the 10th of this month
  the 10th ult. : the 10th of last month
  the 10th prox. : the 10th of next month

A3 거래선 소개의뢰 후 조회

AMS Trading Company

908 Park Avenue
New York, NY 10017 U.S.A.

February 15, 2021

SM Company, Inc.
4501, 45th Floor, Trade Tower
511 Yeongdong-daero, Kangnam-gu
Seoul, Korea 06164

Gentlemen:

We have recently learned through an issue of the "Traders News" bulletin of the New York Chamber of Commerce that you wish to find a distributor for your product line within the United States.

We are very pleased to take this opportunity to introduce our company to you. For over 10 years we have been importing and distributing multimedia speakers from various sources located in Japan and Europe.

We are always looking for opportunities to expand our business activities. It has just now come to our attention that there are similar products available from your country.

We are very interested in reviewing your product line to see how it can fit within our product range. We are especially interested in portable mini speakers for computers and, wireless earphones.

Provided good quality and competitive prices, we can assure you of a large sales volume. Would you please send us samples and a technical bulletin of your products together with trade terms?

We are look forward to your reply.

Very truly yours,

내용 뉴욕 AMS Trading사가 뉴욕 상업회의소의 무역회보를 보고 한국의 SM 사에 수입판매에 대한 문의를 하는 내용의 서한이다.

· 주요 용어 및 표현 ·

- an issue of : 발행물, 인쇄물의 한 부
- bulletin : 회보, 고시
- product line : 제품종류, 제품들(=product mix, product range, products, goods)
- take this opportunity to ~ : ~할 기회를 갖다.
- various sources : 다양한 생산처, 여러 생산지
- business activities : 사업활동(=business operations)
- come to our attention : 우리가 관심을 갖게 되다. 우리의 주의를 끌다.
- available : 구할 수 있는(=obtainable)
- review : 정밀하게 살피다(=take a serious look at)
- portable mini speakers : 휴대용 소형 스피커
- wireless earphone : 무선 이어폰
- a technical bulletin : 기술명세서
- together with ~ : ~와 함께(=along with)
- trade terms : 거래조건(=business terms, trade terms and conditions)

✓	견 본

sample : 견본, 일반적인 의미의 표본
pattern : 직물류, 목형 등 거래에서 사용되는 견본
swatch : 천, 가죽 등의 거래에서 사용되는 조각 견본
specimen : 광물, 동식물의 표본, 인쇄양식의 표본
그 외 shape, type, standard, design 등도 견본의 의미로 사용된다.

✈ A4 거래선소개의뢰에 대한 답신

New York
Chamber of Commerce

1555 Third Avenue
New York, NY 10128 U.S.A.

January 30, 2021

SM Company, Inc.
4501, 45th Floor, Trade Tower
511 Yeongdong-daero, Kangnam-gu
Seoul, Korea 06164

Gentlemen:

In response to your request of January 5, we are pleased to recommend that you contact the following firm which may be interested in establishing a business relationship with your firm.

ABBA Co., Inc.
1156 5th Avenue
New York, NY 10017 U.S.A.

Despite the good reputation of this company, we do not assume any responsibility for their credit. We advise that you contact them directly and pursue all normal due diligence as you deem necessary.

We hope that this arrangement will be helpful to you and assure you of our cooperation at all times.

Very truly yours,

내용 뉴욕 상업회의소가 한국 SM사의 거래선 소개요청에 대하여 미국 ABBA 사를 소개하는 서한이다.

· 주 요 용 어 및 표 현 ·

- firm : 회사, 기업(=company, corporation, concern)
- establish a business relationship with ~ : ~와 거래관계를 개설하다.
- good reputation : 평판이 좋은(=of good repute, of high repute)
- assume : 떠맡다. 책임지다(=take for guarantecd).
- pursue all normal due diligence ~ : ~에 대한 모든 통상적인 조치를 취하다.
- deem necessary : 필요하다고 생각되는
- arrangement : 주선, 마련, 준비

✓	회　사

1. 회사를 나타내는 말로서 company, firm, corporation, concern, company limited (Co., Ltd.), company incorporated(Co., Inc.), 등이 있는데 통상 거의 구별 없이 사용되나 원래 약간의 의미 차이는 있다.
   company : 규모, 내용에 관계없이 회사를 나타내는 일반적인 말
   firm : 2인 이상에 의해 경영되는 회사
   corporation : 주식회사 형태의 법인회사. company limited(Co., Ltd.), company incorporated(Co., Inc.)도 이에 해당한다.

2. 참고로 한국의 회사종류에 대한 영어 이름은 제도상의 차이로 반드시 일치하지는 않지만 대개 다음과 같다.
   개인기업 : proprietorship, sole proprietorship
   주식회사 : company limited, corporation, company incorporated
   합자회사 : limited partnership
   합명회사 : partnership
   유한회사 : private company
   협동조합 : cooperative

3. 기업계열과 관련하여 다음과 같은 말이 사용된다.
   parent company : 모회사
   holding company : 지주회사
   subsidiary company : 기업의 자회사
   affiliated company : 기업의 계열회사
   branch : 지점
   representative office : 대표사무소

Useful Expressions

1 거래선 소개의뢰

📋 자사의 소개

- We are a well-established <u>manufacturer</u> of computers <u>having been in this</u> <u>line of business for over 10 years.</u>

manufacturer exporter importer distributor dealer	having been in this line of business for over 10 years having had 10 years experience in this business and have 10 years experience in this line of business with 10 years experience in this business

- We are <u>one of the leading exporters</u> of electronic products here in Korea.

one of the leading exporters one of the first class exporters well-established exporters a large exporter one of the premier

- Since 1930, we have engaged in the export of textiles of Korean origin and are fully equipped to fulfill your requirements.
- We have been established here for more than fifty years as a general importer and exporter.
- We have been <u>exporting</u> jewelry for more than twenty years and are now interested in <u>making</u> <u>connections</u> with the most reliable <u>firms</u> of your <u>country.</u>

exporting importing manufacturing handling	making establishing opening	connections relations accounts	firms concerns companies	country area territory

- We are exporters and manufacturers of electronics, particularly televisions, refrigerators, radios, etc., but as yet have no connections in your market.

📑 소개의뢰

- We would like to extend our business to your market, but have no good connections there.

- We are especially interested in offering our services to your area manufacturers.

- We would appreciate it if you would introduce us to some reliable importers who are interested in this line of business.

appreciate it greatly appreciate it highly appreciate it	would could will	introduce us to inform us of advise us of

- Please introduce us to competent firms that import automobiles in your country.

competent reliable reputable creditable	import automobiles in your country enjoy good credit in your market as importers of toys deal in cotton textiles

- We are retailers in the silk trade and would like to get in touch with suppliers of silk products.

retailers importers wholesalers	suppliers exporters manufacturers

- We are looking to establish business relationships with firms in your country. We appreciate it if you would introduce us to the ones that are in this line of business.

📋 조회처 제시

■ As for our <u>credit standing</u> and <u>activities</u>, <u>please refer to</u> the Korea Best Bank, Seoul.

credit standing *financial standing* *financial status*	*activities* *reputation*	*please refer to* *we would like to refer you to* *we are permitted to mention*

■ <u>For</u> our financial standing, <u>please feel free to</u> <u>check with</u> ABC Bank, Seoul Branch.

For *As for* *As to* *Regarding* *Concerning* *For information regarding* *For any information on*	*please feel free to* *please* *we advise you to*	*check with* *refer to* *contact*

■ For any information regarding our standing and reputation, we refer you to the Korea Best Bank, Seoul, as a reference.

📋 맺음말

■ We <u>wait for</u> your <u>early reply</u>.

wait for / are waiting for *await / are awaiting* *look forward to* *are looking forward to*	*early reply* *prompt reply* *immediate reply* *speedy answer*

■ Your <u>prompt reply to</u> this matter will be <u>appreciated</u>.

prompt reply to *early reply to* *early attention to* *courtesy in*	*appreciated* *much appreciated* *highly appreciated* *greatly appreciated*

- We hope to receive a favorable reply by return mail.

hope to wish to will be glad to	by return mail promptly immediately soon as soon as possible

- We thank you for your cooperation in advance and await your reply.
- Please let us hear from you as early as possible.
- We would highly appreciate your kind cooperation.
- We hope that through your assistance we will be able to establish mutually beneficial relationships with importers in your country.

2 거래선 소개의뢰에 대한 회신

📄 서 두

- Thank you for your letter of May 5 expressing your interest in establishing agents to handle your products.

Thank you for ~ Many thanks for ~ We have received ~ We are in receipt of ~ We are pleased to acknowledge receipt of ~	letter of May 5 letter of May 5th letter dated May 5 letter dated May 5th letter dated the 5th of May

- In reply to your inquiry of May 1, we recommend the following firms that may be interested in importing the goods you handle.

In reply to In response to In reference to In answer to Replying to	recommend / suggest are pleased to recommend have the pleasure of recommending are pleased to suggest have the pleasure of suggesting	handle desired deal in

📋 소개와 관련된 조치

- We are pleased to recommend that you contact the following firm.
- We mentioned your letter in the May 5th issue of our daily newsletter.
- We advise that you contact them directly.
- Interested firms will be asked to contact you directly.

📋 신용상태에 대한 책임

- Although the above firms are of good repute, we <u>cannot assume any responsibility</u> for their credit.

cannot assume any responsibility
are not responsible for

- While <u>these firms</u> <u>are long established</u> and well-known, and <u>enjoy a good reputation</u>, we, of course, cannot assume any responsibility for them.

these firms	are long established	enjoy a good reputation
the above firms	have long been established	are of good repute
		have been of good repute

- For any information you may <u>desire</u> as to their <u>standing</u>, we advise you to write directly to them, and they will furnish you with references.

desire	standing
want to know	business standing
want to obtain	financial standing
wish to have	status

- We recommend that you pursue all normal due diligence as you deem necessary.
- As for their standing, they will give you their references.
- The company will supply you with references upon request.

🗐 맺음말

- For any further information, please let us know.

For any further information If we can be of further assistance	further additional

- We are hoping that this arrangement will be helpful to you and we assure you of our cooperation at all times.

- We hope our reply will be of service to you, and if we can be of any further assistance, please do not hesitate to let us know.

further assistance additional assistance	do not hesitate to let us know let us know contact us

- If you would like to have any additional information, please do not hesitate to contact us.

- We are glad to recommend these firms and will be happy to supply any further information.

- We hope this information will be helpful to you.

be helpful to be of service to be satisfactory to be of good service to

I

Standard
Trade
English

거래관계의
수립과 유지

1 거래관계의 수립제의

시장조사, 거래선의 물색 등의 과정을 거쳐 거래관계를 설립하고자 하는 대상 기업이 정해지면 이 기업에 대해서 거래관계를 제안하는 것이다.

거래관계의 제의는 한 사람 또는 특정의 몇 사람에 할 수도 있고 불특정 다수 인에게 할 수도 있다. 일반적으로 거래관계의 제의는 자사가 거래관계를 갖기 원 하는 소수의 기업을 선정하고 이 기업들을 대상으로 순차적으로 거래의사를 타 진하게 된다.

이러한 거래관계의 수립제의는 상품의 매매, 매매중개, 판매점, 대리점, 기술 제휴 및 사업협력 등 다양한 형태가 있을 수 있다. 거래관계의 수립 제의를 받는 상대방은 제의해 온 거래조건과 자사의 사정을 검토하여 거래관계수립을 수락하 거나 거절하게 된다. 또한 거래제의가 상대회사의 신용조사나 사업타당성평가 등의 검토를 거쳐야 하기 때문에 당장 결정하기 어려운 경우에는 조건부로 수락 하거나 일정절차나 기간 후에 통보할 것을 약속하기도 한다.

2 거래선에 대한 안내통지

새로운 사업의 시작을 홍보하거나 이미 거래관계가 형성되어 있는 기업과의 관계를 계속적으로 유지 발전시키기 위해서 자사의 주요 변동사항 등에 대한 통 지를 하게 된다. 이러한 통지에 대한 서한을 Circular Letter(안내장)라고 한다.[1] 즉 Circular Letter는 개점, 폐점, 회사의 양도나 인수, 이전, 회사의 개편, 대리인 의 임명, 합병, 지점이나 사무소의 설치, 회사관계인의 이취임과 변동, 사원이동 등의 경우에 이를 알리는 인사장이다. 안내장 중에는 일자나 상대방의 성명, 주 소도 없이 편지의 형식을 갖추지 않은 형태로 보내기도 하는데 이를 Circular Letter와 구분하여 Circulars라고 한다.

---

1) 넓은 의미에서의 Circular Letter는 좁은 의미에서의 일반 안내장 외에 상품판촉장도 포함된 다. 좁은 의미의 일반 안내장은 여전히 Circular Letter라고 하고 상품판촉장은 Sales Letter, Sales Promotion Letter, Sales Circular Letter, 또는 Trade Circular로 불린다.

1 거래제의서

거래제의서는 상대방이 자신의 의도를 쉽게 이해할 수 있도록 간단 명료한 가운데 목적을 명확하게 표현하여야 한다.

거래제의서는 일반적으로 다음과 같은 내용이 포함된다.

1. 상대방을 알게 된 경위
2. 거래관계의 제의
3. 자사 및 자사 취급품목 소개
4. 거래제의 품목 및 거래조건
5. 자사의 신용조회처의 제시
6. 호의적 회답의 기대 문구

2 거래제의에 대한 답신

거래제의에 대해서 이를 수락하는 경우뿐만 아니라 이에 대한 결정에 시간이 필요한 경우나 거절하는 경우에도 이에 대한 내용을 빨리 회신해주는 것이 좋다. 특히 관심이 없는 경우라도 상대방의 입장에서 간략하게 회신을 하는 것이 바람직하다. 거래제의에 대한 회신은 대개 다음과 같은 내용을 포함한다.

1. 거래제의에 감사표시
2. 수락의 경우 기쁨 및 기대
3. 거래조건이나 자료의 요청, 또는 거래조건 제시
4. 거절이나 결정유보의 경우 이에 대한 내용
5. 상호 발전적 관계의 기대 문구

3 안내통지문

안내장은 많은 사람에게 보내는 경우에는 인쇄물을 사용하지만 몇몇 사람에게 보내거나 특정한 친분이 있는 경우에는 편지로 보내게 된다. 안내장은 각 상황별로 그 형식이 대개 정해져 있는데 그 성격상 사교문으로서의 정중하면서도 친밀한 느낌을 주는 표현을 사용하게 된다.

B1 거래관계의 권유

SM Company, Inc.
4501, 45th Floor, Trade Tower
511 Yeongdong-daero, Kangnam-gu, Seoul, Korea 06164

February 17, 2021

ABBA Co., Inc.
1156 5th Avenue
New York, NY 10017 U.S.A.

Dear Mr. Baker:

The NY Chamber of Commerce has recommended you as a possible distributor for our products in the U.S.A.

We are a manufacturer of multimedia speakers which has been in business for more than 20 years. We are one of the few speaker producers that has the capability to completely manufacture speakers from original concept design through final production.

We have an advanced research and development center and are continuously bringing high quality products to the market. Our VOX brand is well known for its high fidelity, reliability, manufacturing quality, and cutting-edge technology.

We would like to know if you are interested in marketing our products in your area. With our extensive technical knowledge and continual research and development, we are confident that we can supply you with high quality products at very competitive prices.

For your reference, we are enclosing an illustrated catalog of our product line. Upon request, we can submit some product samples along with pricing terms.

Should you require any references regarding our business status we suggest that you contact the Kangnam branch of the Korea Best Bank, in Seoul.

We look forward to your kind reply.

Very truly yours,

내용 SM사가 ABBA사에 대하여 자사를 소개하고 자사제품의 판매를 취급할
의향이 있는지를 타진하는 내용의 서한이다.

▫ 이 서한은 새로운 거래관계의 설립을 위한 권유장이다. 권유장이나 조회장에
서는 상대방의 관심과 호감을 줄 수 있도록 하는 것이 중요하다.
자사를 최고의 회사 또는 최대의 회사라고 하는 것과 같은 다소 추상적이고
과장된 느낌을 줄 수 있는 표현은 되도록 삼가고, 대신에 객관적인 지표로
서 좋은 회사임을 알리고, 상대방이 이익을 볼 수 있는 좋은 상품을 공급할
수 있음을 객관성 있게 설명하는 것이 좋다.

• 주요 용어 및 표현 •

- original concept design : 상품의 기본구상, 기본설계
- final production : 최종생산
- research and development center : 연구개발센터
- are bringing : 가져오다. 산출해내다.
- high fidelity : 고성능의(＝Hi-Fi)
- reliability : 신뢰성, 믿음직함
- cutting-edge technology : 최첨단 기술
- at very competitive prices : 경쟁력 있는 가격. 만약 최저가격이라면 at the
  lowest prices 또는 at the lowest prices possible이 된다.
- extensive : 광대한, 넓은, 대규모의
- technical knowledge : 기술지식
- an illustrated catalog : 그림이 든 카탈로그
- submit : 제출하다. 제시하다. 제공하다.
- along with ~ : ~와 함께(＝together with)
- pricing terms : 가격조건
- references : 조회처
- business status : 사업 평판, 영업상의 지위

B2 거래관계 권유에 대한 답신

ABBA Co., Inc.
1156 5th Avenue
New York, NY 10017 U.S.A.

March 3, 2021

SM Company, Inc.
4501, 45th Floor, Trade Tower
511 Yeongdong-daero, Kangnam-gu
Seoul, Korea 06164

Dear Mr. Kim:

Thank you for your letter of February 17, 2021, in which you expressed your willingness to establish business relations with us.

From your letter we have learned that you are especially interested in exporting multimedia speakers to our market. To that end, we are pleased to inform you that we have established a very good marketing network for supporting products which are suitable for our market.

However, before we make a major commitment to market your products within our area of operations, we need to consider carefully whether your products fit our product range.

For that purpose we need to thoroughly test your products as well as conduct a comprehensive market feasibility study.

Therefore, would you please send us a sample set of the products which you would like us to market? Upon completion of our market analysis we will let you know of our recommendations.

We sincerely hope that pleasant business relations will be established between us.

Very truly yours,

내용 SM사의 거래권유에 대한 ABBA사의 회신이다. 거래권유에 대해 긍정적인 입장을 보이면서도 시장조사를 거쳐 확답을 하겠다는 내용을 담고 있다.

• 주요 용어 및 표현 •

- letter of February 17, 2021, in which you expressed your willingness to ~.
 =letter of February 17, 2021 expressing your willingness to ~
- willingness to establish ~.
 =interest in exploring the possibility of establishing ~.
- willingness to : 기꺼이 하고자 하는(=desire to, intention to)
- business relations : 거래관계(=business relationship).
- to that end : 그 때문에, 그러한 목적에 비추어(=toward that end, in consideration of that)
- marketing network : 판매망(=marketing channel)
- make a major commitment : 주요문제에 대한 확약을 하다.
- to market : 시장에 내놓다.
- area of operation : 사업영역, 영업지역(=area of business)
- comprehensive : 포괄적인, 광범위한(=extensive)
- market feasibility study : 시장조사, 시장 타당성조사(=market survey, market research study)
- market analysis : 시장분석
- recommendation : 권고, 충고, 의견서, 추천
- sincerely hope : 진심으로 바란다. sincerely는 보다 강한 의도를 표현한다.

✓ **Hope & Wish & Expect & Want**

hope : 바람직한 일이 실현되리라고 믿고 기대함.
wish : 일의 실현가능 여부에 관계없이 바라는 것.
expect : 결과의 바람직함 여부에 관계없이 일이 일어난다는 확신을 갖고 기대함.
want : 바라다, 원하다의 가장 일반적인 말. 부족하다, 결여되다의 의미 포함.

B3 거래관계 권유에 대한 답신

ABBA Co., Inc.

1156 5th Avenue
New York, NY 10017 U.S.A.

April 12, 2021

SM Company, Inc.
511 Yeongdong-daero, Kangnam-gu
Seoul, Korea 06164

Dear Mr. Kim:

We would like to inform you of the results of our feasibility study. After some very thorough research, we have found that your products indeed meet our high standards of quality and technical capabilities. However our market is an extremely competitive one which means that price is a major factor.

What we have concluded is that for your products to be successfully marketed here, a reduction of price would be needed. Recently, domestic producers such as Zeno and Amco have reduced their prices by 10% on their entire line of products. This puts their prices below yours by about 15%.

Please keep in mind that we must secure a distribution channel of large retailers, and it is imperative that we give these retailers a huge incentive in price in order for them to switch their product lines. We are constantly in touch with a lot of retailers who are in a position to handle large quantities of your products. Once business relations are established, they would order your products continuously and on a large scale.

We suggest that you take up the matter without delay, as we have a few retailers who may be willing to handle your line right away if we give them a price reduction. We leave this matter to you; the results of your decision will determine the future of business in this territory.

We sincerely look forward to your consideration.

Very truly yours,

내용 ABBA사가 SM사 제품에 대한 시장조사를 결과를 통보하면서 상품가격 인하를 강하게 권하고 있다.

• 주요 용어 및 표현 •

- indeed : 실로, 참으로, 정말, 아주
- meet : 충족시키다. 만족시키다.
- capability : 성능, 특성, 능력, 재능, 가능성
- extremely competitive : 매우 치열한(=very competitive)
- reduced their prices by about 10% : 약 10% 인하하다.
  값을 내린다는 표현에는 lower prices, decrease prices, cut down prices 등이 있다.
- entire line of products : 전 제품
- puts their prices below yours by about 15% : 그들의 가격이 당신의 가격보다 약 15% 정도 낮게 되었다.
- please keep in mind that ~ : ~를 유념하십시오.
- imperative : 필수적인, 긴요한, 꼭 해야 할
- huge incentive : 큰 유인, 큰 보상, 큰 인센티브
- switch : 돌리다, 바꾸다, 전환하다.
- in constant touch with ~ : ~와 계속적인 관계를 갖다.
- in a position to ~ : ~할 위치에 있는, ~할 입장인
- once business relations should be established : 한 번 거래관계가 성립된다면
- on a large scale : 큰 규모로
- take up : 처리하다. 시작하다.
- a few : 몇(=a couple of)
- be willing to handle your line : 당신의 제품을 취급하고자 하는
- right away : 즉시(=instantly, at once, immediately, promptly)
- in this territory : 이 지역, 이 시장(=in our market, in our area)

▣ B4 거래관계의 조회

INEM Co., Ltd.

143, Azad Road, Juhu,
Mumbai 700 017, India

March 7, 2021

KSK ELECTRONICS
11 Myongdong-gil, Jung-gu
Seoul, Korea 04534

Gentlemen:

Your name has been recommended to us by CBA Bank, Seoul, as one of the leading manufacturers of business machines in Korea.

We are a large and well established importer of electronics in India. For the past 5 years we have been importing electronic calculators from Japan, and now we are interested in introducing your products into our country.

As we have a wide base of connections among large wholesalers here, we are in a position to handle considerable quantities of your products if they suit our market, and if prices are competitive.

We would, therefore, greatly appreciate it if you send us a full range of samples of your electronic calculators with price quotations on a CIF Mumbai basis and other relevant trade terms in detail, which you deem necessary.

With regard to payment terms, our trade with Japanese companies is conducted on a usance L/C at 90 d/s. All parties concerned have been satisfied so far with these terms. If possible, we would like to have similar terms with your company.

As for our financial standing and business integrity, kindly refer to our bankers, CBA Bank, Mumbai.

We look forward to your favorable reply.

Very truly yours,

내용 인디아의 INEM Co., Ltd.가 한국의 KSK ELECTRONICS사에 대해서 전자계산기 수입과 관련하여 조회하는 내용이다.

• 주요 용어 및 표현 •

- a wide base of connections : 넓은 기반의 연고, 넓은 기반의 거래관계
- be in a position to ~ : 의 입장에 있다. ~할 수 있다.
- handle : 취급하다(=deal in).
- a full range of samples : 전 종류의 샘플들
- price quotations : 가격, 가격표
- on a CIF Mumbai basis : CIF 뭄바이 조건으로(=on the basis of CIF Mumbai)
- relevant trade terms : 관련 거래조건
- in detail : 상세히
- deem necessary : 필요하다고 생각되는
- with regard to payment terms : 가격조건에 대해서는(=regarding payment terms / for the terms of payment)
- conducted : 거래해 오다(=carried on).
- on a usance L/C at 90 d/s : 일람 후 90일불 기한부신용장 방식으로
- 90 d/s : 일람 후 90일(=90 days after sight)
- parties concerned : 관계당사자들
- financial standing : 재무상태, 재무적인 위치
- business integrity : 사업상의 성실성
- refer to ~ : ~에 조회하다. ~에 문의하다.
- 자기회사의 신용조회처 제시는 다음과 같은 방식으로도 한다.
  We would be happy to give you any reference should you so desire.
  For our business standing, CBA Bank, Seoul will provide you with the necessary information.
  Should you require any references regarding our financial standing we suggest that you contact the following bank:

⬚ B5 거래관계 조회에 대한 답신

KSK ELECTRONICS

11 Myongdong-gil, Jung-gu
Seoul, Korea 04534

March 24, 2021

INEM Co., Ltd.
143, Azad Road, Juhu,
Mumbai 400049, India

Gentlemen:

We would like to express our thanks for your deep interest in our electronic calculators.

As you may have been informed by CBA Bank, we have been established as a manufacturer of business machines for more than 15 years and have been exporting to several countries. We have a good reputation for supplying high quality products at a reasonable price.

As you requested, we have sent today a full range of samples of our products together with a copy of the illustrated catalog and price list. We are sure that you will find our products to be outstanding, especially when compared to our competitor's in terms of quality and design.

Regarding the terms of business, it is our policy to trade on a Banker's Irrevocable Letter of Credit, under which we draw a draft at sight.

We hope that our products will meet your requirements. Your trial order will get our immediate attention to ensure prompt shipment.

Yours very truly,

내용 한국의 KSK ELECTRONICS사가 인디아의 INEM사의 전자계산기 수입 관련 조회에 대하여 회신하는 내용이다.

• 주요 용어 및 표현 •

- to express our thanks : 고마움을 표하다.
- electronic calculators : 전자계산기
- business machine : 사무용 기계
- have a good reputation : 좋은 평판을 누리고 있다.
- high quality products : 고급 품질 제품
- at a reasonable price : 합당한 가격으로, 과하지 않은 가격으로, 싼 가격으로
- a full range of : 전 범위의
- together with ~ : ~와 함께(=along with)
- illustrated catalog : 그림 또는 사진이 들어있는 제품 목록
- price list : 가격표
- outstanding : 눈에 띄는, 걸출한, 우수한
- competitor's : 경쟁회사의 상품, 경쟁회사의 것
- in terms of quality and design : 품질과 디자인 면에서
- the terms of business : 거래조건
- policy : 회사 방침, 정책
- trade on ~ : ~방식으로 거래하다.
- banker's irrevocable letter of credit : 은행 취소불능신용장. 오늘날은 대부분 은행신용장이지만 원래 은행 이외의 개인이나 기관에서 발행하는 신용장도 있기 때문에 은행에서 발급하는 신용장을 Banker's L/C라 한다.
- draw a draft : 어음을 발행하다.
- a draft at sight : 일람출급환어음
- meet your requirements : 당신의 요구조건을 충족시키다.
- trial order : 시주문, 시험적 주문(=initial order, first order)
- prompt shipment : 조속한 선적

B6 거래관계의 조회

Fuji Trading Co.
33-12 Hitotsubashi
Chiyoda-Ku Tokyo, Japan.

March 10, 2021

SM Company, Inc.
511 Yeongdong-daero, Kangnam-gu
Seoul, Korea

Dear Mr. Kim:

Through the courtesy of the Korea Trade-Investment Promotion Agency, we have obtained your name and we would like to introduce ourselves with the hopes of establishing a good business relationship.

We have been importing various kinds of multimedia speakers for TVs, radios, toys, cars, computers, etc., as one of the major speaker importers in Japan. We provide our goods to about 50 wholesalers nationwide and our average annual combined sales volume is approximately US$ 50 million.

Among your products, we are interested in model DS-123A and DS-213F. Could you please supply us with your best terms of trade for these items on a CIF Kobe basis? If possible, please send us a brochure for each of the above mentioned items and a few samples for evaluation and demonstration to our end-users here. Should the terms of trade be satisfactory, we will be able to place fairly large orders with you.

For any information regarding our financial standing and business reputation, please refer to the Fuji Bank, Tokyo.

Your early and favorable reply would be greatly appreciated.

Very truly yours,

내용 Fuji Trading사가 SM사에 대하여 멀티미디어 스피커의 수입의 거래조건 을 조회하는 내용이다.

• 주 요 용 어 및 표 현 •

- Korea Trade-Investment Promotion Agency : 대한무역투자진흥공사
- with the hopes of ~ : ~를 희망하며
- for our mutual benefit : 우리 공동의 이익을 위해, 우리 서로의 이득을 위해
- various kinds of : 다양한 종류의(=various sorts of, a variety of)
- wholesalers nationwide : 전국의 도매상들
- average annual combined sales volume : 평균 연간 총매출 규모
- amounts to ~ : ~에 이르다. ~에 달하다.
- supply us with ~ : 우리에게 ~을 제공하다.
- best terms of trade : 최상의 거래조건
- on a CIF Kobe basis : CIF 코베 조건으로
- brochure : 소개용 소책자, 팜플렛
- above mentioned items : 상기 물품
- demonstration : 실험, 전시
- end-users : 최종소비자, 실수요자
- place large orders with : 많은 주문을 하다(=furnish large orders with)
- fairly : 꽤, 어지간히(=moderately)
- should the terms of trade be satisfactory : 만약 거래조건이 만족스럽다면

✓	금액(1. 숫자 표시와 읽기)

USD 50 million : fifty million US dollars
$ 45.67 : forty-five dollars (and) sixty-seven (cents)
£ 76.80 : seventy-six pounds (and) eighty (pence)
¥ 234.50 : two hundred (and) thirty-four yen (and) fifty sen
* pence는 penny의 복수이며, yen, sen은 원래 -s를 붙이지 않는다.

✚ B7 거래관계 조회에 대한 답신

SM Company, Inc.

4501, 45th Floor, Trade Tower
511 Yeongdong-daero, Kangnam-gu, Seoul, Korea 06164

March 25, 2021

Fuji Trading Co.
33-12 Hitotsubashi
Chiyodaku Tokyo, Japan.

Dear Mr. Yoshida:

Thank you very much for your inquiry of March 10, 2021 regarding our Speaker Models DS-123A and DS-213F. We are glad to learn that you are interested in distributing our products in your territory and hope that this will be the beginning of a mutually beneficial business relationship.

Please find enclosed our general terms of trade and price quotations. You will find our prices to be very competitive and we are forgoing our normal profit in order to develop sales in your market.

According to your request, we have already shipped some samples and catalogs by DHL.

The Models DS-123A and DS-213F are two of the latest models which are in great demand in the overseas market as well as the domestic market. The number of these in stock is decreasing rapidly and so we cannot guarantee to fulfill your order unless it is placed promptly.

We wish to receive your order by return mail.

Very truly yours,

내용 Fuji Trading사의 스피커 수입 거래조건 조회에 대한 SM사의 답신이다.

• 주 요 용 어 및 표 현 •

- in your territory : 당신 지역, 귀 지역에(=in your area, in your country)
- a mutually beneficial business relationship : 상호이익이 되는 거래관계, 상호호혜의 거래관계
- beneficial : 유익한, 이익이 되는(=profitable)
- Please find enclosed ~ : ~을 동봉합니다. ~을 보냅니다.
  =We are enclosing ~, Enclosed are ~
- general terms of trade : 일반 거래조건, 개괄적인 거래조건, 통상의 거래조건
- price quotations : 가격, 가격표
- you will find competitive : 우리의 가격이 경쟁력 있음을 알 것이다.
- competitive : 경쟁력 있는(=가격이 낮다고 하는 경우에는 low)
- forgoing : ~ 없이 지내다. 삼가하다(=sacrificing).
- normal profit : 정상이윤(=usual markup)
- shipped : 발송하다(=dispatched).
- DHL : 서류나 화물의 특급배달회사 이름. DHL은 설립자 세 사람 이름에서 따온 것. DHL 외에 FedEx(Federal Express)나 UPS(United Parcel Service)가 유명하다. 한국의 우체국, 미국의 USPS 등 과 같이 국영기관 우편서비스를 이용할 수도 있다. 여기서 서류배달서비스를 courier service라 하고 소화물 배달서비스를 small package service라 한다.
- latest models : 최신모델(=recent models)
- great demand : 수요가 많은(=large demand, good demand)
- overseas market : 해외시장
- domestic market : 국내시장
- stock : 재고(* out of stock : 재고부족)
- guarantee : 보장하다. 보증하다. 약속하다.
- fulfill order : 주문을 이행하다.

B8 대리점지정 조회

Asia Trading Company

212 Yoi-daero, Youngdeungpo-gu
Seoul, Korea 07325

March 2, 2021

BASB Company, Ltd.
1 Hammersmith Grove
London W6 ONB, U.K.

Dear Mr. Smith:

We have learned from our friends, Messrs. Johnson Brothers Company, of New York, that you are a well established electronics manufacturer producing high quality electronic components. We understand that you have not yet been represented here and so we would like to offer our services as the exclusive distributing agent marketing your fine products in Korea.

We have established a large presence here for the last ten years, during which time, we have imported a wide range of electronic components and have supplied numerous end products manufacturers in Korea. We also have had a lot of experience in representing foreign manufacturers including several internationally well known companies.

The electronic components market in Korea is expanding rapidly. We estimate the demand for electronics will increase continuously for several years to come; on the other hand the competition in this field will be more and more intense. Considering these facts, we feel that the best way for you to penetrate our market is to take advantage of our sales network which we have spent the past several years developing.

Should you be willing to make an arrangement with us, the Johnson Brothers Company of New York will give you information regarding our business standing, and ABC Bank in Seoul will give you any information you need with regard to our financial standing.

We look forward to your favorable response, and trust that a mutually pleasant relationship may shortly be established.

Very truly yours,

내용 한국의 Asia Trading사가 영국의 BASB사에 보내는 한국 대리점을 맡고
싶다는 내용의 조회서한이다.

• 주요 용어 및 표현 •

- well established electronics manufacturer : 견실한 전자제품 제조업자
- electronic components : 전자부속품(＝electronic parts)
- have not yet been represented here : 이곳에 대리점을 두고 있지 않다.
- exclusive distributing agent : 독점 판매대리점(sole distributing agent)
- a large presence : 큰 규모로 영업하는
- numerous : 수많은
- end-products : 완제품, 최종품
- a wide range of : 폭넓은 범위의, 넓은 영역의
- well known companies : 잘 알려진 기업들
- on the other hand : 반면에
- in this field : 이 영역, 이 분야
- intense : 치열한, 심한(＝keen)
- penetrate : 침투하다. 스며들다. 진입하다.
- sales network : 판매망, 판매경로(＝distribution network, sales channels)
- arrangement : 협정, 합의
- with regard to ～ : ～에 관하여
- information on ～ : ～에 대한 정보
- mutually pleasant relationship : 상호간 좋은 관계

✓	Maker, Manufacturer, & Producer
	① maker : 제작자, 소규모적인 생산업자
	② manufacturer : 대규모의 제조업자, 제조회사
	③ producer : 생산자, 넓은 의미의 상품을 산출하는 업자

B9 대리점지정 조회에 대한 답신

BASB Company, Ltd.
5th Floor, St. Martin's House
1 Hammersmith Grove, London W6 ONB, U.K.

March 26, 2021

Asia Trading Company
212 Yoi-daero, Youngdeungpo-gu
Seoul, Korea 07325

Dear Mr. Lee:

We are pleased to learn from your letter of March 2 that you would like to act as our agent for Korea. We would like you to know that we are very much interested in your proposition since we have wanted to expand into the Korean market for a long time. We truly hope that this will give us the opportunity to do so.

We would like to discuss the possibility of establishing sole agency ties with your company. Mr. Jim Baker, our marketing manager in charge of overseas markets, plans to visit the East Asian region including China, Japan, and Korea in the middle of April. He will be available to call on your company to discuss this proposition in detail.

In the meantime, we are sending you a catalog describing our entire line of products as well as a copy of our company profile. We shall be very pleased if you will inform us of the details of the products you are especially interested in, and provide us with an outline of the general terms of business you have in mind.

We trust that this will be the beginning of a cordial and mutually beneficial relationship.

Very truly yours,

내용 영국의 BASB사가 한국의 Asia Trading사의 한국 대리점을 맡고 싶다는 조회에 대하여 호의적인 회신을 하는 내용이다.

• 주요 용어 및 표현 •

- act as our agent : 대리점으로 일(직무)을 맡다. 대리점으로 대리인 일을 하다.
- expand into : 진출하다. 확장하다.
- for a long time : 오랫동안(=quite some time)
- sole agency ties : 독점 대리점 협정
- in charge of ~ : ~을 맡고 있는, ~을 담당하는
- plans to visit : 방문할 계획이다. 방문할 작정이다.
- China, Japan and Korea : 국가명은 알파벳순으로 하는 것이 국제관행이다.
- provide us with ~ : 제공하다. 주다(=give us).
- in the middle of : 중순에
- be available to call on : 방문할 수 있을 것이다.
- in detail : 상세히, 자세히
- in the meantime : 그 동안에, 한편(=meanwhile)
- company profile : 회사소개
- details : 상세한 설명(=particulars)
- an outline of the general terms : 일반 조건의 개요
- in mind : 생각하고 있는, 염두에 두고 있는
- cordial : 성심성의의(=sincere, hearty)
- mutually : 상호간에, 서로
- a cordial and mutually beneficial relationship와 같은 취지로 pleasant and agreeable business connections to our mutual advantage로도 쓸 수 있다.

✓	~ 하고 싶다는 표현	
would like to ~	want to ~	wish to ~
desire to ~	be desirous of ~	be anxious to ~

⊞ B10 대리점지정 조회에 대한 답신

BASB Company, Ltd.

5th Floor, St. Martin's House
1 Hammersmith Grove, London W6 ONB, U.K.

March 26, 2021

Asia Trading Company
212 Yoi-daero, Youngdeungpo-gu
Seoul, Korea 07325

Dear Mr. Lee:

Thank you for your letter of March 2 expressing your desire to act as our agent in Korea. Although we very much appreciate your interest in our products, we are sorry that we are unable to accept your offer.

The reason is simply that we already have an agent who handles all our products in your area. This agent has been handling our products on an exclusive basis covering the entire East Asia region for many years. To date, we are thoroughly satisfied with their services. Therefore, we have no immediate plans to make any changes.

If you have any further interest in our products, we would like to refer you to our agent in your region:

Mr. Taro Tanaka
SHINKO Co., Ltd.
21 Marunouchi, 3-Chome, Chiyoda-Ku
Tokyo, Japan

Thank you very much for your inquiry.

Very truly yours,

내용 영국의 BASB사가 한국의 Asia Trading사의 한국 대리점을 맡고 싶다는 조회에 대하여 이미 이 지역 독점대리점이 있음을 알리는 내용이다.

· 주 요 용 어 및 표 현 ·

- handles : 취급하다(=deal in, represent).
- all our products : 우리의 모든 제품(=our full product line)
- on an exclusive basis : 독점계약으로
- covering : 담당하는, 커버하는
- to date : 지금까지(=until now)
- further interest : 더 이상의 관심, 더 많은 관심
- we would like to refer you to our agent : 우리 대리점에 문의하십시오.
- refer you to ~ : 당신이 ~에게 문의하도록 하다(=ask you to contact).
- East Asia region : 동아시아지역(=East Asia area)
- We have no immediate plans to make any changes. : 같은 취지로 보다 완곡하게 We are not in a position to nominate any agency in your territory for the time being.으로 표현할 수도 있다.

✓ **Distributor, Agency, & Broker**

Distributor : 본사와는 독립적인 관계에서 자신의 계산과 위험부담으로 거래하는 판매대리점이다.

Agent : 본사의 대리인으로서 본사의 계산과 위험부담으로 거래하는 판매대리점이다.

Broker : 거래중개의 서비스를 제공하고 중개수수료를 받는 사람으로서 거래의 당사자는 아니다.

독점판매대리점은 Exclusive Distributor 또는 Sole Distributor라 하는데, 일반적으로 Exclusive Distributor는 해당지역에 본사도 판매할 수 없는 반면에 Sole Distributor는 본사는 판매할 수 있는 경우를 말한다.

✉ B11 지점개설 인사

SM Company, Inc.
4501, 45th Floor, Trade Tower
511 Yeongdong-daero, Kangnam-gu, Seoul, Korea 06164

May 15, 2021

AMS Trading Company
908 Park Avenue
New York, NY 10017 U.S.A.

Gentlemen:

We are pleased to announce that we have opened a new branch in New York City. Due to the rapidly expanding demand for our electronic products in the eastern area of the U.S.A., we have decided to open a branch office to serve you better. This means that we will be able to process your orders more efficiently. Our branch is at the following address:

SM Company, Inc.
New York Branch
1203 Park Avenue
New York, NY 10017 U.S.A.

We have appointed Ms. H. S. Jung as the new branch manager. She has been with us for many years and is highly experienced in international trade. We ask you to favor us, either through our area branch or directly, with brisk orders which will always receive our best attention.

We look forward to your continued patronage.

Very truly yours,

내용 SM사가 미국지역의 거래선에 뉴욕지점의 개설사실을 알림과 동시에 앞으로도 계속적인 후원을 부탁하는 지점개설인사서한이다.

• 주요 용어 및 표현 •

- due to ~ : ~로 인하여, ~ 때문에(=because of, owing to)
- rapidly expanding demand : 급속히 증대하는 수요
- process orders : 주문을 처리하다.
- has been with us : 우리와 함께 근무해왔다.
- either through our area branch or directly : 지역지점을 통하거나 직접
- brisk orders : 활발한 주문(=substantial orders)

회사 부서와 직위의 영어명칭

부 서	사장실	Office of the President
	비서실	Secretariat
	기획	Planning
	총무	General Administration
	인사	Personnel
	경리	Accounting
	재무	Finance
	영업관리	Sales Administration
	마케팅	Marketing
	자재	Materials
	구매	Purchasing
	생산	Production
	물류	Logistics
	수출	Export
	수입	Import
	해외사업	Overseas Operation
	연구개발	Research and Development
	고객지원	Customer Support
	홍보	Public Relation
직 위	회장	Chairman, Chairperson
	사장	President
	부사장	Vice President
	전무이사	Senior Managing Director
	상무이사	Managing Director
	이사	Director
	감사	Auditor
	고문	Senior Advisor
	본부장	General Manager
	지점장	Branch Manager
	부장	Department Manager
	차장	Associate Department Manager
	과장	Section Manager
	계장	Assistant Section Manager

Useful Expressions

1 거래관계의 제의

📋 상대방을 알게 된 경위

- Your name has been recommended to us by ABC Company.

> Your name has been recommended to us by ABC Company.
> We have learned your name from ABC Company.
> From ABC Company, we have come to learn about your company.
> You were introduced to me by ABC Company.
> ABC Company has introduced your company to us.

> We have learned from ABC Company that you are ~.
> ABC Company has recommended you as ~.

> ABC Company has informed us to get in touch with you about ~.
> ABC Company suggested that we wrote to you concerning ~.

- Your name has been recommended to us by the New York Chamber of Commerce as one of the most reliable importers of electronic appliances.

Your name	recommended to us
Your address	given to us
Your name and address	mentioned to us
	supplied to us

- Through the courtesy of JETRO,[2] we have heard your name and address.

Through the courtesy of	heard / learned of /
From	came to learn / acquired /
Through	obtained / found

---

2) 일본무역진흥기구(Japan External Trade Organization): 한국의 대한무역투자진흥공사(KOTRA) 에 해당하는 일본의 무역지원기관이다.

- We have learned from the Korea Chamber of Commerce and Industry that you are <u>one of the leading exporters</u> of electric shavers.

  > *one of the leading exporters*
  > *one of the first class exporters*
  > *a large exporter*

- We have <u>seen</u> your advertisement in "Korea Trade News" and are interested in your <u>broad range of</u> foodstuffs.

seen	*broad range of*
noticed	*extensive line of*
read	*entire line of*

- Having found your name in Kelly's Directory of Merchants, we learned that you <u>are interested in importing</u> general merchandise.

  > *are interested in importing*
  > *are looking for reliable exporters of*
  > *are seeking reliable exporters of*
  > *are in the market for*

- Your name has been given to us by the KCCI and we would like to know whether you can supply electric ovens to us.

- The local Trade Bulletin <u>referred</u> your firm as a potential supplier.

  > *referred*
  > *recommended*

- During a recent visit to Los Angeles, I saw a sample of your new model K-123.

- While attending the exhibition, I saw some samples of your products.

- We are interested in the electronic appliances you advertised in the February issue of "Electronics."

- We hear from KOTRA that you have recently introduced a digital camera and we would appreciate it very much if you would send us full details by return mail.

📄 자사소개

- We have over twenty years of experience in the field of electronic appliances and can offer you the finest quality goods.

- We have been established here for over 10 years as a general importer and distributor.

- We are <u>manufacturers</u> of wooden toys, with well-established <u>business contacts</u> in Japan and the USA.

manufacturers *suppliers*	*business contacts* *distribution networks*

- We are doing <u>an extensive business</u> in the manufacture and exportation of tableware, and <u>hope you will give us a trial order</u>.

an extensive business *a high volume business*	*hope you will give us a trial order* *trust you find our prices very competitive*

- We are importing electronics, particularly car accessories, for distribution throughout this country.

- For the past 10 years, <u>we have enjoyed a good reputation for exporting various types of toys</u>.

we have enjoyed a good reputation for exporting various types of toys *our firm has been engaged in exporting various types of toys* *our company has been a leader in exporting various types of toys*

- We handle the highest quality goods and export over US$ 1 million per year.

- Our office staffs are well trained and can answer all questions concerning export.

📋 거래개설의사

- We would like to do business with you.

> to do business
> to trade
> to open an account

- We would like to enter into business with you.

> | would like to | enter into business with |
> |---|---|
> | are anxious to | enter into a business relationship with |
> | are keen to | open an account with |
> | desire to | establish business with |

- We are interested in extending our export trade of silk clothing into your market with the introduction of these products.
- We would very much like to offer our services to you as an agent.

📋 세부 관심사항

- We are interested in your new personal computer and would like very much to have a catalog and price list.

> are interested in
> are interested in importing
> are interested in the import of

- We are now seriously considering the possibility of commencing business with you, if your terms and conditions are acceptable.

> considering
> investigating
> examining

- We are particularly interested in your products, and would like to have more detailed information on your entire product range.

particularly *especially*	*product range* *product line*

- We wish to know whether you can supply the goods specified in the list below.
- We are looking for reliable wool textile producers.

looking for *in the market for* *in urgent need of*

- We have recently received an inquiry from our customer for your new model K-123.

📄 자료송부

- We are sending our samples, price list and full promotional materials for you to examine.
- For your reference, we have enclosed our latest catalog and price list, which we believe you will find to be very competitive.
- Upon receipt of your drawings, we will submit counter samples with our best prices.
- We send you our catalog under separate cover and welcome your specific inquiries for any of our lines and assure you that we will make every effort to meet your requirements.

under separate cover *by separate post* *separately*	*lines* *products*

📄 자사제품소개

- Our products enjoy a good reputation.

> *enjoy a good reputation*
> *are commanding very good sales*
> *are selling well*

> *good reputation*
> *wonderful reputation*
> *excellent reputation*

- Our products have been well received by buyers in Europe and we are interested in supplying our quality products to you on favorable terms in order to diversify our market.

> *have been well received by*
> *are in much demand by*

- We are sure that they are the highest quality products and are supplied to you at the very lowest price.

- If you are interested in our proposal and send us details concerning your special requirements, we will be able to supply you with quality products at competitive prices.

📄 대리점 및 판매점 지정 조회

- I wish to offer my services as a distributor for your auto glass in the Indonesian market.

- We would like to distribute your products in Korea.

> *distribute*
> *handle*

- We found the proposal to be attractive and would like to discuss it in detail with you.

- We have heard from our correspondent in New York that you are looking for an agent in this area, We would very much appreciate it to be chosen for the position.

- We would like to know if you would be interested in working with us on a consignment basis.

- We have a lot of experience with representing several leading companies in your country, and are fully confident of meeting your requirements if you will <u>entrust us with your agency</u> in Thailand.

> *entrust us with your agency*
> *appoint us as your agent*

- We are pleased to inform you that we have decided to appoint you as our sole sales agent for the Indonesian market.
- Regarding the terms of being an agent, we would like to make the following proposals, which we hope will be agreeable to you.
- We are willing to appoint you as an agent for a one-year trial period, and if your performance is satisfactory, we will then enter into further negotiations to give you a more permanent status.
- We are ready to commence doing business with you, subject to your consent to give us 4% commission on all transactions up to US$ 50,000, and 3% above that amount.
- As we are already represented in Malaysia, we <u>are unable to take advantage of your offer</u> for the time being. We will, however, contact you if your services are required in the future.

> *are unable to take advantage of your offer*
> *are not in a position to accept your offer*

🗎 신용조회처의 제시

- For our credit standing and business reputation, <u>please refer to ABC Bank</u>.

> *please refer to ABC Bank*
> *please feel free to refer to ABC Bank*
> *you may refer to ABC Bank*
> *our reference is ABC Bank*
> *please make an inquiry to our bankers, ABC Bank*

- As to our standing and reputation, we would like to refer you to the Korea Best Bank, Seoul.
- For <u>information</u> <u>on</u> our financial standing, please feel free to check with ABC Bank, Seoul.

For information As for information As to information	on regarding

- For our credit standing, CBA Bank, Seoul Branch will supply necessary information.

📋 맺음말

- Your <u>prompt reply</u> will be <u>much appreciated</u>.

prompt reply prompt answer immediate response	much appreciated highly appreciated greatly appreciated

- We <u>look forward to</u> your <u>response</u> <u>as soon as possible</u>.

look forward to hope to have expect to receive wish to receive	response reply answer favor	as soon as possible soon promptly immediately at your earliest convenience

- Your <u>attention to this matter</u> will be highly appreciated.

attention to this matter cooperation kind consideration.

- We look forward to the pleasure of serving you.
- We hope this will meet your immediate attention.
- We <u>await</u> your prompt reply.

> *await*
> *are waiting for*
> *are expecting*
> *are looking forward to*

- We are hoping to hear from you soon.
- We will appreciate your prompt reply by e-mail.
- We hope to receive your reply by return mail, and trust we can do business to our mutual benefit.
- We hope that this opportunity will lead us to a prosperous business relationship in the future.
- We trust you will be interested in this proposal and hope that a mutually profitable relationship will soon be established.

2 인사장

- We are pleased to inform you that on the 1st of June, we established our company in this city as a dealer of electric car under the name of Hansung Company.
- We are pleased to inform you that we have opened a Tokyo branch office on May 1, 2021, which enables a steady supply in the market.
- For the convenience of our customers, we have decided to open a new branch in Paris, and have appointed Mr. H. S. Lee as our manager.
- We are pleased to inform you that we will open a Tokyo branch office on Monday, August 27, 2021 in an effort to improve our service to you.
- We have entrusted the management of the branch to Mr. J. J. Kim, who is thoroughly familiar with all details of trade management.
- We have pleasure in announcing that, <u>as of</u> the 1st of May, our two firms of SG Co., Ltd. and Samil Company will <u>be amalgamated</u> under the name of SS Co., Ltd.

as of on and after	be amalgamated be merged be combined

- We are pleased to inform you that we have recently moved to the above address. We hope to be favored with your inquiries and also hope that all communication will be sent to us at the new address.

communication correspondence

- The change of the company name will entail no changes in personnel or business operations.

Standard
Trade
English

신용조회

무역업무의 주요 내용

1 신용조회의 의의

새로운 거래선과 거래를 하게 될 때는 반드시 그에 대한 신용조사를 하게 된다. 국제상거래에는 신용상의 위험이 매우 크기 때문에 거래상대방의 신용에 대한 철저한 조사와 분석이 필요하다. 국제거래에서는 상대방의 신용상태 파악이 더 어려울 뿐만 아니라 신용사고가 발생하면 국내거래에서 보다 훨씬 큰 어려움에 직면하게 되고 결국 치명적인 손실을 입을 수 있기 때문이다.

2 신용의 평가와 조사 내용

일반적으로 조사대상 기업의 신용상태를 판단하는 주요 요소로서 3C′s라고 하여 Character, Capital, Capacity를 평가의 중요한 요소로 둔다.
① Character : 회사의 연혁 및 사업성격, 경영자의 성실성, 계약이행자세, 평판
② Capital : 자산, 부채 등의 재정상황
③ Capacity : 거래량, 영업영역, 시장점유율 등의 영업능력
여기에 4C′s 라고 하면 이상의 3C′s에 상대국의 정치, 경제적 상황을 의미하는 Condition이 추가된다. 또, Collateral(담보능력), Currency(통화가치), Country(소속국가) 등의 요소를 추가하여 여러 가지 C′s를 설정하기도 한다.

3 신용조회의 방법

신용조회는 자신의 해외지사나 대리점 등 기존의 해외영업망을 이용할 수도 있다. 그러나 이러한 내부적인 정보망이 없어 외부의 기관을 이용할 때 상대기업과 거래하는 현지의 은행이나 회사에 조회하게 된다. 이 때, 은행에 하는 조회를 은행조회(Bank Reference)라 하고 회사에 하는 조회를 동업자조회(Trade Reference)라 한다.

또, 신용에 대한 조사와 평가를 보다 전문적으로 하는 신용보증기금, 수출보험공사, 대한무역투자진흥공사, Dun and Bradstreet Inc.와 같은 신용조사평가 전문기관에 조회할 수도 있다.

무역영문통신의 주요 사항

1 신용조회

　신용조회의 서신은 상대회사의 거래은행 또는 상대회사와 거래경험이 있는 업자에게 내는 경우가 일반적이다. 은행조회는 비교적 객관적인 반면, 동업자조회는 주관적 경험에 의존하고 같은 업자에 대해 호의적으로 회신하기 쉽다는 점을 감안하여 객관적인 신용평가요소에 기초하여 자신이 잘 판단하여야 한다.

　조회회신 내용에 대해 회신자에게 책임을 물을 수 없으며, 또 의뢰자는 받은 정보에 대해서 비밀을 지켜야 하고, 당해 거래목적 외에 사용해서는 안 된다는 일반적인 관례 속에서 조회와 회신을 하게 됨을 염두에 두어야 한다.

2 신용조회 서신

　신용조회를 의뢰하는 조회장은 상대방이 회신하기 쉽도록 간결하고 명료해야 한다. 회신용 질문지를 첨부하는 것도 하나의 방법이며, 반신용 봉투를 첨부하는 것이 좋다. 조회서신은 대개 다음과 같은 내용으로 구성된다.

　1. 조사하고자 하는 회사 및 주소
　2. 조사하는 이유
　3. 특히 알고 싶은 부분이 있는 경우에는 그에 대한 내용
　4. 회신내용에 대한 비밀엄수 약속
　5. 조사 비용에 대해서는 부담하겠다는 내용

3 신용조회 답신

　신용조회 답신은 신속하고 객관적이고 간결한 회신을 하는 것이 중요하다. 부정확한 정보나 불필요한 내용을 포함시키지 않도록 해야 한다.

　신용조회 답신은 대개 다음과 같은 내용으로 구성된다.

　1. 기업에 대한 객관적인 정보
　2. 알고 있는 대로의 해당기업에 대한 평판 및 자사의 의견
　3. 회신내용에 대한 책임은 지지 않는다는 내용
　4. 회신내용의 비밀취급 요청
　5. 도움이 되길 바란다는 취지의 맺음말

C1 은행신용조회

SM Company, Inc.

4501, 45th Floor, Trade Tower
511 Yeongdong-daero, Kangnam-gu, Seoul, Korea 06164

April 2, 2021

International Trade Dept.
CBA Bank
1133 Park Avenue
New York, NY 10017 U.S.A.

Gentlemen:

Your bank has been given as a reference by the following company, in their proposal to open a new business connection with us.

SEMTECH Corporation
1224 Park Avenue
New York, NY 10016 U.S.A.

We would be much obliged if you would furnish us with such information as you may deem necessary for us to evaluate their credit worthiness.

We are particularly interested in knowing what line of business they are mainly engaged in and, if possible, your candid opinion regarding their financial responsibility, their mode of doing business, and the reputation they enjoy in your community. We would also be grateful for any other pertinent information you could furnish us.

Please be assured that any information you may give us will be held in strict confidence, and any expenses to be incurred in connection with this inquiry will be gladly paid by us upon receipt of your bill.

We would very much appreciate it if you would give prompt attention to this matter.

Yours very truly,

내용 한국의 SM사가 미국의 CBA은행에게 미국 SEMTECH 회사의 신용조회를 의뢰하는 내용이다.

• 주요 용어 및 표현 •

- referencc : 조회처, 문의처, 참조처
- the following company : 다음의 회사
- proposal : 제의, 제안
- be obliged : 감사하다(be appreciated).
- furnish us with ~ : 우리에게 ~을 제공하다(=supply us with, give us).
- may deem necessary : 필요하다고 생각하는
- to evaluate : 평가하다.
- credit worthiness : 신뢰성
- line of business : 업종
- are mainly engaged in : 주로 종사하는
- if possible : 가능하다면
- candid opinion : 솔직한 의견
- financial responsibility : 재무적인 책임감, 재무적 지불능력, 재정적 신뢰성, 여기서 responsibility는 주로 지불능력을 의미한다.
- mode of doing business : 사업운영방식(=way of doing business)
- community : 같은 업계, 지역사회 공동체
- pertinent information : 관련 정보
- Please be assured that ~ : ~에 대해서는 안심해도 좋다. ~를 꼭 하겠다.
- be held in strict confidence : 엄격한 비밀로 지키겠다(=be treated in(as) strict confidence, be kept as strict confidence).
- in connection with ~ : ~와 관련하여
- upon receipt of your bill : 청구서를 받는 즉시
- prompt attention : 신속한 배려, 즉석의 조치

C2 은행신용조회 답신

CBA Bank
1133 Park Avenue
New York, NY 10017 U.S.A.

April 30, 2021

SM Company, Inc.
511 Yeongdong-daero, Kangnam-gu
Seoul, Korea 06164

Gentlemen: RE : SEMTECH Corporation

As per your request of April 2nd, 2021, we are pleased to furnish you with the following summary of SEMTECH Corp.

The company you inquired of is one of the most well established firms within their industry here in the U.S.A. Commencing operation in 1970 as manufacturers of electronic appliances, the company has been doing business on a large scale and has many good business relations both at home and abroad.

They have had an account with us since December, 1970. Since then we have been maintaining an excellent business relationship with them to our complete satisfaction. The managing staff of the company is well-known to us and we have high confidence in their character, integrity, and financial responsibility.

We consider that SEMTEC Corp. is a respectable company of good standing and quite reliable for normal business engagements.

We wish it to be understood that the above information is supplied confidentially without any responsibility on our part and any opinion expressed herein is subject to change without notice.

We trust this information will prove helpful and assure you of our pleasure in being of assistance.

Yours very truly,

내용 한국의 SM사가 요청한 미국 SEMTECH 회사에 대한 신용조회에 대하여 미국 CBA은행이 회신하고 있는 내용이다.

• 주요 용어 및 표현 •

- as per ~ : ~에 대해서(=in compliance with, according to)
- summary : 요약
- operations : 사업운영, 사업(=business)
- good business relations : 좋은 거래관계(=good business relationship, excellent business relations, cordial business relations)
  좋은 정도 : fair(괜찮은) < good(좋은) < excellent(매우 좋은)
- to our complete satisfaction : 우리는 아주 만족하여, 우리가 만족스럽게
- character : 인격, 품성. character는 도덕적, 윤리적인 측면을 중심으로 하는 반면, personality는 신체적, 정신적, 감정적 측면을 중심으로 하는 성격 또는 인격을 의미한다.
- integrity : 성실성, 진실성
- we consider that ~ : 우리의 의견으로는 ~하다(=in our opinion).
- company of good standing : 이름 있는 회사, 명망 있는 회사
- quite reliable : 아주 믿을 만한(=very reliable)
- normal business engagement : 통상적인 거래약속, 일반적인 거래
- ~ is supplied without responsibility on our part : 정보에 대해 제공자가 책임지지 않음을 표현하는 대표적인 문구이다. 같은 의미의 문구로서 we assume no responsibility in ~ / we are not responsible for ~도 사용된다.
- confidentially : 대외비로, 비밀로(=privately, secretly)
- ~ is subject to change without notice : 변동적이고 현재까지에 대한 것이며 이후의 것에 대해서는 자신이 알게 되어도 통보하지 않겠다는 것이다.
- opinion expressed herein : 여기에 밝힌 의견, 여기서 표명한 의견
- prove helpful : 도움되기를
- our pleasure in being of assistance : 도움이 되었으면 기쁘겠습니다.

⊞ C3 동업자신용조회

SM Company, Inc.

4501, 45th Floor, Trade Tower
511 Yeongdong-daero, Kangnam-gu, Seoul, Korea 06164

April 10, 2021

ANC Co., Ltd
32 Walker Street, North Sydney,
N.S.W. 2060 Australia

Gentlemen:

We have recently received an order for US$ 50,000 worth of our products on a D/A basis from Jason Co. which is located in your city. They have given us your company as a reference.

We would appreciate it if you will kindly furnish us with information regarding the means and standing of the above mentioned firm. Furthermore, we wish to know whether, in your opinion, they would qualify for credit of US$ 50,000.

You may be assured that any information you may furnish us will be used with all discretion and that we should be pleased to reciprocate a similar service for you if the occasion arises.

Yours very truly,

내용 SM사가 호주 Jason회사와 같은 업계에 있는 호주의 ANC사에게 Jason회사의 신용상태에 대한 동업자조회를 의뢰하는 서신이다.

• 주 요 용 어 및 표 현 •

- on a D/A basis : D/A 조건으로
- the means and standing : 자력과 명망, 재산과 명성
- above mentioned firm : 상기 회사, 위에 언급한 회사
- would qualify for ~ : ~할 자격이 있는, ~해도 괜찮은(＝would prove good for ~)
- credit of US$ 50,000 : 50,000달러의 외상판매
- any information you may furnish us : 당신이 제공해주는 어떠한 정보도
- with discretion : 신중하게, 분별 있게, 주의하면서(＝with caution, with care)
- reciprocate a similar service : 같은 서비스로 보답하다. 상대회사가 우리 회사에 신용조회를 요청하는 경우에 우리도 기꺼이 해주겠다는 뜻
- if the occasion arises : 기회가 있으면, 기회가 주어진다면

✓	금액(2. 문자표시)

1. 금액을 문자로 표기할 때는 읽는 대로 쓴다.
2. 화폐단위는 앞 또는 뒤에 쓴다.
3. 영수증, 어음과 같이 금액을 정확하게 표현해야 하는 경우는 숫자표기와 문자표기를 동시에 하는 경우가 많다. 이 때 문자표기 금액의 앞에는 "SAY"를, 뒤에는 "ONLY"를 붙인다. 즉, "SAY"는 우리나라의 "일금", 또는 "금"에 해당하고 "ONLY"는 "정"에 해당한다.

   예 ₩ 25,142(일금 이만 오천 일백 사십 이원 정)
   US$ 25,142.50(US Dollars SAY Twenty-Five Thousand, One Hundred Forty-Two And Cents Fifty ONLY)

   or

   US$ 25,142.50(SAY Twenty-Five Thousand, One Hundred Forty-Two US Dollars And Fifty Cents ONLY)

4. 착오로 문자표시와 아라비아숫자표시를 다르게 표시한 경우에는 일반적으로 문자표시가 우선적 효력을 갖는다.

⊞ C4 동업자신용조회 답신

ANC Co., Ltd
32 Walker Street, North Sydney,
N.S.W. 2060 Australia

April 29, 2021

SM Company, Inc.
4501, 45th Floor, Trade Tower
511 Yeongdong-daero, Kangnam-gu
Seoul, Korea 06164

Gentlemen:

We are writing in response to your letter dated April 10th inquiring about Jason Co. which had furnished us as a reference to you.

At this time we are sorry to say that our transactions with this firm have been so small and infrequent that we are not in a position to make any recommendations regarding their financial standing and creditworthiness one way or the other.

Once again, we regret that we could not furnish you with any concrete information that may encourage you to commence doing business with them.

If you feel we may be of further assistance, please don't hesitate to ask.

Sincerely yours,

내용 한국의 SM사가 요청한 호주 Jason회사에 대한 신용조회에 대하여 호주의 ANC사가 회신하고 있는 내용이다.

• 주요 용어 및 표현 •

- We are writing in response to your letter dated ~

  =In response to your letter of ~

  =As per your letter of reference inquiry dated ~

- furnished us as a reference to you : 당신회사에게 우리 회사를 조회처로 제시한

- infrequent : 드문, 좀처럼 없는

- be not in a position to ~ : ~할 입장이 아닌

- furnish you with ~ : ~를 제공하다(=supply you with ~, give you ~).

- financial standing : 재정상태, 재무능력(=financial status, financial position)

- creditworthiness : 신용도, 신뢰성(=trustworthiness, reliability)

- one way or the other : 어떻게 해서더라도

- concrete information : 구체적인 정보

- encourage : 권하다. 격려하다. 조장하다.

- commence : 시작하다.

- we may be of further assistance : 우리가 더 도움이 될 수 있다면, 우리가 더 도와줄 일이 있으면

- please don't hesitate to ask : 주저 마시고 물어 보십시오. 어려워 마시고 물으세요.

✓	금액(3. 통화표시)

금액에는 반드시 통화표시를 해야한다. $의 경우는 $를 통화이름으로 하는 국가가 많으므로 국제시장에서는 다음과 같이 구분한다.

US$(미국)	C$(캐나다)	R$(브라질),
A$(오스트레일리아)	HK$(홍콩)	M$(말레이지아)
T$(타이완)	NZ$(뉴질랜드)	S$(싱가포르)

Useful Expressions

① 신용조회 의뢰

📖 서두

- Asia Company has referred us to your bank.

> Asia Company has referred us to your bank
> Your bank has been referred to us by Asia Company.
> Your bank has been given as a reference by Asia Company.
> Asia Company named you as a reference
> Asia Company has given your name as a reference

- Messrs. Brown & Co. of your city has given us your name as a reference.

> of your city
> located in your city
> in your city

> your name
> your bank

- Your bank was given as a reference by SAS Co. which wishes to enter into business relations with us.

> wishes to
> desires to

- GMS Co., Ltd. desires to open an account with us, and has given us your address as a reference.

> desires / is desirous of ~ing
> is anxious of ~ing
> approached with a view to

> open an account with
> enter into business relations with

- I would be much obliged if you would obtain information to the present financial position of the firm named on the attached slip.

📄 신용정보 요청

- Would you please <u>furnish us with</u> information regarding their financial standing?

furnish us with
supply us with
give us

- Would you please inform us <u>confidentially</u> of your opinion <u>as to</u> their <u>financial standing?</u>

confidentially	as to	financial standing
privately	about	financial status
in confidence	regarding	reliability
in private	concerning	solvency

- We would be very grateful if you would let us have the following information.
- Please inform us in confidence your opinion regarding their financial standing.
- We will very much appreciate it if you would give us such information as their capital assets and liabilities, turnover, and number of employees.
- We will be grateful for any information you can give us.
- As we are at the point of transacting some important business with them, we would like to know exactly how their credit stands.
- Will you kindly inform us if, in your opinion, we may safely credit them, say, to the extent of US$ 50,000?
- <u>Please inform us</u> objectively of <u>your opinion</u> as to their <u>business integrity</u> and <u>mode of doing business.</u>

		business integrity
		trustworthiness
Please inform us		reputation
Would you please advise us	your opinion	reality
Would you please inform us	your objective view	

> *mode of doing business*
> *way of doing business*

▤ 비용부담 의사 표시

- Any expenses connected with this inquiry will be promptly paid by us <u>upon receipt of your bill.</u>

> *upon receipt of your bill*
> *as soon as we receive your bill*

- Please charge to our account any expenses connected with this inquiry.
- Any expenses will be gladly paid upon receipt of your bill.

▤ 동일한 보답 의사표시

- We shall be glad to <u>reciprocate</u> the courtesy <u>on any similar occasion.</u>

| *reciprocate*
return | *on any similar occasion.*
should a similar occasion occur |

- It will be a pleasure for us <u>to</u> <u>do</u> a similar service for you at any time.

| *it will be a pleasure for us to*
we shall be pleased to
we will be pleased to
we shall be happy to | *do*
render |

- If at any time we can assist you with information, we shall welcome the opportunity.
- We will be pleased to reciprocate your courtesy.
- We will be of a similar service to you when requested.
- We will be pleased to render you a similar service <u>upon request.</u>

> *upon request*
> *when requested*

- Please avail yourself of our service on a similar occasion.
- We shall be pleased at any time to be able to render you a like service.

▣ 비밀엄수 약속

- Any information you may give us will be kept absolutely confidential.
- <u>Any information</u> will <u>be held in strict confidence.</u>

| Any information | be held in strict confidence |
Any information	be held in strict confidence
All information	be kept in strict confidence
Any information you can give us	be treated as strictly confidential

- Your reply will, of course, be treated in strict confidence.

▣ 맺음말

- We assure you of our sincere <u>thanks</u> and absolute confidence.

thanks
gratitude

- Please accept our thanks in advance <u>for any help you can give us.</u>

for any help you can give us
for your assistance in this matter

- We thank you in anticipation for your reply, and assure you that we shall be pleased at any time to be able to render you a like service.
- We hope to receive a favorable reply by return mail.
- Your kind cooperation will be greatly appreciated.
- We would highly appreciate your kind assistance.
- We thank you for your cooperation in advance and await your reply.

② 신용조회에 대한 답신

🔲 서두

- In reply to your inquiry of May 1, we have the pleasure of supplying you with the following information.

In reply to	of supplying you with
In reference to	of furnishing you with
In response to	of giving you

- We are pleased to report on the firm referred to in your letter of May 7 as follows:
- In reference to your credit inquiry of March 12, we welcome the opportunity to report favorably on Pacific Trading Co., Ltd.
- We regret to say that we are unable to give favorable information regarding the firm referred to in your letter of May 10.
- We regret that we cannot give as favorable a report as we would like to give.
- In response to your inquiry about Mr. Brown's financial standing, we regret to inform you that our reply must be in the nature of a warning.
- This is a strictly confidential reply to a request made by your firm.

🔲 조회대상회사의 현황

- The company you inquired about was established in 1980 as a distributor of electronic appliances.
- They operate as an importer and exporter of various types of goods, trading principally with Japan and China.
- Their annual sales are estimated in the amount of US$ 30,000,000 and their payments have been often made irregularly.
- Officers of the company are : James Baker, President, who is well regarded

in the trade ; Harry Hoof, vice-president, who was formerly associated with the NIT company. The founder of the company was John Smith who passed away a few years ago.

📄 신용이 좋은 경우

■ We have done good business with this company for more than seven years, and consider it to be amongst our most valuable clients.

have done good business with have had good relations with	clients customers

■ They are enjoying a good reputation within business circles for their punctuality for meeting obligations.

a good reputation an excellent reputation an absolute confidence	business circles the business world the business community

■ We have every confidence to recommend to you the firm you inquire about as one of the most reliable importers in our district.

reliable reputable creditable

■ According to our records, they have never failed to meet our bills since they opened an account with us.

According to our records, they ~ Our records show that they ~

■ The company is composed of men of integrity and responsibility.

integrity honesty

- They deserve their reputation for <u>reliability</u> as businessmen.

reliability
trustworthiness

- The firm is highly esteemed.
- The balance with the bank has averaged in the low nine-figures,[1] and the account has always been handled in a satisfactory manner.
- They have always paid their account regularly, and we would not hesitate at all to extend to them credit for the amount you mention.
- The firm enjoys <u>an excellent reputation in</u> the business circles here.

an excellent reputation	*in*
an absolute confidence	*among*
an almost unlimited credit	*within*

- The firm carries on a substantial business and the owners are known to us to be reliable, and liabilities have been met regularly and punctually.
- The firm has maintained a current account with us for more than ten years always to our satisfaction and its latest financial statements are enclosed for your information.
- As far as we know, they are sound enough, but we have no certain knowledge of their true financial position.

신용이 좋지 않은 경우

- We regret that we have to give you unfavorable information about the firm.
- We regret to inform you that the company is known to be in poor financial condition.
- They are said to be slow in settling their bills.

---

1) 1, 2억원대. nine-figures는 아홉자리 숫자, 즉 억대를 의미하고, low는 억대 중 낮은 수준의 억대를 뜻한다. 이같이 수치를 대략적으로 표현할 때 다음과 같은 단어를 사용한다.
   1, 2 : low   3, 4 : moderate   5, 6 : medium   7, 8, 9 : high

- You would run some risk entering into a credit transaction with it.
- We would therefore hesitate to extend credit for the amount you mentioned.
- The firm in question has recently suffered heavy losses, so it would be advisable for you to take every precaution in dealing with it.
- If the report in circulation is true, they are losing considerable reputation.
- He has caused us considerable trouble with respect to his payment.
- We had to press him for payment many times, and once we were obliged to take legal proceedings to recover his debts.
- We would advise cash transactions only.
- We would advise you to proceed with caution in your dealings with the firm in question.
- We still remember the bitter experience we had with the company regarding its settlement of account.

알지 못하는 경우

- We cannot understand why this gentleman should refer you to us.
- We are sorry that we cannot give you sufficient information regarding the credit standing of the firm.
- Our relation with the firm is small, so we cannot give you an accurate opinion.
- We regret our inability to inform you of anything concerning the firm mentioned.

> mentioned
> in question

- We are very sorry that we are unable to give you the information you require.
- We are sorry to express our inability to assist you in this matter.
- It would be advisable for you to instruct an inquiry agency to investigate the matter.

📋 조회비용의 청구

■ Enclosed please find our statement of the expenses connected with this inquiry.

■ A debit note for this reply is enclosed and we shall be glad to receive it by T/T.

■ We hand you our account on the expenses connected with inquiry, amounting to US$ 500, which kindly pass to our credit.

📋 신용제공자의 면책

■ This information is for your own use only and without any responsibility.

> *any responsibility*
> *any assumption of responsibility*

■ We supply you with this information for your files only and without any responsibility on the part of our bank.

■ We decline all personal responsibility.

■ We cannot be held responsible in this matter.

■ This is, of course, without assumption of responsibility on our part.

■ Please note that this information is furnished without any responsibility on our part.

> | *furnished* *given* | *on our part* *by us* *on the part of our company* |

■ Any statement on the part of this bank or any of its officers as to the standing of any person, firm, or corporation, is given as a mere matter of opinion for which no responsibility, in any way, is attached to this bank or any of its officers.[2]

---

2) 개인, 상사, 또는 법인의 신용 상태에 관하여 은행 또는 그 직원이 말씀드리는 것은 단지 하나의 의견에 지나지 않습니다. 당행 또는 그 직원은 이에 대해서 어떠한 책임도 지지 않습니다.

🗐 비밀준수 요청

- This information is private and confidential for your use only.
- No mention of our name should be made with regards to this matter.
- Please use this confidential information with every discretion.
- This information is given in strict confidence, and entirely without prejudice and no assumptions of responsibility by us.
- We ask you to consider this information as given in strict confidence.

🗐 맺음말

- We hope this information will be helpful to you.

> will be helpful to you
> will be satisfactory and of good service to you

- We shall be pleased to render you any further services.

> render
> give

- We are hoping that this information will be helpful to you and assure you of our cooperation at all times.
- We wish our reply will be helpful and of service to you.
- We are sorry we cannot give you as favorable a report as we would like to.
- We hope to be better able to assist you on the occasion of your next inquiry.
- We regret our inability to assist you in this matter.

Standard
Trade
English

매매거래의
권유 및 조회

무역업무의 주요 내용

① 거래의 권유와 조회

거래 권유 및 조회는 특정상품을 대상으로 거래를 권유하고 문의하는 것이다. 거래관계의 권유 및 조회와 개별상품거래의 권유 및 조회는 같이 이루어 질 수 있기 때문에 실무적으로 명확히 구분되지는 않는다. 그러나 무역 영어에서는 구분하는 것이 편리하므로 앞 단원의 거래관계의 권유 및 조회와 본단원을 구분하여 여기서는 상품거래의 권유 및 조회를 중심으로 다룬다.

② 거래의 권유

상품거래의 권유는 적극적인 거래관계의 제의이다. 상품거래의 권유는 하나 혹은 몇몇 특정인에게 보내거나 불특정 다수인을 대상으로 하게 되며 그 대표적인 것이 Sales Letter(상품판촉장)이다. Sales Letter에서는 독자로 하여금 자신이 원하는 대로 행동하도록 만들어야 한다는 점에서 독자의 심리와 행동방식을 염두에 두고 설득력 있게 작성되어야 효과를 발휘할 수 있다.

③ 거래의 조회

상품거래의 조회는 상품과 거래조건에 관하여 문의하는 것이다. 조회는 때에 따라 Sales Letter와 같은 거래의 권유를 비롯한 매도자 측의 조회도 포함된다. 즉, 거래에 대한 문의나 제의를 매수인이 할 때는 buying inquiry라고 하고 매도인이 할 때는 selling inquiry라 한다. 또, offer 이전의 모든 교섭단계를 조회라고 부르기도 한다. 따라서 조회를 크게 보면 그 범위가 매우 넓다.

그러나 조회는 매수인이 매도인에 대하여 하는 경우가 많으므로 일반적으로 buying inquiry만을 조회라고 부른다. 조회는 거래성립을 위한 중요한 계기가 되기 때문에 조회를 받는 상대방은 회신과 함께 샘플, 카탈로그, 가격표 등의 자료를 제공하거나 offer를 내어 거래를 진전시켜 나가게 된다.

1 Sales Letter

Sales Letter는 단순한 의사전달이 아니라 설득력 있는 글이어야 한다. 그래서 앞에서 본 AIDA, ABCD와 같은 원칙이 특히 중요하게 된다. 즉 자신의 입장에서 일방적으로 호소하기 보다는 상대방의 입장에서 이득이 되는 점을 들어 이해시키도록 해야 한다. Sales Letter에는 대개 다음과 같은 내용이 포함된다.

1. 상대방을 알게 된 경로, 2. 희망하는 거래의 내용, 3. 자사에 대한 소개, 4. 자사제품의 내용과 우수한 점의 소개, 5. catalog, sample 등을 동봉하거나, catalog, sample 또는 offer를 보낼 수 있다는 내용, 6. 자사에 대한 신용조회처의 제시

2 조회장

조회는 상대방이 회답해야 할 사항이 무엇인지 쉽게 빨리 알 수 있도록 명확하고 간략하게 작성한다. 그렇게 해야만 원하는 답변을 받기 쉽고 회답을 받을 가능성도 높아지게 된다. inquiry에는 대개 다음과 같은 사항이 포함된다.

1. 상대방을 알게 된 경로, 2. 자사에 대한 소개, 3. 문의사항 또는 자료의 요청

3 조회에 대한 답신

조회답신은 신속하고 친절해야 한다. 상품의 과장선전보다 객관적인 평가 속에 장점을 알리며, 거래를 할 수 없는 경우라도 좋은 인상으로 다음의 거래기회를 남기도록 한다. 조회에 대한 답신은 대개 다음과 같은 내용이 포함된다.

1. 조회에 대한 감사표현, 2. 문의사항에 대한 회답 내용, 3. 상품과 거래조건에 관해서 전문적인 지식에 기초하여 명확하게 제시, 4. catalog, sample의 동봉 사실, 5. 상품공급을 못할 경우 대안 제시, 6. 거래성사 및 빠른 답신 기대 표시, 또는 상품공급 못할 경우는 차후의 거래희망 표시

⊞ D1 제품조회

AMS Trading Company

908 Park Avenue
New York, NY 10017 U.S.A.

April 15, 2021

SM Company, Inc.
4501, 45th Floor, Trade Tower
511 Yeongdong-daero, Kangnam-gu
Seoul, Korea 06164

Dear Mr. Kim:

We are interested in your new model Sound Systems GA-33T you advertised in the April 1 issue of "Electronics World".

We would like to have your quotation for this article together with a catalog and a descriptive literature for it. At the same time please let us have the terms of trade in detail including the earliest shipping date, discount policy, and minimum order quantity.

If your prices are competitive and other conditions are acceptable, you can be assured of our repeated orders in the near future.

We look forward to your early reply.

Very truly yours,

내용 AMS Trading사가 잡지에서 SM사 신제품의 광고를 보고 거래조건에 대하여 조회하고 있다.

• 주 요 용 어 및 표 현 •

- April 1 issue of "Electronic World" : "전자세계" 4월 1일호
- quotation : 가격, 시세, 견적
- descriptive literature : 설명서 cf) illustrated catalog(그림이 있는 카탈로그) 회사 및 상품의 안내인쇄물로는 다음과 같은 용어들이 큰 구분 없이 사용된다.

  literature : 인쇄물

  catalog : 제품의 목록을 담은 인쇄물

  booklet : 소책자

  brochure : 업무안내 등의 소책자

  pamphlet : 소책자

- discount policy : 할인정책, 할인제도(=discount schedule)
- terms of trade : 넓은 의미로는 거래 전반의 조건을 의미하고 좁은 의미로는 가격조건을 의미한다.
- minimum order quantity : 최소주문수량
- you can be assured of our repeated orders : 당신은 계속적인 주문을 보장받는다. 즉, 우리가 계속적으로 주문하겠다.
- in the near future : 가까운 장래에, soon이 수 시간, 수 일, 수 주의 단기임에 비해 수 주, 수 개월, 수 년의 장기적 의미 내포

✓	품질에 대한 표현
최상등품	extra fine article / extra-superfine article / highest quality / finest quality / most excellent quality
상 등 품	first grade(class/rate) article / fine quality / superior quality
중 등 품	medium goods / common goods / usual goods / second class goods / average / fair average quality(FAQ)
열 등 품	inferior article / low grade goods / bad goods / poor goods / low goods / third class goods / inferior quality / below standard

D2 제품조회에 대한 답신

SM Company, Inc.

4501, 45th Floor, Trade Tower
511 Yeongdong-daero, Kangnam-gu, Seoul, Korea 06164

May 10, 2021

AMS Trading Company
908 Park Avenue
New York, NY 10017 U.S.A.

Gentlemen:

Thank you for your letter of April 15 inquiring about our Sound System GA-33T. We are glad to hear that you have learned about our new products through the magazine advertisement.

The model GA-33T is far advanced in quality compared to other models by adapting new technology, and is one of our articles which has a good reputation all over the world at present.

We are enclosing for you a complete set of descriptive literature and a catalog for our Sound System, along with a copy of our latest price list.

We can ship one month after receipt of an irrevocable letter of credit. We offer a 5% discount for orders of over 500 sets. Our minimum order quantity is 50 sets. In addition, we can allow you a cash discount of 3% off the total amount if payment is made by T/T on or before delivery.

If you have any questions or need more information, please let us know. We look forward to hearing from you soon.

Very truly yours,

내용 SM사가 자사의 신제품광고를 보고 문의를 해온 AMS Trading사의 조회
에 대하여 거래조건을 답신하는 내용이다.

• 주요 용어 및 표현 •

- a complete set of : 전체 세트(＝a full set of, an entire set of)
- descriptive literature : 설명서
- latest price list : 최신 가격표(＝recent price list)
- after receipt of : 수령 후(＝upon receipt of)
- offer a 5% discount : 5% 할인을 제공하다
  "정상 가격 100달러에서 5%를 할인해 주겠습니다"는 "offer a discount of 5%
  off the regular price of US$ 100"로 한다.
- over 500 sets : 500세트 이상
- minimum order quantity : 최소주문수량
- allow you a cash discount of 3% off the total amount : 현금지불의 경우 총
  액에서 3% 할인을 제공하다.
- quantity discount : 수량할인, 일정수량 이상의 대량구매에 대한 할인
- cash discount : 현금할인, 현금구매에 대한 할인
- 할인의 용어는 discount, lowering, reduction 등이 사용된다. 그 외 allowance
  (파손, 품질미달 등의 보상으로 할인), deduction(총액에서 공제) 등이 있다.
- T/T : telegraphic transfer, 전신환, 전신에 의한 외환송금
- on or before delivery : 인도 전이나 인도 시에

✓	할인에 대한 표현

to discount a price / to make a discount off a price / to allow a discount on
the price / to reduce a price / to make a reduction in price / to abate a price /
to rebate a price / lower a price / cut down a price /bring down a price /
make it cheaper / knock off / take off

⊞ D3 제품조회

Asia Trading Company

212 Yoi-daero, Youngdeungpo-gu
Seoul, Korea 07325

May 2, 2021

NPN Company, Ltd.
12-1, Marunouchi, 3-Chome
Chiyoda-Ku, Tokyo, Japan

Gentlemen:

We would appreciate it if you would send us an estimate for a supply of approximately 1,000 units of NPN MONITOR 531F.

The prices quoted should include delivery to here, Seoul, Korea, and please state 1) the earliest possible date of deliver, 2) discount allowable, 3) minimum order quantity, and 4) warranty period.

Please send us the information immediately so that we will be able to place an order no later than June 10.

Very truly yours,

내용 Asia Trading사가 일본의 NPN사에 대하여 MONITOR 1,000개에 대한 견적을 요청하는 내용이다.

• 주요 용어 및 표현 •

- estimate : 견적서(quotation)

  quotation도 같은 의미이나 estimate는 어림잡아 산정하는 의미가 있다.

- approximately : 대략, 약(=about, around, circa, cir., c.)

- the earliest possible date of delivery : 가능한 가장 이른 선적일

- discount allowable : 가능한 할인, 허용되는 할인

- no later than ~ : ~ 이전에(=not later than)

✓	상품, 물품, 화물
goods	상품, 화물, 물품, 물자, 재화, 동산, 자재(가장 넓은 의미로 사용)
	high quality goods 고급품 / finished goods 완제품 / ad valorem goods 종가품 / standard goods 표준품 / seasonal goods 계절품 / sundry goods(miscellaneous goods, general goods) 잡화 / proceed goods 가공품 / household goods 가정용품 / domestic goods 국산품
article	물품, 품
	necessary article 필수품 / first grade article 상등품 / coarse article 조잡품 / domestic article 국산품 / household article 가정용품
merchandise	집합적인 의미의 상품(특히 공산품)
	general merchandise 잡화 / merchandise warehouse 상품창고
commodity	상품, 물품, 물자, 물산(특히 곡물, 식료품 등 일차상품)
	commodity broker 상품브로커 / commodity market 상품시장
produce	물산, 물자, 작물, 산출물(특히 농산품 등 산출된 물자)
	produce broker 상품브로커 / field produce 농작물
product	산출물, 생산물, 제작품, 제품, 작품
	industrial products 공업제품 / agricultural products 농산물 / foreign products 외제 / natural products 천연산품
ware	제품, 세공품, 상품, 물품(합성어로 잘 사용됨)
	hardware 철물 / handmade ware 수제품 / ceramic ware 도자기 / woodenware 목기 / tableware 식기 / luxury ware 사치품
line	품목, 업종, 거래처, 노선
	line of business 업종 / grocery line 식료품상 / banking line 은행업 / airline 항공로

D4 제품조회에 대한 답신

NPN Company, Ltd.

12-1, Marunouchi, 3-Chome
Chiyoda-Ku, Tokyo, Japan

May 15, 2021

Asia Trading Company
212 Yoi-daero, Youngdeungpo-gu
Seoul, Korea 07325

Gentlemen:

Thank you very much for your inquiry for the supply of approximately 1,000 units of NPN MONITOR 531F. We are pleased to quote as follows:

Item : NPN MONITOR 531F
Payment : irrevocable L/C or T/T
Shipment : June
Destination : Seoul
Unit price : US$ 250
Warranty : 24 Months after Purchase

Please note that the above information is a statement of price only and not a firm offer.

We can ship by the beginning of June if you order by the end of this month. We are prepared to allow you a discount of 5% off the invoice value for cash, 2% if paid within 30 days, or net 60 days.

We thank you for your inquiry and look forward to receiving your order at an early date.

Very truly yours,

내용 NPN사가 Asia Trading사의 요청에 응하여 NPN MONITOR 1,000개에 대한 견적을 보내는 내용이다.

• 주요 용어 및 표현 •

- not a firm offer : 확정오퍼로서가 아니라
- by the beginning of June : 6월 초순까지
- by the end of this month : 이 달 말까지
- at an early date : 멀지 않아서
- to quote : 가격을 제시하다. 견적을 내다(＝to estimate).
- discount of 5% off the invoice value for cash, 2% if paid within 30 days, or net 60 days : 현금에 대해서는 송장가격의 5% 할인, 30일 내 지불에 대해서는 2% 할인, 60일 내 지불에 대해서는 무할인. 이는 다음과 같은 형식으로 표시할 수 있다.
  Price terms : 5% COD, 2% 30, net 60.
  여기서 COD는 cash on delivery 또는 collect on delivery, 즉 대금상환인도.

✓	가격의 오르내림에 대한 표현
가격을 내리다.	lower a price / lessen a price / cut down a price / bring down a price / beat down a price / knock down a price / cheapen a price / shave a price / come down on a price
가격을 올리다.	raise a price / increase a price
시장가격이 오르다.	the prices jump abnormally / the prices rise suddenly / the prices shoot up / the prices go up
시장가격이 내리다.	prices fall / prices go down / prices slump / prices decline heavily
가격을 결정하다.	quote a price 가격을 매기다. / make a price 값을 매기다. / fix a price 값을 정하다. / offer a price 값을 제의하다. / limit a price 값을 제한하다.

D5 제품소개

SM Company, Inc.

4501, 45th Floor, Trade Tower
511 Yeongdong-daero, Kangnam-gu, Seoul, Korea 06164

March 3, 2021

AMS Trading Company
908 Park Avenue
New York, NY 10017 U.S.A.

Gentlemen:

You will be pleased to hear that we have just introduced a new speaker. Our new DD-9920 mini speaker has achieved the goal of highest performance, and will be the first speaker to fully exploit the potential of digital audio system.

Our research team has finally solved the problems of sound quality that exists with mini speakers. The DD-9920 mini speaker ensures realistic and precise sound equal to that of large speakers, unlike other mini speakers in its price and size class.

As you have been placing steady orders for our audio systems, we thought you would be interested in this new model. With assurance that the DD-9920 will be one of best selling models in the mini speaker market before long, we recommend that you introduce this new item in your market.

We are enclosing a copy of the brochure showing detailed information about the DD-9920 mini speaker. We would be glad to furnish you with any additional information.

We look forward to your reply soon.

Very truly yours,

내용 SM사가 거래사인 AMS Trading사에 자사가 출시한 신제품을 소개하고 주문을 권유하는 내용이다.

• 주요 용어 및 표현 •

- highest performance : 최상 성능, 최고 성능
- fully exploit : 충분히 개발한, 완전히 개발된
- potential : 가능성, 잠재력
- digital audio system : 디지털방식의 음향장치
- come up with : 따라잡다. 고안하다.
- ensures : 보증하다. 확보하다.
- realistic and precise : 생생하고 정확한
- equal to ~ : ~에 상응하는
- size class : 동급, 같은 크기의
- place steady orders : 지속적으로 주문하다.
- with assurance : 확신을 갖고, 틀림없이
- to introduce this item : 이 제품을 도입하다. 들여오다. 처음으로 수입하다.
- additional information : 추가적인 정보, 더 많은 정보

✓	시장 동향에 대한 표현
상 승	strong(강세의) / bullish(상승하는) / advancing(전진하는) / stiff(오름세의) / improving(개선되고 있는)
하 락	weak(약세의) / bearish(약세의) / declining(완만한) / depressed(하강하는)
활 발 한	active(활발한) / animated(활기 있는) / brisk(활발한) / excited(활기 있는) / feverish(열광적인)
활기 없는	inactive(활발하지 않는) / flat(활기 없는) / slack(부진한) / sluggish(불경기의) / dead(침체한) / dull(침체한)
기 타	firm(견고한) / quiet(평온한) / unchanged(변하지 않는) / irregular(불규칙한) / panicky(공황 상태의)

🔲 D6 제품조회

AMS Trading Company
908 Park Avenue
New York, NY 10017 U.S.A.

April 12, 2021

SM Company, Inc.
4501, 45th Floor, Trade Tower
511 Yeongdong-daero, Kangnam-gu
Seoul, Korea

Gentlemen:

Thank you very much for your letter of March 3 along with the brochure of your new model DD-9920. Some of our customers have recently expressed interest in this item and inquired about its price.

From the description in your brochure we think that your new model may sell quite well if the price is competitive. Provided the price is right we are willing to place a test order for 10 gross.

We will appreciate it if you could make for us your best offer for the DD-9920 for the earliest possible shipment. We particularly stress the importance of price since the principal market here is not for the high quality goods at higher prices.

Very truly yours,

내용 AMS Trading사가 SM사의 신제품에 대하여 오퍼를 내줄 것을 요청하는 서신이다.

· 주 요 용 어 및 표 현 ·

- description : 설명, 해설
- new model sells well : 새 모델은 잘 팔린다(=new model enjoys a ready sale / new model is a good seller).
- provided the price is right : 가격이 적절하다면(=if the price is right)
- be willing to : 기꺼이 하다(=be ready to).
- test order : 시험주문(=pilot order).
- place an order : 주문을 하다(=furnish you with an order).
- gross : 12 dozen(144개). great gross는 12 gross(1,728개).
- make for us your best offer : 최상조건의 오퍼를 내주십시오.
- for the earliest possible shipment : 가장 빠른 선적
- principal market : 주종의 수요, 주종의 거래

✓	가격관련 표현
비싸다	expensive, dear, high, steep
싸다	cheap, inexpensive, moderate
중간이다	modest, moderate, affordable
높은 가격	high(highest) price / maximum price / excessive price / extravagant price / exorbitant price / unreasonable price / ridiculous price / absurd price / prohibitive price / padded price
중간 가격	moderate price / reasonable price / normal price / fair price / right price / usual price
낮은 가격	low(lowest) price / reduced price / minimum price / rock-bottom price / bed-rock price / popular price
기 타	competitive price 경쟁가격 / introductory price 보급가격 / favorable(handsome/fine/good/best) price 호가 / remunerative price 수지맞는 가격 / actual price 실제가격 / present price 현재가 / fixed price 정가 / list price 표기가격 / current price 시가 / tag price 정찰가 / cost price 원가 / spot price 현물가격 / credit price 외상가격 / contract price 계약가격 / special price 특가 / bid price 입찰가격, 매수호가 / offered price 매도호가 / firm price 확정가격 / wholesale price 도매가 / retail price 소매가 / unit price 단가

Useful Expressions

① 거래의 조회

📄 상대방을 알게 된 경위

- We have seen your advertisement in the "Electronics Journal" and would be glad to have your price lists and details of your terms.
- Your name has been given by the Seoul Chamber of Commerce & Industry and we would like to inquire whether you are interested in these lines.
- The British Consulate General in Seoul has recommended you to us, and we wish to know the monthly quantity of "MG #3" steel plate you could supply to us.
- While staying in Paris a week ago, I visited the Trade Fair there and was strongly impressed with the articles demonstrated in your booth.

📄 거래일반

- How soon can we expect your answer to our proposal?
- We are ready to give you a good deal.

> *give you a good deal*
> *make you a good bargain*

- We are especially interested in the computers exhibited at the May, 2021, Seoul Comdex, and would be glad to have full details of your export terms.

📄 상품문의

- When are you going to put out new model?

> *put out*
> *come out with*

- We would appreciate receiving full particulars of your "GGO" sedan.
- We are enclosing specifications and drawings of our gas gauge and ask you to submit your estimate with details including the possible time of shipment.
- Please inform us whether you are able to supply the articles as per the enclosed sample.
- We require 300 sets of steel cabinets approximately 30″ wide, 50″ high, and 30″ deep.
- We are interested in any type of auto accessories, and would be glad to have full details of your product.

가격조건

- We shall be grateful if you will quote us your lowest possible prices CIF Busan for the leather jackets.
- We would like to receive your <u>best quote on</u> your model K-123 color television.

> best quote on
> best price FOB L.A. for
> lowest quote CIF Busan for

- Would you please quote us for the following items:
- Please let us know by return e-mail your <u>best</u> <u>quotation</u> for 1,000 sets of color televisions.

> best
> lowest   quotation
> rock-bottom price

- Please quote us your lowest price based on CIF Busan for the following goods.
- We would appreciate your sending us your quotations.
- Please give us the best quotations possible for the goods.
- Your prices are too <u>steep</u> to be competitive in this market.

> *steep*
> *expensive*
> *high*

- The price is to include export packing in wooden cases.
- We effect insurance on your goods, and you may quote CFR Hamburg or FOB your port in U.S. Dollars.
- Please let us have your prices in US dollars for the model M-22 Color TV.
- Please quote prices CIF&C(3%) Bangkok as usual.

가격할인

- Can't you quote us anything cheaper?

> *quote us anything cheaper*
> *make it cheaper*
> *lower the prices*

- May we ask you for a 10% reduction in price?

> *May you allow us a 10% reduction in price?*
> *May you allow us a discount of 10% off the price?*
> *May you bring the price down by 10%?*

- How much discount can you offer if we purchase 1,000 more units?
- Do you make any allowance for large quantities?
- Please inform us what special discount you could allow us.
- Would you please give us your best discount off your list prices for this quantity?

인도시기문의

- When can we expect the delivery?
- Please let us know how soon you can deliver the goods.

> *let us know*   *deliver the goods*
> *inform us as to*   *execute the order*
> *advise us as to*   *fulfill the order*

- How long will it take for merchandise to arrive here after an order has been placed?
- Please inform us whether you can guarantee shipment by August 10 at the latest.
- Please let us know whether you can deliver within two weeks after receipt of our order.
- Please inform us of the earliest possible date you can effect shipment.

| the earliest possible date |
| the earliest time |

- We require the goods in the middle of March. Punctual shipment is essential.

수량

- We expect to obtain orders for at least 50,000 yds. of each item for shipment during August/September.
- We are highly interested in your brand-new S9 Phone, and are in a position to buy this item in large quantities.
- If you can supply us with goods of superior quality at reasonable prices, we are prepared to give you an order for 2,000 units.

| supply | superior | reasonable prices/competitive prices |
| furnish | excellent | satisfactory prices |

- As we expect a large demand for these products, we can place orders of a considerable size with you if your quality is exactly per sample and the price competitive enough.

As we expect a large demand	exactly per
As we anticipate a large demand	(right) up to
As there is a large demand	same as
	in accordance with

- As we are in a position to handle large quantities, we can place orders of a considerable size with you if your quality is right and the price competitive enough.

| *are in a position to* | *large quantities* |
| *are able to* | *considerable quantities* |

재고

- We need 2,000 dozen pencils, can you <u>fill</u> this order immediately?

| *fill* |
| *handle* |
| *take care of* |
| *accept* |
| *take up* |

- Will you please let us know whether you could supply these from <u>stock</u>. If you cannot, please inform us how long it would take to complete an order for the quantity required.

| *stock* |
| *inventory* |

- We received an inquiry for textiles and would be glad if you would send us the patterns of the qualities you have in stock.

카탈로그, 가격표 요청

- We will be very happy to receive your latest price list and catalog.
- Please let us have your price list.
- We would appreciate receiving your <u>illustrated catalog.</u>

| *illustrated catalog* |
| *descriptive literature* |

- We will be very happy if you would send us your present price list for electronic calculators and state your best terms.
- We would much appreciate it if you would send us a copy of your illustrated

catalog and a price list covering your men's suits to show our customers your latest models.

- We would <u>be pleased to</u> <u>receive</u> your <u>latest</u> catalog and price list for the laptop computer you advertised in the April 13th issue of Computer Magazine.

be pleased to be glad to	receive have	latest recent

- Please send us samples of your leather gloves as advertised, with the lowest prices and best terms.
- We would be much obliged if you would submit to us the catalogs and prices of your products.

샘플의 요청

- We will be pleased if you would send us the samples of your recent products.
- Will you please send us various samples of the "COW" brand shirts.
- We have a considerable demand here for golf balls and would appreciate some samples sent by airmail.
- Please supply to us some samples of warm-up suits in navy blue and rust brown.
- We are especially interested in your wool textiles and ask you to let us have a pattern book.
- We enclose a few samples of imitation silver necklaces and would greatly appreciate it if you would send us samples of similar product you could offer from stock.
- Will you please send us samples of the silk scarfs you displayed at the recent Seoul International Trade Fair?

여러 가지 요청 및 문의

- Will you please send us your catalog and full details of your export prices and terms of payment, together with any samples?

- We would be glad to receive your latest catalog and any technical literature you may have recently issued, as well as your lowest possible export prices on the basis of CIF Busan.

- We are interested in the "SBX" auto radios and would be obliged if you would send us your samples together with terms of payment and the largest discount you can allow us.

- We would appreciate it if you would quote your best prices CIF Busan for the Wireless Headphones you advertised in The Electronics World and let us know the earliest possible shipment date.

- Would you please send us further details of your earphones together with a delivery schedule and your CIF export prices.

- Please give us your best quotations in US Dollars for immediate shipment together with pro-forma invoices and samples.

- Please quote your best prices CIF Mumbai for 500 each of these coats in medium and small sizes and let us know if you could ship them within two weeks on receipt of an order.

- Please send us samples with your lowest prices and best discount for cash.

- All your quotations should be as completely detailed as possible in order to avoid unnecessary further inquiries.

거래의 가능성 시사

- If your price is competitive and the quality <u>matches</u> the sample, we will <u>give you a big order.</u>

matches *comes up to* *agrees with* *corresponds to*	*give you a big order* *give you a very substantial order* *place large orders with you*

- If your <u>prices</u> are <u>satisfactory,</u> we shall give you <u>an order.</u>

prices quotations terms	satisfactory attractive competitive reasonable	an order a substantial order a trial order regular orders a steady stream of orders

- Please let us have full details of your products so that we can place regular orders with you.

- If you can quote us your best quality goods at competitive prices, we are prepared to enter into business relations with you.

- Being closely connected with reliable wholesalers here, we should be able to do a considerable import business with you.

- As we have <u>extensive business connections</u> here in the field of industrial rubber products, we look forward to your best terms.

> extensive business connections
> a nationwide business network

- Your machines should command a ready sale in our market if they are up to the specifications.

- You may expect a constant flow of sizable orders if your pricing is acceptable.

- If you can guarantee regular supplies, we will push sales as strongly as possible.

- If you can supply your goods strictly in accordance with our specifications, we will be prepared to place a prompt trial order.

- Should your <u>aftersales services</u> prove prompt and efficient, your products would find a <u>ready sale here</u>.

aftersales services aftersale service aftersales service	ready sale here very receptive market here market here

맺음말

- We look forward to hearing from you soon.
- May we expect your reply soon?
- If the samples meet with our approval, we shall give you a large order.
- If you give us special terms, we shall do our best to sell the goods.
- If you let us have the lowest prices, we may place considerable orders with you.
- If you give us the most favorable terms, we will push sales to the best of our ability.

2 조회의 답신

서 두

- Thank you for your inquiry of March 20 regarding our compact disk player.

Thank you for your inquiry. We have received with thanks your inquiry We appreciate your inquiry Many thanks for your inquiry	regarding concerning about

- In reply to your letter of April 7, we are pleased to send you by separate cover our revised catalog and a price list.

In reply to In answer to In reference to In response to In regard to	letter inquiry fax e-mail

- Thank you very much for the interest you have shown in our 2XD car radio in your letter of April 17.

- We are pleased to learn from your letter of April 3 that our calculators are well received in your market.

📄 상품

- The article you inquired <u>is a good seller</u> at present.

> *is a good seller*
> *sells well*
> *is selling well*

- We are certain that our product would meet your customer's needs.

- We have already had big demand for this model from Europe.

- The most special feature of this product is that it is small in size and high in quality.

- We have just <u>put out</u> a new model

> *put out*
> *released*
> *come out with*

- Our product is the best as far as performance is concerned.

- We are confident that you will be impressed with the quality of our products.

- Would you let us know what size you have in mind?

- We could introduce a less expensive model if you wish.

- The quality of our goods is the finest available at this price.

- The Model you inquired about is no longer in production and has been replaced by a new model.

- We are glad to say that we can supply copper wire to the exact specifications of your samples.

- The T-shirt you mentioned has been a great success wherever it has been introduced, and we are exporting it to several tropical countries.

📋 수량

- We have around 500 units of the product in stock at present.
- We would like to know what quantity you have in mind?
- We have no minimum quantities for orders.
- We have minimum order quantities to ensure that we can safely ship your order.
- We can not take orders fewer than 100 units.
- Our quotations include packing in export cases of 100 doz., with a minimum order of 200 doz. required, but are available for minimum orders of 50 doz. per design.
- Prices quoted apply only to quantities of 100 dozen or more. Any order under 100 dozen is subject to 10% increase.

📋 재고

- Due to the increased demand for this type of shoe, our inventory has run very low.
- We are out of stock on the model T-21 at present, and no longer produce it.

are out of stock have no inventory	produce manufacture

- The goods you want are out of manufacture at present, and we regret being unable to quote on them.

want required inquire	manufacture stock

- As soon as our present stock has run out, we will have to revise our prices.

📋 샘플, 카탈로그, 가격표 등 송부

- We enclose our samples together with a catalog of our products.

> *We enclose our samples*
> *We are enclosing our samples*
> *We are pleased to enclose you*
> *We have the pleasure of enclosing you*
> *Enclosed are our samples*
> *Enclosed, please find our samples*

enclose	*together with*
send	*along with*
submit	*with*

- We are sending you <u>a full set of our samples</u>.

> *a full set of our samples*
> *a complete range of types and sizes*
> *a fine collection of our latest designs*
> *an entire range of our samples*
> *an assortment of our product line*

- All details are given in our enclosed price list.
- We are pleased to send you <u>under separate cover</u> our latest catalog.

under separate cover	*our latest catalog*
separately	*our most recent catalog and price list*
by express mail	*our illustrated catalog*

- <u>As instructed</u> in your inquiry of October 3, we are forwarding to you the samples, catalogs, and sales promotional materials for our underwear.

> *As instructed*
> *As desired*
> *As requested*
> *As you requested*
> *In accordance with your request*

- We are pleased to enclose our prices for the goods that you inquired about.
- The enclosed catalog illustrates part of the vast range of our products. A trial order will convince you of the excellence of our goods and services.
- Our illustrated export catalog will be sent to you today, with a range of samples of the various skins used in the manufacture of our gloves and shoes.

- A full range of patterns has been sent to you by express mail today.
- Mr. Lee, our resident representative, will be in New York next week, and he will be pleased to call on you with an assortment of our hand-made lines.

📋 가격조건

1. 일반적 가격조건

- Our <u>prices</u> are based on FOB Busan.

> *prices*
> *quotations*

- We can quote you <u>@US$ 30 CIF</u> Hong Kong.

> *@US$ 30 CIF*
> *a unit price of US$ 30 CIF*
> *US$ 30 per piece CIF*

- The price is US$ 100 per case FOB Busan.
- On the enclosed price list, we quoted our prices FOB Busan.
- Our quotations include your commission of 5%.
- These are our best prices we can give you at present.
- Our price is about 5% lower than that of other makers.
- Our prices are <u>subject to change without prior notice</u>.

> *subject to change without prior notice*
> *subject to market fluctuations*
> *subject to 2% discount for cash*
> *subject to a 2% cash discount*
> *subject to 2% discount for quantities of 2 gross and more*

- We reserve the right to modify the prices in accordance with market fluctuations.
- Our prices are all subject to change on October 2 because there is every indication that the cost of materials is increasing.

- We have given our best quotations in the attached Price List No. 125.
- The prices vary slightly according to the finish you prefer.
- The prices are valid subject to your reply reaching us on or before March 15.
- Regretfully, there is no room to negotiate the price.
- We carefully reviewed your estimate and concluded that the price is a little on the high side.

reviewed	on the high side
gone through	rather stiff
check through	too high

2. 가격할인 등 특별조건

- For quantities of 10 gross and over, we can offer a discount of 10% off list prices.

offer	
make	
allow you	a discount of 10% off list prices
grant you	a 10% reduction in the prices

- As noted on the price list, we offer discounts according to the size of the order.
- We will take 5% off the list price if you place an order for 300 or more units.

take 5% off
make a 5% discount
allow you a 5% discount

- The prices for smaller and for larger quantities are noted in a separate list, which may be used as an order form.
- We would be pleased to give you a discount of 3% from our list prices for quantities of over 100 doz. for each item.

> *for each item*
> *per item*

■ Could you reduce the total amount to USD 2,000.

■ Unfortunately, a further discount is not possible since our price is already low.

3. 가격 및 시황

■ Prices have gone up steadily since October, but we have not revised our quotations as of yet.

■ We are convinced that our goods represent the best values in the market at these figures.

■ As you may know, prices have risen sharply during the last few weeks. This is a very moderate increase and we hope that you will take advantage of our offer.

■ While your market is quiet, ours has been very active with a recent rush of orders from Europe. Under these circumstances, we have quoted the very best prices with deliveries as near March as possible.

■ There is a tendency of prices rising very rapidly and if you miss this opportunity, you may not be able to obtain this article even at higher prices.

■ The market has been steadily rising, and we have no further stock available to offer even at a higher price.

4. 경쟁력

■ We are sure that our prices are competitive enough to attract your customers.

■ These articles are in high demand.

■ Demand of this item in world markets greatly exceeds its supply.

■ We have quoted our best terms in the enclosed offer sheet and trust that you will agree that the price is extremely reasonable for this excellent quality.

- A comparison with other similar makes will convince you that there is no copier of comparable performance available on the market at this price.

📋 인도조건

- We quote you as follows and can <u>promise delivery</u> within 3 weeks <u>upon receipt of your order</u>.

promise delivery	*upon receipt of your order*
guarantee delivery	*from receiving your order*
promise shipment	*after confirming your order*

- We are able to deliver in 30 days after receiving your order.
- You may be assured that we will ship your goods by the end of July if your order reaches us by the end of this week.
- The goods <u>you have in mind</u> are out of stock, so it would take three months to make shipment.

you have in mind
you mentioned
you require

- We <u>can deliver</u> from stock at once.

can deliver
are ready to supply

- Delivery can be made from stock immediately.
- We will be able to deliver the goods in 3 weeks.
- Delivery takes 3 weeks after we receive your order.

🗒 대금결제조건

- To cover our shipment, we should require you to open an irrevocable credit in our favor for the invoice amount with a first class bank.
- For payment, please arrange for an irrevocable credit in our favor valid until November 15th.
- An irrevocable letter of credit at sight must be opened within 2 weeks after the date of the contract.
- We accept subject to a covering credit being received by us not later than September 30.
- Payment will be made by check.

> *by check*
> *in cash*

- Our usual terms are cash with order (C.W.O.).

> *cash with order (C.W.O.)*
> *cash on delivery (C.O.D.)*
> *documents against payment (D/P)*
> *documents against acceptance (D/A)*

- Goods are sold on open account.

> *on open account*
> *on sight draft*
> *on time draft*
> *on L/C*
> *on consignment*

- We normally effect payment by letter of credit.

> *effect*
> *make*
> *accept*

- We deal with our usual transactions on an L/C basis.

- As for payment, we ask you to <u>open</u> an Irrevocable Letter of Credit <u>at sight</u> in our favor for the full invoice value immediately upon confirmation of sale.

open establish issue	at sight at 30 days after sight

- Our terms of payment are irrevocable letter of credit, under which a draft will be drawn at 90 days after sight.
- Drafts will be drawn at sight, documents attached, under the L/C opened in our favor.
- <u>In regard to</u> the terms of business, <u>it is our policy to</u> trade on an at sight irrevocable credit.

In regard to With regard to As to Regarding Concerning	it is our policy to it is customary to

- We usually do business on an L/C basis, but if you insist we may accept D/P.
- We should be pleased to supply you on a consignment basis.

📋 상품의 설명, 홍보, 권유

- One great advantage of our new system is its simple installation, which reduces the initial cost considerably.
- We would like to draw your attention particularly to the new specialities as shown on pages 28~30 and which made a great sensation at the 2021 Exhibition in Rome.
- It is designed along modern lines and gives, without any increase in fuel consumption, 20% more heat than other makes.

- In particular, we would recommend item No. 5 developed by our own research department. It is a synthetic substance with features as shown in the attached certificate issued by the National Institute of Technology of India.

맺음말

1. 상품 설명, 견본 및 자료 제공시의 맺음말

- We hope that these samples will <u>prove satisfactory to you.</u>

> *prove satisfactory to you*
> *prove attractive to you*
> *meet your requirement*
> *meet with your approval*

- We hope that this sample will prove satisfactory to you and that we may receive your order.

- We hope that our offer will induce you to place an order with us at an early date.

- We hope that you will find the article you want in our catalog, and we are looking forward to receiving your order.

- We hope that our sample will be approved and orders follow.

- We trust that the samples will <u>sufficiently interest</u> you to give us a trial order soon.

> *sufficiently interest*
> *be of sufficiently interest to*

- We are sure that these goods will meet your requirements, and look forward to your prompt instructions.

- If there is any further information we can provide you on any of our goods, please refer the matter to us; we shall be only too pleased to respond immediately.

- If you do not find just what you want among the range of samples we sent, please let us know the full details of your requirements.

2. 거래조건제시 경우 거래기대 맺음말

- We hope to have the pleasure of serving you.

the pleasure of *the opportunity of*

- We look forward to receiving your early decision.
- We hope we shall have the pleasure of receiving your early order.
- We appreciate your confidence in our products and assure you of our best efforts to deserve it.
- Any order that you may place with us will have our prompt and careful attention.
- We hope the prices and quality will be satisfactory.

hope *are confident that*

- Your soonest reply will make us deeply grateful.

soonest *immediate* *earliest*

- Your immediate attention to this matter will be greatly appreciated.
- We hope that we may hear from you within the next few days.
- We hope that you will find our prices sufficiently attractive to send us your order soon.
- You may rely on us to give your order our best attention.
- We suggest that you place an order promptly as our stock is quickly running low.

- We thank you for your inquiry and hope that you will follow it with an order.
- We await your reply by return mail.
- If our proposal is acceptable to you, please confirm by e-mail.
- As we are booking heavy orders every day, we advise you to place an order soon.

> *soon*
> *without delay*
> *without loss of time*
> *at your earliest convenience*

Standard
Trade
English

청약과 승낙
그리고 주문

무역업무의 주요 내용

무역계약은 청약(Offer)에 대하여 승낙(Acceptance)을 함으로써 성립된다. 즉 당사자 일방이 구체적이고도 확정적인 거래제의를 하고 이에 대하여 상대방이 이의 없이 동의함으로써 성립된다.

1 청 약

1) 청약의 의의

청약(Offer)은 일정한 조건으로 물건을 팔거나 사고 싶다는 확정적인 의사표시이다. 확정적인 의사표시이기 때문에 이후에 이를 변경하거나 철회 또는 취소하지 못한다. Offer는 일반적으로 그 속에 승낙기간을 제시하게 되는데, 승낙기간을 정하지 않은 경우에는 그 거래에 타당한 합리적인 기간(reasonable time)이 승낙기간으로 된다.

2) Counter Offer

Offer를 받은 상대방이 Offer를 한 사람에게 Offer의 내용을 변경하여 되돌려 거래제의를 할 때 이를 Counter Offer라 한다. Counter Offer는 원래 Offer의 거절이며 자신이 새로운 Offer로 된다. 상거래에서는 양당사자 간에 Counter Offer가 오고 가는 가운데 의견수렴이 되고 이러한 과정을 거쳐 거래가 성립되는 경우가 보다 일반적이다.

3) 조건부 Offer

특정한 사항이 충족될 것을 전제로 하는 조건부 청약(Conditional Offer)을 내기도 하는데 다음과 같은 문구를 삽입하게 된다.
- subject to our final confirmation
- subject to being unsold
- subject to prior sale
- subject to change without notice

이러한 Offer는 확정성이 없기 때문에 이는 엄격한 법적 의미에서는 Offer가 아니고 거래의 조회 또는 유인에 해당되지만 보통 Offer라고 부른다.

2 승 낙

승낙(Acceptance)은 Offer를 수락하는 의사표시이다. 계약이 성립되기 위해서는 청약자의 의사와 승낙자의 의사가 합치해야 하므로 승낙은 청약에 대한 중요한 거래조건에서 이의가 없는 무조건적인 동의이어야 한다. 승낙은 청약과 마찬가지로 철회나 취소할 수 없고, 청약에 대해 승낙으로서 계약은 성립된다.

청약에서 승낙기간을 제시하기 때문에 그 기간 안에 승낙했느냐의 문제가 있는데 이것이 승낙효력 발생시기문제이다. 당사자간 의사전달이 즉시 이루어지는 대화나 전화의 경우에는 문제가 없으나, 편지와 같이 의사표시를 보내고 나서 일정한 시일 이후에 받게 되는 경우는 발송시점을 승낙한 시점으로 보느냐(발송주의), 도달한 시점을 승낙한 시점으로 보느냐(도달주의)의 문제가 있다. 법에서 정하기 나름인데 아래에서 보는 바와 같이 국가마다 다르다.

✓		승낙의 효력발생시기	
준거법	구분	한국법, 일본법, 영국법, 미국법	독일법, CISG
의사표시 일반		도달시점	
승낙 의사표시	대화자간		
	격지자간	발신시점	도달시점

1) 의사표시 일반은 일반적인 의사표시에서의 효력을 말함.
2) 대화자, 격지자 구분은 시간적 개념임. 따라서 국제전화는 대화자간임.
3) CISG : United Nations Convention on Contracts for the Int'l Sale of Goods(국제물품매매계약에 관한 유엔협약)

무역영문통신의 주요 사항

1 Offer Sheet(물품매도확약서)

Offer는 매도자가 내는 Selling Offer와 매수자가 내는 Buying Offer가 있지만 실제 Selling Offer가 대부분이기 때문에 보통 Offer Sheet를 물품매도확약서라고 부른다. Offer는 계약성립의 한 부분이 되는 중요한 문서이기 때문에 미리 인쇄된 양식을 많이 사용하는데 그 형식에 관계없이 내용상으로 그 요건을 갖추고 있으면 된다. Offer는 일반적으로 다음과 같은 내용으로 구성된다.

1. 조회에 대한 감사표시 및 Offer한다는 내용
2. 조건의 제시 : 거래가 바로 성립할 수 있을 정도로 구체적인 조건,[1] 즉 상품명세, 수량, 선적일, 포장, 대금결제방법, 원산지 등 일반적 조건
3. 승낙유효기간[2]
4. 승낙을 유도하기 위한 제품의 장점 소개와 수락을 권유하는 내용
5. 승낙 또는 회신을 기대한다는 취지의 맺음말

2 Counter Offer

Counter Offer는 원래의 Offer를 변경한 자신의 수정안에 대하여 상대방의 동의를 얻어야 하므로 조건변경의 내용을 알리거나 수정의 필요성을 상대방에 설득하게 된다. Counter Offer는 대개 다음과 같은 형식으로 된다.

1. 오퍼를 받았다는 내용
2. Offer 조건 중 해당조건은 수락할 수 없음과 이에 대한 이유
3. 자신의 조건 제시

또는

1. 오퍼에 대하여 Counter Offer한다는 내용
2. 자신이 제기하는 조건을 포함한 전체 거래조건 명시

---

1) 상대방이 이미 합의하고 있거나 알고 있는 부분에는 이에 대한 내용이 없어도 승낙시에 의사의 합치에 문제가 없기 때문에 생략할 수 있으나 가급적 명확하게 명시하는 것이 좋다.
2) 승낙시점을 발송한 시점과 도착한 시점 둘 중 언제를 기준하느냐의 문제가 있으므로 "~ your acceptance reaching(arriving) here(to us) by May 4, 2021"과 같이 승낙기간과 함께 기준장소도 명시하는 것이 좋다.

3 승 낙

승낙은 Offer 위에 주어지는 것이기 때문에 "I accept your offer"라는 간단한 표시로 가능하다. 또는 상대방의 Offer를 승낙한다는 의사표시와 함께 Offer에서의 거래조건들을 그대로 명시해도 된다.[3]

4 주 문

주문(Order)은 Offer나 Acceptance와 달리 법률상의 용어는 아니며 거래를 위한 의사표시이다. 따라서 상대의 청약이 있는 상태에서 주문을 하게 되면 그 주문은 법적으로 승낙이기 때문에 이로써 바로 계약이 성립되고, 청약이 없는 상태에서 주문하게 되면 청약이 되기 때문에 상대방의 승낙인 주문확인(Confirmation of Order)이 있어야 계약이 성립하게 된다. 주문에 포함되는 내용은 대개 다음과 같다.

1. 주문한다는 내용
2. 거래조건의 명시(상품명세, 수량, 선적일, 포장, 대금결제, 원산지, 등 일반적 조건[4])
3. 확인통지의 요청[5]

5 주문의 승낙

주문을 받으면 바로 답신을 하여야 한다. 주문을 수락하지 못하는 경우에는 이에 대한 이유, 대체품의 권유, 다음 거래의 희망 등을 내용으로 하는 답신을 하게 된다. 주문승낙시 주문확인서에 포함되는 사항은 대개 다음과 같다.

1. 주문승낙 및 감사의 표시
2. 상대방의 주문서 참조번호 및 주문내용
3. 거래조건의 확인
4. 주문품에 대한 배려약속과 계속적인 거래희망

---

3) 승낙의 효력발생시기와 관련하여 승낙기간을 넘기지 않도록 우편일수가 오래 걸리는 편지보다는 즉시 의사전달이 되는 전화, fax, 또는 e-mail을 이용하는 것이 좋다. 이로써 국가마다 승낙의 법적 효력발생시점이 다른 데서 생길 수도 있는 문제를 사전에 예방할 수 있기 때문이다.
4) 상대방이 이미 오퍼를 한 경우에는 승낙에서와 같이 거래조건을 모두 명시하지 않아도 되나 가급적 명확하게 명시하는 것이 좋다.
5) Offer에 대한 Order인 경우에는 확인이 필요 없으나 이 때에도 확인요청을 하는 경우가 많다.

E1 오퍼

SM Company, Inc.

4501, 45th Floor, Trade Tower
511 Yeongdong-daero, Kangnam-gu, Seoul, Korea 06164

OFFER SHEET

Date : May 5, 2021

Messrs. : AMS Trading Company
908 Park Avenue
New York, NY 10017 U.S.A.

Gentlemen:

We are pleased to offer you the following goods on the terms and conditions described as follows:

Origin : Republic of Korea
Payment : By an irrevocable L/C at sight
Shipment : Within two months after receipt of the L/C
Packing : Export standard packing
Destination : New York
Inspection : Seller's inspection to be final
Validity : June 15, 2021 subject to receipt of your acceptance

H.S. No.	Description	Quantity	Unit Price	Amount
8518	Speaker System Model : DD-9920	1,000	US$ 135.50 FOB Busan	US$ 135,500

Very truly yours,

Accepted by

_____

Jin-ho Kim

Jin-ho Kim
General Manager

내용 SM사가 AMS Trading사에 제시하는 스피커 수출판매에 대한 물품매도
확약서이다.

• 주요 용어 및 표현 •

- 왼쪽 offer 양식의 내용이나 형식상의 구성을 보면 보통 편지와 큰 차이가 없음을 알 수 있다.
- 오퍼문은 We offer you the goods at US\$ 10와 같은 형식을 취하게 된다. offer 대신에 make an offer, submit an offer, offer firm, make a firm offer 등이 사용된다.
  offer는 "subject to our final confirmation"과 같은 확정력을 배제하는 문구가 없는 한 항상 확정 오퍼이다. 따라서 firm의 용어가 들어 있고 없음이 효력에 영향을 미치지 않는다.
- the following goods : 다음의 상품, 아래 상품(=goods described below, goods undermentioned)
- terms and conditions : 거래조건
- as follows : 다음과 같이
- after receipt of L/C : 신용장 수령 후(=upon receipt of L/C)
- irrevocable L/C at sight : 일람출급취소불능신용장
- export standard packing : 표준 수출포장
- seller's inspection to be final : 수출자의 검사를 최종적인 것으로 함.
- subject to receipt of your acceptance : 승낙 도착을 조건으로, 즉 승낙의 효력발생시점을 도착 기준으로 설정하는 문구이다.
- description : 명세, 종류, 물품의 설명, 상품명(=specification, item, goods, commodity)
- 왼쪽과 같은 offer를 2통 작성하여 우하단에서와 같이 서명하여 보내면 상대방이 좌하단에 서명하고 이 중 1통을 반송함으로써 각자 1통씩 갖게 되고 이로써 양당사자의 의사합치를 입증하는 계약서가 되는 것이다.

⊞ E2 반대 오퍼

AMS Trading Company

908 Park Avenue
New York, NY 10017 U.S.A.

May 25, 2021

SM Company, Inc.
511 Yeongdong-daero, Kangnam-gu
Seoul, Korea 06164

Dear Mr. Park:

Thank you very much for your offer of May 5 and for samples of the digital speaker system DD-9920 which you kindly sent us.

We are favorably impressed with the quality of your products which we believe are perfectly suited to the needs of the customers here.

However, we feel that the prices of your products seem to be somewhat on the high side with regard to the market here. Please understand that the market here is very tight because there are so many speaker systems imported from Japan, Europe, and Southeast Asian countries. In order for us to maintain competitiveness in this type of market, we need a steady supply of products at prices which are appropriate for the market.

May we ask you to reduce the unit price to US$ 120.00? This would greatly facilitate our ability to introduce your products to our customers. Should you be able to meet our request we are confident that we will be able to place orders with you on a regular basis.

We hope that you will take advantage of this occasion so that you will benefit from the expanding market.

We are awaiting your consideration and favorable reply.

Very truly yours,

내용 SM사의 오퍼에 대해서 상품가격의 인하를 요청하는 AMS Trading사의 counter offer이다.

• 주 요 용 어 및 표 현 •

- favorably impressed with ~ : ~에 좋은 인상을 받다.
- the needs of the customers : 고객의 수요, 고객의 취향
- somewhat : 다소간, 약간
- on the high side : 높은 편, 즉 비싼 편
- the market here is very tight because there are so many speaker systems
  = the market here is somewhat saturated with speaker systems
- very tight : 경쟁이 치열한(=very competitive)
- steady supply : 안정된 공급, 계속적인 공급
- appropriate : 적합한, 적당한
- reduce the unit price to ~ : ~로 단가를 낮추다.
- facilitate : 촉진하다. 쉽게 하다.
- meet our request : 요구에 응하다. 요구를 들어주다.
- on a regular basis : 규칙적으로, 계속적으로
- take advantage of ~ : ~을 이용하다.
- expanding market : 시장확대, 시장개척

✓	이전, 이후, 부터, 까지		
~ 이전	~ 이후	~ 부터	~ 까지
before ~ not later than ~	after ~	from ~ as from ~	till ~ / until ~ by ~ / to ~

1) 해당일의 포함여부를 명확히 할 필요가 있는 경우에는 on or before, till and including과 같이 on이나 including을 사용하여 해당일이 포함됨을 표시한다. 또 inclusive(including), exclusive(excluding)을 사용할 수 있다.

   예 from May 5(exclusive) to June 5(inclusive).

2) till, until은 ~시점까지 계속을, by는 ~시점까지 완료를 나타낸다.

E3 반대오퍼에 대한 반대오퍼

SM Company, Inc.

4501, 45th Floor, Trade Tower
511 Yeongdong-daero, Kangnam-gu, Seoul, Korea 06164

June 14, 2021

AMS Trading Company
908 Park Avenue
New York, NY 10017 U.S.A.

Dear Mr. Collins:

Thank you very much for your letter of May 25 requesting a price reduction for our offer.

Unfortunately, we are not able to meet the price which you suggested for our Model DD-9920, speaker system. Please understand that we would very much like to help you in this matter but we have already cut the price down to the absolute minimum.

As an excellent substitute for the article, we recommend our Model DD-9910 which is very similar to Model DD-9920 in quality but at a lower price. We are ready to offer you a special discount of 5% on our Model DD-9910 to help you introduce it to the market. That would lower the price to US$ 118.75 per unit.

We truly hope you will take advantage of this offer, which we will gladly honor until the 30th of July.

Very truly yours,

내용 상품가격의 인하를 요청한 AMS Trading사의 counter offer에 대해서 SM사가 다시 상품을 변경하여 제시하는 counter offer이다.

• 주요 용어 및 표현 •

- requesting a price reduction ~ : 가격할인을 요청한(=in which you request a price reduction ~)
- meet the price : 가격을 맞추다. 가격을 충족시키다.
- cut the price down : 가격을 낮추었다. 가격을 인하하였다.
- to the absolute minimum : 아주 최소한의 수준으로
- substitute : 대체품, 대용품
- article : 물품(=goods)
- be similar to ~ : ~와 유사한
- be ready to ~ : 기꺼이 ~하다. ~할 준비가 되어 있는
- lower the price to ~ : ~로 가격을 낮추다.
- will gladly honor until the 30th of July : 7월 30일까지 받아들이겠다. 즉 유효기간을 7월 30일까지로 한다는 뜻. 여기서 honor는 받아들인다는 의미

✓	무역에서의 날짜관련 전치사의 해석

1. to, until, till, from : 해당일자를 포함한다(신용장통일규칙 47조).
   예 from the 2nd of May to the 7th : 2일에서 7일 사이(2일과 7일 포함)

2. after : 해당일자를 제외한다(신용장통일규칙 47조).
   예 after the 15th of May : 15일 이후(16일부터)
   따라서 not after의 경우 해당일을 포함한다.
   예 not after the 15th of May : 15일 이전(15일 포함)

3. by : 해당일자를 포함한다(일반적인 관례).
   예 by the 15th of May : 15일까지(15일 포함)

4. before : 해당일자를 제외한다(일반적인 관례).
   예 before the 15th of May : 15일 이전(14일까지)

5. on or about : 해당일 이전 5일부터 해당일 이후 5일까지의 기간 내로 해석(신용장통일규칙 46조)
   예 on or about the 15th of May : 10일부터 20일 사이(11일간)

⌨ E4 승낙

AMS Trading Company

908 Park Avenue
New York, NY 10017 U.S.A.

June 29, 2021

SM Company, Inc.
4501, 45th Floor, Trade Tower
511 Yeongdong-daero, Kangnam-gu
Seoul, Korea 06164

Dear Mr. Park:

We are pleased to accept your offer of June 14 for 1,000 units of Model DD-9910, speaker system, at a unit price of US$ 118.75 FOB Busan. Enclosed please find our Purchase Order No. 1332.

In order to cover the amount of this purchase we will arrange with our bankers an irrevocable sight letter of credit to be opened in your favor within a week. When the goods are ready for shipment, please inform us, and we will send you detailed instructions.

Since this transaction is very important for us, we would like to ask you to give it your utmost attention.

Very truly yours,

내용 가격을 인하한 SM사의 counter offer에 대하여 AMS Trading사가 승낙하는 내용이다.

• 주요 용어 및 표현 •

- at a unit price of US$ 29.00 CIF New York :
가격의 금액 뒤에는 Incoterms의 가격조건이 수반된다. 같은 액수로 표기되었다 하더라도 EXW의 경우는 buyer가 생산지에서 물건을 인수하여 이후에 발생하는 운송, 보험, 통관 등의 모든 비용을 부담해야 하는 반면, DDP의 경우는 반대로 seller가 모든 비용을 부담하여야 하기 때문에 실제가격은 달라지게 된다. 그렇기 때문에 incoterms의 조건들은 가격조건이 되는 것이다. 그리고 incoterms 뒤의 지명은 FOB와 같은 선적지 조건의 경우는 선적항이 표시되고, CIF와 같은 목적지 조건은 양륙항이 표시된다.

- unit price : 단가
 at a unit price of US$ 10
 =US$ 10 per piece
 =@US$ 10

- to cover the amount : 대금지급을 위하여, 대금분에 대하여

- arrange with our bankers : 은행에 주선하다. 은행에 마련토록 하다.

- an irrevocable sight letter of credit : 취소불능 일람출급 신용장
신용장은 취소가능여부에 따라 revocable L/C와 irrevocable L/C로 나누어진다. 신용장통일규칙 제6조는 신용장에 이에 대한 내용을 명시하도록 권장하고 있고, 이에 대한 명시가 없는 경우는 취소불능신용장으로 간주하도록 하고 있다. irrevocable L/C는 취소가 전혀 안 되는 것은 아니고 신용장거래의 세 당사자인 개설의뢰인, 개설은행, 수익자의 합의하에서는 취소하거나 수정할 수 있다.
또 sight L/C는 일람출급의 환어음을 발행하도록 하는 L/C로서, L/C at sight로도 표기된다.

- in your favor : 당신에게 지불되도록, 당신을 수취인으로 하여(=in favor of you)

- detailed instructions : 상세한 지시

- utmost attention : 최대한의 배려, 최상의 관심

☐ E5 오퍼

Asia Trading Company

212 Yoi-daero, Youngdeungpo-gu
Seoul, Korea 07325

May 12, 2021

ABBA Co., Inc.
1156 5th Avenue
New York, NY 10017 U.S.A.

Dear Mr. Brown:

Thank you for your letter of April 24 inquiring about our men's jackets.
As to your inquiry, we are pleased to offer you as follows:
Item : Men's Jacket (S/T # LLG-822)
    Shell : 65% Polyester, 35% Cotton
    Body Lining : T/C 186T
    Sleeve Lining : 100% Nylon
Quantity : 3,000 PCS
Unit price : $ 25.50
Total Amount : $ 76,500 FOB Busan
Shipping : Within 30 days upon receipt of order.
Packing : Each packed in a poly bag, 50 pieces in a cardboard carton.
Destination : New York, U.S.A.
Payment : By 100% irrevocable L/C at sight

Owing to the sharp rise of manufacturing costs, we are planning to adjust the price and will be issuing a new price list before the end of next month. Therefore, the price quoted above is valid subject to your acceptance received here by June 30.

We are confident that the conditions we offer are fully competitive with those of other manufacturers and hope you will take advantage of this opportunity.

We look forward to your favorable reply.

Very truly yours,

내용 한국의 Asia Trading사가 미국의 ABBA사에 Men's Jacket의 판매에 대해서 offer하고 있는 내용이다.

· 주요 용어 및 표현 ·

- 오퍼는 앞 [E1]과 같이 인쇄양식화 된 offer sheet를 많이 사용하나 왼편과 같이 서신의 형태로 해도 된다. 모든 법률문서는 그 내용이 중심이며 형식에 구애받지 않는다.
- as follows : 다음과 같이. "위와 같이" 또는 "아래와 같이" 라면 "as above" 또는 "as below"로 한다.
- item : 품목
- each packed : 낱개로 포장되어, 개별로 포장되어
- poly bag : 폴리비닐 포장
- cardboard carton : 마분지 상자
- by June 30 : 6월 30일까지(=prior to June 30, no later than June 30)
- by 100% irrevocable L/C : 상품대금전액에 대해서 신용장을 개설한다는 것이다. 상품대금의 일부에 대해서만 신용장을 개설하고 나머지는 다른 방법으로 대금을 지급할 수도 있다.
- owing to ~ : ~ 때문에
- manufacturing costs : 제조원가, 제조비용
- issue : 발간하다. 배포하다.
- valid : 유효한
- subject to your acceptance received here by November 30 : 승낙이 11월 30일까지 여기에 도착하는 조건으로, 즉 승낙효력발생 시점을 도착지 기준임을 나타내는 문구이다.
- opportunity : 기회, 호기. 여기서는 this opportunity 대신에 this offer라고 해도 된다.

⟦⟧ E6 반대오퍼

ABBA Co., Inc.
1156 5th Avenue
New York, NY 10017 U.S.A.

May 30, 2021

Asia Trading Company
215 Yoi-daero, Youngdeungpo-gu
Seoul, Korea 07325

Dear Mr. Lee:

We would like to thank you for your offer of the 12th of May for men's jackets.

We consider your offer to be quite acceptable for the most part. However, we regret to inform you that the prices you quoted are far higher than we expected.

Although we feel your products have some advantage with respect to quality, the quoted prices leave us no margin. We are sure that we will not be able to successfully market your products at such a high price because the primary demand here is for products in the mid-price range.

We like the quality of your products and also the manner in which you handled our inquiry and would very much welcome the opportunity to do business with you. We would be pleased to place an order with you if you lower the price by 10% to US$ 22.95 per piece. We will place our first order with you as soon as we receive a reply granting the discount.

We cordially await your reply with great anticipation.

Very truly yours,

내용 Asia Trading사의 offer에 대해서 ABBA사가 가격인하를 요청하는 counter offer를 내고 있다.

• 주요 용어 및 표현 •

- acceptable : 받아들일 수 있는, 만족스러운
- for the most part : 대부분, 대체적으로
- far higher than ~ : ~보다 훨씬 높은
- with respect to ~ : ~에 관해서는(=as regards ~)
- advantage : 우위, 유리한 점, 이점, 강점
- leave us no margin : 우리에게 마진을 남기지 않는다. 우리는 남는 게 없다 (=leave us no profit).
- market products : 제품을 팔다(=sell products).
- primary demand : 주요 수요(=principal demand)
- mid-price range : 중간 가격 범위, 중간 가격대(=medium price category)
- handle : 다루다. 취급하다.
- welcome the opportunity : 기회를 환영하다. 기회를 맞이하다.
- place an order with you : 주문하다.
- lower the price by 10% to US$ 22.95 per piece : 가격을 10% 낮추어 개당 22.95달러로 하다.
  =bring the price down to US$ 22.95 per piece with an allowance of 10%
- first order : 첫 주문, 시주문(=initial order, test order, pilot order)
- granting the discount : 할인을 허용하다. 할인해 주다.
- cordially : 진심으로(=sincerely, heartily)
- anticipation : 예상, 기대

✓	per
① ~당, ~단위로 : per piece / per ton / per capita / per annum	
② ~편으로 : per ship / per rail	
③ ~에 따라서 : as per	
④ 대리하여 : per pro	
⑤ 백분율로 : per cent, percent	

⊞ E7 반대오퍼에 대한 승낙

Asia Trading Company

212 Yoi-daero, Youngdeungpo-gu
Seoul, Korea 07325

June 15, 2021

ABBA Co., Inc.
1156 5th Avenue
New York, NY 10017 U.S.A.

Dear Mr. Brown:

We are glad to accept your counter offer of May 30 for a quantity of 3,000 of our men's jacket, S/T # LLG-822, at a unit price of US$ 22.95 FOB Busan. To confirm this transaction, we are sending you our sales contract No. FZ-AT-0412.

This price is virtually at rock-bottom and barely covers the cost of production. However, we are willing to offer this price to you with the expectation of continued orders.

Upon the receipt of your letter of credit, we will immediately make every arrangement necessary to clear the goods by the first available vessel to New York.

We feel certain that you will find our products satisfactory in every way and we hope to be favored with further orders.

Very truly yours,

내용 ABBA사의 가격인하를 요청하는 counter offer에 대해서 Asia Trading사가 승낙하는 내용이다.

· 주요 용어 및 표현 ·

- at rock-bottom : 최저의, 바닥의. cf) rock-bottom price(최저가격)
- barely covers the cost : 비용을 겨우 보상하는, 비용을 거의 커버하지 못하는
- ~ the expectation of continued orders : 후속주문을 기대하면서
  = ~ the expectation of receiving further orders from you
  = ~ the expectation of more orders on a continued basis
- upon the receipt of your letter of credit : 신용장을 받고, 받자마자
  = As soon as we receive your letter of credit
- first available vessel : 첫 배, 가장 먼저의 뱃편
- clear : 출항절차를 밟다. 통관하다.
- vessel : 대양을 항해하는 큰 배. 이에 대해서 boat는 작은 배, ship은 배에 대한 일반적인 말로 사용된다.
- continued orders : 계속적인 주문(=steady stream of orders)
- be favored with further orders : 후속주문을 받다.

✓	이상, 이하, 미만, 대략			
~ 초과 (해당수 포함않음)	~ 이상 (해당수 포함)	~ 이하 (해당수 포함)	~ 미만 (해당수 포함않음)	대략 ~ ※
more than ~ over ~ exceeding ~	not less than ~ ~ or more ~ or over	not more than ~ ~ or less not exceeding ~	less than ~ below ~	about ~ / around ~ approximately ~ ~ or so / circa ~
※ 신용장 통일규칙 제39조는 수량의 과부족에 대하여 금지를 명시하지 않은 한 정한 양에서 ±5% 이내의 과부족을 허용하고 있다. 그러나 수량의 표시 앞에 about와 같은 「대략」의 표현을 붙이고 있는 경우, 이는 과부족의 범위가 보다 클 것을 예상하고 있으므로 ±10% 이내의 과부족을 허용하 는 것으로 하고 있다.				

E8 물품매도계약서

Asia Trading Company

212 Yoi-daero, Youngdeungpo-gu
Seoul, Korea 07325

Sales Contract

Date : June 15, 2021
Contract No. : FZ-AT-0412

MESSRS. : ABBA Co., Inc.
1156 5th Avenue
New York, NY 10017 U.S.A.

Gentlemen:

We, as Seller, hereby confirm having sold to you, as Buyer, the following goods on the terms and conditions as stated below and on the back hereof:

ITEM NO	COMMODITY & SPECIFICATION	QUANTITY	UNIT PRICE	AMOUNT
H.S. NO. 5407	Men's Jacket (S/T # LLG-822) Shell : 65% Polyester, 35% Cotton Body Lining : T/C 186T Sleeve Lining : 100% Nylon	3,000 PCS	US$ 22.95 FOB Busan	US$ 68,850

Shipment : Dispatched within 1 month upon receipt of order.
Packing : Each packed separately in a poly-urethane bag, 50 pieces per cardboard carton.
Destination : New York, U.S.A.
Payment : By 100% irrevocable L/C at sight
Remarks : Please insert "INSPECTION CERTIFICATION" on L/C

Kindly sign and return the duplicate after confirming the above. If you find anything herein not in order, please let us know immediately, by e-mail, fax, cable, or telegram. Unless we are advised of any amendment to these terms and conditions, this contract shall be considered as ultimately confirmed by you.

Accept by :   Asia Trading Company

By : _____   By : *K. H. Lee* _____

                                      K. H. Lee Manager
                                      Export Department

    On _____   On June 15, 2021

내용 Asia Trading사의 ABBA Trading사에 대한 남자용 상의 판매에 대한 물품매도계약서이다.

• 주 요 용 어 및 표 현 •

- 상품의 판매시에 일반적으로 사용하는 매도계약서이다. Sales Contract, Sales Note, Contract 등으로 인쇄되어 사용되는데 이름과 형식에 상관없다.
  본문상단에 계약조건은 아래 기재된 사항과 뒷면에 기재된 사항이라고 표시하고 있다. 즉 앞면에 계약조건을 기재하게 되는 계약서 양식의 뒷면에는 대개 거래의 일반적 조건에 관한 약관을 함께 인쇄해 두고 있다(다음 페이지의 일반거래조건 참조). 계약서에서 만약 미리 인쇄된 부분과 계약시에 작성된 내용부분이 서로 상충될 때는 계약시 작성된 것을 우선으로 한다.
- as seller : 매도인으로서, 매도인 자격으로
- terms and conditions : 거래조건
- as stated below and on the back hereof : 아래와 이 계약서의 뒷면에 명시된 대로. 여기서 as는 생략되기도 한다.
- specification : 명세, 명세사항, 설명
- each packed separately : 각 물품 개별로 포장되어, 개별 별도 포장
- poly-urethane : 폴리우레탄
- cardboard carton : 마분지 박스
- please insert "INSPECTION CERTIFICATION" on L/C : 신용장상의 요구서류 중에 검사증명서를 넣을 것
- kindly sign and return : 서명하여 반송하여 주십시오.
- duplicate : 부본. 계약서 두 통 중의 하나를 의미한다.
- the above : 상기사항
- find anything herein not in order : 여기에 이상이 있다면
- amendment : 정정, 개정, 수정
- be considered as ultimately confirmed by you : 당신회사에 의해서 최종 확인된 것으로 간주되다.

[✦] E9 일반거래조건

General terms and conditions

(1) Basis : All business shall be transacted between the Buyer and the Seller on a Principal to Principal basis.

(2) Quantity : Quantity is subject to a variation of five percent (5%) plus or minus at the Seller's option.

(3) Shipment : The date of the Bill of Lading shall be taken as the conclusive date of shipment and partial shipment and/or transshipment shall be permitted, unless otherwise stated on the face hereof. The Seller shall not be held responsible for non-shipment or late shipment in whole or in part by reason of Force Majeure or any other circumstance beyond the Seller's control.

(4) Price : The price(s) is/are on the rate of freight and/or insurance premium prevailing at the time of accepting the order, and any increase in the rate of freight and/or insurance premium at the time of shipment shall be borne by the Buyer.

(5) Inspection : Inspection performed by the Seller shall be final in respect of quality and/or conditions of the contracted goods, unless otherwise stated on the face hereof.

(6) Claim : Any claim by the Buyer must be made in writing within fourteen (14) days upon receipt of the goods at the destination stated on the face hereof.

(7) Trade Terms : The trade terms used in this Contract shall be governed and interpreted by the provisions of Incoterms 2020, unless otherwise specifically stated.

(8) Infringement : The Buyer shall hold the Seller harmless from liability for any infringement with regard to patents, trademark, design, and/or copyrights originated or chosen by the Buyer.

(9) Arbitration : All disputes, controversies, or differences which may arise between the Seller and the Buyer, out of or in relation to or in connection with this Contract, or for the breach thereof, shall be finally settled by arbitration in Seoul, Korea in accordance with the Commercial Arbitration Rules of The Korea Commercial Arbitration Board. The award rendered by the arbitrator(s) shall be final and binding upon both parties.

(10) Governing Law : Both the conclusion and the performance of this Contract shall be governed by Korean law.

내용 매매계약서 뒷면에 인쇄되어 있는 일반거래조건의 내용이다.

• 주요 용어 및 표현 •

- on a Principal to Principal basis : 본인 대 본인간에. 본인 대 본인간이란 계약당사자 각자가 자기 책임과 비용을 스스로 부담하는 독립된 당사자로서 계약한다는 것이다. 이와 달리 만약 on a Principal to Agent라고 한다면 본인과 대리인간의 계약, 즉 본사와 대리점간의 계약에서의 문구이다. 대리계약에서는 대리인은 비독립적으로 본인의 지시에 따르는 반면, 대외거래에서의 모든 책임과 비용을 본인이 부담하고 대리인은 부담하지 않는다.

- variation of five percent (5%) plus or minus at Seller's option : 수량과부족 조항이다. 수량이 조금 초과하거나 미달하여도 ±5% 범위 내에서는 허용된다는 것이다. 물론 초과 및 미달부분에 대해서 값을 치루게 된다. 이 때 양의 단위로 하는 것에 해당되며 개수 단위로 하는 것에는 해당되지 않는다.

- as the conclusive date of shipment : 선적일을 기준일(결정하는 날)로

- partial shipment and transshipment : 분할선적과 환적

- unless otherwise stated : 달리 명시되지 않는 한

- on the face hereof : 이 계약서의 문면에

- Force Majeure ~control : Force Majeure (p. 233 참조)나 any other circumstance beyond Seller's control이나 같은 의미이지만 불가항력에 대한 범위를 포괄적으로 명시하기 위해서 동일의미를 중복 표현하고 있다.

- be governed and interpreted by the provisions of Incoterms 2020 : Incoterms 2020의 규정이 적용되고 해석된다.

- The Buyer shall hold the Seller harmless from liability ~ : Buyer는 Seller가 ~책임으로 인하여 피해를 보지 않도록 해야 한다.

- out of or in relation to or in connection with this Contract : 계약과 관련하여. out of, in relation to, in connection with 모두 "계약과 관련하여"라는 말이지만 계약과 관련된 여러 측면을 포괄적으로 명시하기 위하여 중첩적으로 용어를 사용하는 것이 법률 및 계약 조항문의 한 특성이다.

- award rendered by the arbitrator : 중재인의 판정

- be final and binding upon both parties : 최종적인 것이며 양당사자를 구속한다.

- conclusion and the performance : 체결과 이행

- be governed by Korean law : 한국법이 적용된다.

E10 주문서

HK Trading Inc.

12/Floor, St. John's Building
33 Garden Road, Central, Hong Kong

Date : May 24, 2021

Our P/O No. : 09/00
Your Offer No. : 711F-1935

SM Company, Inc.
511 Yeongdong-daero, Kangnam-gu
Seoul, Korea 06164

PURCHASE ORDER

Gentlemen:
We are pleased to place an order to you based on the terms and conditions specified hereunder:

Item #	Description	Quantity	Unit Price	Amount	Remarks
2543-71	2-Piece Speaker System Model : J-2130	400	US$ 35.50	US$ 14,200	
2543-81	Digital Speaker System Model : DD-9910	300	US$ 125.00	US$ 37,500	
	TOTAL			US$ 51,700	

Price Terms : CIP, Hong Kong
Date of Shipment : During July, 2021
Payment : By an irrevocable L/C at sight
Packing : Each piece to be separately packaged, 20 pieces packed in an export carton.
Origin : Korea

Please note that we make this order on a trial basis as per your confirmation offer of April 30, 2021. We will rush to open an L/C upon receipt of your final confirmation.

Very truly yours,

Chen Chang

Chen Chang, President

내용 HK Trading사가 SM사에 내는 스피커 수입 주문서이다.

• 주 요 용 어 및 표 현 •

- based on the terms and conditions specified hereunder : 아래에 명시한 조건
  으로
- description : 상품명세, 물품설명
- CIP : Carriage and Insurance Paid to, 운송비 보험료 지급조건
- please note that ～ : ～를 유념하십시오.
- make an order : 주문을 하다. 주문을 내다.
- trial basis : 시험적으로, 즉 trial order라는 의미이다. 사보고 좋으면 다음에
  많이 혹은 계속적으로 주문하겠다는 것.
- rush to open : 개설을 서두르다. 빠른 시간 내 개설하다.
- as per your confirmation offer : 당신회사의 확인조건 offer에 따라.
  확인조건 offer는 오퍼에 "subject to our final confirmation"와 같은 단서가
  붙은 offer로서 offer를 받은 사람이 승낙을 하더라도 계약이 성립되지 않고
  이에 다시 offer를 낸 사람이 승낙해야만 계약이 성립한다. 따라서 확인조건
  offer를 비롯한 조건부 offer는 구속력이 없기 때문에 법적인 측면에서 엄격
  하게 보면 오퍼가 아니다.
- your final confirmation : 당신회사의 최종확인.
  여기서는 확인조건부오퍼에 대해서 주문하는 것이기 때문에 반드시 상대방의
  확인이 있어야 계약이 성립하게 된다.
  일반적으로 볼 때 만약 order가 상대방의 offer가 있는 상태에서 주어졌다면
  이 order는 승낙이 되므로 상대방의 주문확인이 필요 없다. 그러나 상대방의
  offer가 없는 상태에 주어졌다면 이 order는 offer가 되므로 상대방의 승낙인
  confirmation이 있어야 계약이 성립한다. 그러나 상대방의 offer가 있었다고
  하더라도 확실히 하기 위해서 이 같은 주문확인을 요청하기도 한다.

E11 주문의 확인

SM Company, Inc.

4501, 45th Floor, Trade Tower
511 Yeongdong-daero, Kangnam-gu, Seoul, Korea 06164

June 10, 2021

HK Trading Inc.
12/Floor, St. John's Building
33 Garden Road, Central, Hong Kong

Dear Mr. Chang:

We want to thank you for your initial order for our speakers, models J-2130 and DD-9910 and want to welcome you as one of our valued customers.

We are confirming that the items ordered are in stock and available at the terms stated in your order so we have already made arrangements for shipment. The goods should reach you by the end of August, provided there aren't any unforeseen delays.

We are confident that you will be completely satisfied with the products and with the overall manner in which we handle this order.

We sincerely hope this will be the beginning of a long and prosperous business relationship.

Very truly yours,

내용 SM사가 HK Trading사의 스피커 수입 주문에 대하여 보내는 주문확인서
한이다.

• 주 요 용 어 및 표 현 •

- initial order : 첫 주문, 시주문(=first order)
- want to welcome : 환영하고자 한다. 환영한다.
- valued customers : 귀빈, 귀한 고객
- be in stock : 재고가 있는
- made arrangements for shipment : 선적을 위한 준비를 하였다.
- by the end of August : 8월 말까지
- provided : 만약에(=if)
- unforeseen delays : 예기치 않은 지연
- completely satisfied with : 완전히 만족하는, 아주 만족하는
- the overall manner in which we handle this order : 주문에 대한 우리의 전
  반적인 일처리
- a long and prosperous business relationship : 오랫동안 번성하는 거래관계

✓	order

1. 명사표현
initial order / first order 첫 주문   regular order 정기주문
trial order / test order 시험주문   substantial order 대량주문
repeat order 재주문   large order 대량주문
additional order 추가주문   original order 원주문

2. 동사표현
to order 주문하다.
to place(give, put in, submit, send) an order 주문을 하다.
to accept(receive, take, get) an order 주문을 받다.
to execute(fill, fulfill, carry out, attend to, complete) an order 주문을 이행하다.
to confirm an order 주문을 확인하다.
to cancel(countermand) an order 주문을 취소하다.
to book(note, enter) an order 주문을 기장하다(받다).

E12 주문의 거절

SM Company, Inc.
4501, 45th Floor, Trade Tower
511 Yeongdong-daero, Kangnam-gu, Seoul, Korea 06164

June 10, 2021

HK Trading Inc.
12/Floor, St. John's Building
33 Garden Road, Central, Hong Kong

Dear Mr. Chang:

We want to thank you very much for your order of May 24 for our speaker system, Model DD-9910. However, we regret to inform you that we are unable to fulfill your order for the time being.

Currently we have no stock available for the items requested and cannot say with certainty when we will be able to make a delivery.

However, as a substitute we can offer to you our new model DD-9920 which is far superior to the DD-9910 in quality and performance. The price of the DD-9920 is only a little higher at US$ 135.50. At present it is the best selling model in our home market.

Should you feel somewhat uneasy about the price of the DD-9920, we would like to recommend our model DD-9900 which is similar in features, performance, and overall quality but at a much lower price of US$ 105.00.

We await any further requests you may have.

Very truly yours,

내용 SM사가 HK Trading사의 스피커 주문에 대하여 재고가 없어 응할 수 없음을 알리고 대체상품의 주문을 권유하는 내용이다.

• 주 요 용 어 및 표 현 •

- are unable to fulfill your order : 당신의 주문에 응할 수 없음을
- for the time being : 당분간
- currently : 지금(=now, at present)
- have no stock available : 재고가 없는(=be out of stock, be no longer in stock, be exhausted, be sold out, sell out, inventory shortage)
- with certainty : 확실히(=certainly)
- make a delivery : 인도하다.
- as a substitute : 대체품으로서
- is far superior to ~ : ~보다 훨씬 우수한
- in quality and performance : 품질과 성능면에서
- a little higher at US$ 135.50 : 약간 높아서 135.50달러이다.
- should you feel somewhat uneasy about ~ : ~면에서 다소 곤란하다면
- we would like to recommend ~ : ~을 추천하고자 합니다.
- overall quality : 전반적인 품질, 품질전반

✓	달의 부분적 기간 표시

1. 달의 초순, 중순, 하순
   the begining of May : 초순(1일부터 10일까지)
   the middle of ~ : 중순(11일부터 20일까지)
   the end of ~ : 하순(21일부터 말일까지)

2. 달의 전반과 후반
   the first half of ~ : 전반(1일부터 15일까지)
   the second half of ~ : 후반(16일부터 말일까지)

Useful Expressions

1 청 약

📋 오퍼의 제시

- We are pleased to offer you as follows:
- We <u>offer you</u> the goods on the terms and conditions <u>specified below</u>.

offer you	*specified below*
make an offer for	*below*
are pleased to offer you	*following*
have pleasure in offering you	*as follows*
have the pleasure of offering you	*stated below*
take pleasure in offering you	*described as follows*

- In reply to your inquiry of May 15, we have the pleasure of offering you as follows:
- We are pleased to offer to you the compact disk model No. 777 as follows:
- We are pleased to offer you 5,000 sets of model CM-8000 Headphones at US$ 65.50 per set FOB Busan for September shipment subject to your acceptance reaching us by June 30.
- We have faxed you the following offer as per the enclosed confirmation.
- We confirm our e-mail sent this morning offering you the following goods.

📋 오퍼의 유효기간의 제시

- We are pleased to <u>make a firm offer</u> for 50 M/T copper sheets subject to your <u>acceptance</u> received here by May 10.

make a firm offer	*acceptance*	*received here by May 10*
offer to you	*reply*	*reaching us by May 10*
	confirmation	*being received here by May 10*

- This special offer is subject to your reply reaching us by June 10.
- This offer is <u>open for</u> your acceptance <u>on or before June 10.</u>

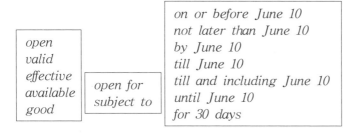

- This offer is effective till May 1, 2021.
- Our offer <u>holds good</u> until the end of May.

> holds good
> is valid
> is in effect

- We offer you subject to your acceptance reaching us by noon May 20 as follows:
- We take pleasure in offering you the following goods, subject to your reply received here by May 25.
- Unfortunately, we cannot keep these prices effective more than 3 weeks from the date of this letter and we wish to receive your order by return mail.

📋 조건부오퍼의 제시

- We submit the following offer <u>subject to our final confirmation.</u>

> subject to our final confirmation
> subject to being unsold
> subject to prior sale

- The price is subject to change without notice.
- All prices are subject to change without notice, in accordance with exchange fluctuations.

- We offer you the below mentioned goods subject to our final confirmation.

📑 승낙 권유를 위한 부가설명

1. 가격상황

- As for the above offer, it is extremely probable that prices will <u>rise even more</u>, and it would, therefore, be <u>to your interest</u> to place your orders without delay.

rise even more increase yet again continue to rise	to your interest to your advantage in your best interest

- We can not guarantee that these prices will be available next month, because the cost of materials is steadily increasing.

- As prices <u>are rising</u>, we <u>advise you to order</u> without delay.

As Since	are rising are steadily increasing are going up are trending upward are on the rise	advise you to order suggest you place an order urge you to place an order quickly

- Although prices have been going up since the beginning of this year, we have not yet raised our prices, but may have to do so soon.

- In view of the increase in wages and raw materials, the price may rise before long.

- We are clearing our stock now, so these prices are 20% lower than those of other manufacturers.

2. 재고상황

- Large orders are rushing in from your country, therefore our inventory is running out very quickly.

- Our <u>inventory is</u> limited due to increased demand for this type of article.

inventory is
stock is
supplies are

■ We are afraid that our stock will be exhausted.

■ Due to the inventory <u>being short</u> and an unfavorable outlook for the new crop, it is most likely that the prices will go up before long.

being short
running short
being low
being out

3. 시장상황

■ The market has been steadily rising, and so we have no further inventory available to offer <u>even at a higher price.</u>

even at a higher price
at any price

■ We cannot guarantee these offers will be repeated once their time limit has elapsed, due to the very heavy demand and the orders that we are booking everyday.

■ We expect <u>no further drop in price</u> in the near future.

drop	*no further drop in price*
decline	*the price won't go down any more*

■ If our offer is not acceptable, we must <u>switch to other</u> clients in China, where large quantities are now being imported at a higher price. You are urged to accept this best price before the date of expiry.

switch to other
seriously consider other

■ The market is very <u>brisk</u> with a strong upward trend.

> *brisk*
> *active*
> *viable*
> *strong*

- The market for cotton <u>has made a sudden advance</u>.

> *has made a sudden advance*
> *has rapidly advanced*

- The market is in a very strong position.
- The great demand for raw silk caused a turn in market.
- There is a promising market for good quality office machines.
- <u>In view of</u> recent <u>heavy demand</u> for this type of article, we would recommend you to place an order without delay.

> *In view of*
> *Viewing*
> *In consideration of*
> *Considering*
> *In light of*
> *Due to*

> *heavy demand*
> *big demand*
> *keen demand*
> *increased demand*

맺음말

- Your prompt acceptance of this offer would be highly appreciated.
- We await your acceptance of this offer by return mail.
- We hope that you will accept this offer and that this may be the beginning of our business relations.
- We suggest that you take advantage of this most competitive offer right away.
- We trust that the above offer is excellent in both price and delivery.
- We are certain these goods will <u>meet</u> your <u>requirements</u>, and hope to receive your <u>first order</u>.

| meet
fill
satisfy | requirements
wants
needs |

| first order
initial order |

- We are confident that a trial order will give you <u>full satisfaction.</u>

| full satisfaction
complete satisfaction |

- We are confident that you will be completely satisfied.
- We trust that you will be able to accept our offer.
- We trust that this offer will meet your acceptance.
- It is always a pleasure to serve you.
- We stand ready <u>to be at your service,</u> awaiting your order.

| to be at your service
to be of service to you
to serve you |

- Awaiting your acceptance of this offer, and hoping that this may be the beginning of a venture that will be <u>of profit to both of us.</u>

| of profit to both of us
mutually beneficial |

- We very much look forward to receiving an order from you.
- We hope you will take full advantage of our offer.
- We hope you will find our quotation satisfactory and look forward to <u>receiving your order.</u>

| receiving your order
booking your order |

- <u>We assure you that</u> any order you place with us <u>will have our prompt and careful attention.</u>

We assure you that ~ *Be assured that ~* *You may be sure that ~*	*will have our prompt and careful attention* *will receive our full attention* *will be handled quickly and efficiently*

② 승 낙

🗎 서두 및 본문

- <u>Thank you for</u> your letter of June 10 offering silk jackets.

> *Thank you for*
> *We acknowledge with thanks*
> *We appreciate*
> *We received*

- We appreciate your offer of the hand tools with the catalog.

- We are pleased to accept your firm offer of the 18th June for 4,000 cases of floppy diskettes at US$ 5 per case.

- We accept your offer in full and are going to instruct our bank to open an L/C in your favor.

- Thank you for your offer of February 12 which is receiving our full attention.

- We have received your offer for our canned food subject to your final confirmation.

- Please <u>forward</u> the following goods:

> *forward*
> *deliver*
> *supply*

- Thank you for your offer of May 20, which we accept <u>on the terms quoted</u>.

> *on the terms quoted*
> *as follows*

- We have accepted your offer in appreciation of your past services though we have similar offers from other sources.
- We are pleased to enclose our Order No. 123 for your offer of May 3.

📋 승낙의 맺음말

- We trust that you will pay particular attention to our acceptance.
- We are looking forward to your confirmation of this acceptance and also the sales note.
- If your goods are satisfactory, we may be able to place substantial orders.
- Your prompt attention to this order will be highly appreciated.

③ 청약에 대한 거절

- We are not in a position to accept your offer at the moment.
- We are unable to accept your offer <u>at present.</u>

> *at present*
> *for the time being*

- We thank you very much for your offer of June 10 for cameras but regret our inability to accept it as we are overbooked at present.
- We thank you for your offer, but regret to say that your prices do not allow us to accept the offer.
- Unfortunately we cannot accept your offer because another supplier in your <u>district</u> offered us a similar article at a 5% lower price.

> *district*
> *area*
> *region*

- We appreciate your offer of June 10 for "Hankuk" bags, but regret our inability to accept it as we are already above our production capacity to meet demand.

■ The price you offered is about 15% higher than the level workable for us, so we refrained from even making a counter offer.

4 Counter offer

■ We would like to make the following counter offer.

■ We wish to make a counter offer to your offer of June 10 for blue jeans.

■ We accept your offer with the following modification.

■ We can accept your offer if you can shorten the delivery period.

> *shorten the delivery period*
> *move up the delivery date*

■ We suggest the following modification to your offer of May 3 for the Wireless Headphones.

■ We would like to make a firm counter offer at US$ 110 per piece subject to your reply arriving here by May 3.

■ In view of the prevailing prices in this market, your price is a little expensive.

■ The price is rather high considering tight market conditions here; could you please quote a little lower.

> | *high* | *please quote a little lower* |
> | *stiff* | *please go a little lower* |

■ Please shave just a little more off your price.

■ One of our important customers is ready to buy 5,000 yards for a September shipment if you can reduce the price to 30 cents per yard C.I.F. Jakarta.

■ We would be pleased to place an order with you if you could grant us a 5% discount.

■ We can place an order if you can give us a price reduction of 10%.

- For an order of this large quantity we would expect a wholesale discount off your list prices.
- We will accept your offer if you can guarantee shipment during June, not July as stated in your offer.
- A comparison of your offer with that of our regular suppliers <u>shows</u> that their figures are more competitive.

shows
reveals

- The market is so <u>slow</u> at present that we need to ask you to <u>come down</u> a bit on your pricing.

slow	come down
slack	do down
dull	lower
poor	make low

- We would like to do business with you but find your prices a little high according to the current market situation. Therefore, if you can give us a 6% discount, we would place an order for 5,000 units.
- The order must be shipped <u>not later than July 18</u>.

not later than July 18
no later than July 18
within 2 weeks after receipt of order

- Due to the increased supply of similar products, it is certain that prices will <u>fall</u> before long. Considering this situation, we believe you can <u>allow</u> us a special discount of 10%.

fall / drop / slump / decline / go down / slide hit bottom / reach a new low	allow grant give

- Please confirm this order subject to the above-mentioned modifications should you find the terms acceptable.

5 Counter offer에 대한 답신

- We have duly received your counter offer for laser printers.
- We have carefully considered your counter proposal of July 18 concerning our offer for P-IV computers.
- We accept your offer and decide to <u>reduce the price</u> to US$ 10 per piece as you requested.

> reduce the price
> drop the price
> cut the price
> bring down the price

- We <u>are glad to accept</u> an extra discount of 2% over and above the usual trade discount in consideration of a quantity of 5,000 M/T.

> are glad to accept
> are willing to agree to

- Regretfully, the minimum price we could accept would be US$ 12 per piece.
- At the moment, the best reduction we could <u>grant</u> you would be 3%.

> grant
> extend to

- Our calculation is so close that it is simply impossible for us to make any further concessions.
- We are very sorry we cannot give you any discount because the price is fixed.

- We have quoted special prices and therefore the offer cannot be subject to the usual discounts.
- We regret that we are unable to <u>allow</u> even the smallest <u>reduction</u> in price.

allow *make* *give*	*reduction* *concession* *deduction* *cut*

- Our goods are quite reasonable in price considering their superior quality and their production costs.

6 주 문(매수오퍼)

📋 서 두

- We are pleased to <u>place an order with you</u> for your auto radios on the terms and conditions set forth below:

place an order with you *give you an order* *make an order with you*

- With reference to your letter of March 10, we are pleased to give an order for the following:
- We have the pleasure of sending you an order for 5,000 pieces of leather handbags based on your sample and price list you sent us on June 5.
- We are pleased to submit to you an order for 500 pcs. of "GAG" fancy panels.
- Would you <u>send us</u> 50 units of radio as soon as you can?

send us *furnish us with*

- Please let us know whether you could <u>fill</u> our order.

> *fill*
> *take up*
> *accept*
> *take care of*

- We enclose our order sheet for fountain pens with detailed instructions.
- We find your terms satisfactory and are now sending you an order for the following items:
- We have received with thanks your letter of September 10 together with samples of silk neckties, and are now pleased to place the following order with you <u>as a trial</u>.

> *as a trial*
> *to start with*

- Please <u>deliver</u> the product Model #3 <u>as listed in your catalog</u>.

> | | *as listed in your catalog* |
> |---|---|
> | *deliver* | *in accordance with your offer* |
> | *ship* | *as per particulars given* |
> | *send* | *as specified below* |
> | *forward* | *under the following terms and conditions* |

- Please <u>book</u> the following order.

> *book / take /*
> *receive / enter /*
> *complete*

- Enclosed, you will find our purchase order No. 3 under your offer.
- We are enclosing our Order Sheet No. 1234 for SG color televisions and would appreciate having your Sales Note as usual.
- We highly appreciate your offer of September 10 and enclose our order No. 1122 for 100 dozen toys.

🗐 주문조건 및 지시사항

1. 상품의 규격 및 품질

■ The goods must <u>agree with</u> <u>our specification</u> in every respect.

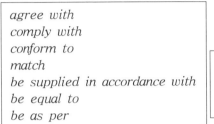

■ If pattern No. 123 is not available, please <u>send</u> a substitute, but the price must not <u>exceed</u> US$ 30 per unit.

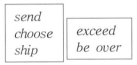

■ Weights and colors must be as per the samples you sent us.

■ Please supply in assorted colors, preferably 20 doz. each of dark brown, navy blue, light green, and orange.

■ The alcohol content must not be under 15%, and we place this order subject to this guarantee.

■ The over-all length must not exceed 6 ft. and the total weight must not be above 200kgs.

■ <u>We need to point out that</u> the machine tools must be guaranteed to be to our own specifications.

> *We need to point out that*
> *We need to make it very clear that*
> *Please note that*

■ The minimum quantity required is three tons, and we would take up to a maximum of five tons if the quality is high enough.

2. 인도시기

- The order must be <u>shipped</u> without delay.

> *shipped*
> *executed*
> *completed*

- The delivery date must be strictly kept. Please note the delivery date.
- Please confirm that you can supply this quantity by the required date.
- Unless the goods can be shipped by October 30, we will have to <u>cancel</u> the order.

> *cancel / annul*
> *revoke / withdraw*
> *countermand*

- As our stock is running short, we must have the goods by the end of September at the latest.
- We have accepted this offer because the delivery date is so attractive. We would like to ask you, therefore, to do everything possible to ensure an on time delivery.
- We would ask you to do everything possible to ensure punctual shipment.
- We request you to make shipment so that the goods may arrive here not later than August 31.
- We must have the goods <u>by the end of</u> November as our stock is running short.

> *by the end of*
> *by the middle of*
> *by the beginning of*

- If you cannot make shipment by May 30, please cancel our order and refund the money.

- We reserve the right to cancel this order if the goods are not shipped on or before March 17.

3. 선적지시

- Shipping instructions and the L/C will be airmailed.
- Please inform us when the order is ready for shipment.
- When the goods are ready for shipment, please inform us, and we will send you detailed instructions.
- Shipping instructions will be airmailed upon receipt of your acceptance of the order.
- We would like to have them sent by the first vessel possible as our customers require them as soon as possible.
- Punctual shipment is essential.

4. 포 장

- Please pay special attention to packing and the time of shipment.
- Please limit the weight of any one carton to 30 lbs.
- Packing in sturdy wooden cases is essential. Cases must be nailed, battened and secured by overall metal strapping.
- Overall measurements of each case must not exceed $4' \times 2' \times 2'$.
- Please make up our order into bales of about 5 cwt., covered with waterproof sheets and strapped vertically and horizontally with metal bands.
- Please mark all boxes as usual, but number them consecutively from No. 001 upwards.
- Detailed instructions regarding marks and numbers will follow.

5. 보 험

- Insure on ICC(C) and Breakage for 110% of the invoice amount.
- War Risks to be covered by you for our account.
- Please insure for 10% over the invoice amount on an All Risks policy.

- Please effect insurance on ICC(B) including War Risks and prepay the premium and freight.

6. 대금지급

- Please draw a draft at 90 days after sight on us for the amount of your invoice.
- We propose to pay by Bill of Exchange at 60d/s, D/A. Please confirm if this is acceptable to you.
- For reimbursement, we have applied to our bankers for an irrevocable credit to be issued in favor of your company.
- We have today instructed our bankers here, The DBM Bank, Ltd., to open an irrevocable credit in your favor, for US$ 65,000.⁻ valid until November 15.

📑 주문확인, 지시사항준수, 기타

- Please confirm the receipt of this order as soon as possible.
- Please inform us whether you can accept this order on these terms and conditions.
- Please execute the order in strict accordance with our instructions.

execute / carry out *deliver / ship* *fill / fulfill*	*in strict accordance with* *in strict conformity with* *according to* *agreeably to* *as*

- Instructions for designs and assortment will be sent to you as soon as we receive them from our clients.

📑 맺음말

- We shall appreciate your prompt attention to this order.

prompt attention   *careful attention*   *best attention*

- We shall expect you to execute this order in due course.
- We hope that this order will meet your immediate acceptance and careful execution as usual.
- We expect a careful execution of this order.

expect
rely on

- Please give this order your prompt and best attention.
- If this order is satisfactory, we may be able to place substantial orders.

satisfactory	substantial / regular
completely acceptable	large / further

- This special order is very important for our company, so we would like to ask you to pay your closest attention to the quality of the goods.
- You may be assured that we will place a repeat order should the present order be executed in a satisfactory manner to us.

⑦ 주문의 수락

📄 서 두

- Thank you very much for your Order No. 345 for DVD players.

Thank you very much for
We appreciate
We have the pleasure of receiving
We are pleased to accept
We are pleased to confirm
We are grateful for
It is a pleasure to receive
We have received with pleasure

- Thank you for your order No. 121 of April 6 for leather handbags which we confirm as follows:
- We acknowledge your order of May 20 for which we thank you.
- We appreciate your kind acceptance of our offer for color televisions.
- We want to say how pleased we were to receive your order of May 20, and welcome you as one of our valued customers.
- We thank you for your letter of May 10 enclosing your order No. 123 which is now being processed.

> *is now being processed*
> *has been processed immediately*
> *has been already passed on to our manufacturers*
> *has been given our immediate attention*

- Thank you very much for your order No. 30 of October 10. We are pleased to accept it and are sending herewith our Sales Note No. 20.
- We are pleased to confirm our sale to you of the following goods on the terms and conditions set forth below.

> *set forth*
> *stated*
> *stipulated*

- We appreciate your order dated June 11 and would like to inform you that your goods will leave here by the M.S. "Pacific" on June 28.

📑 주문이행에 대한 사항

- You can rest assured of our best attention to your order.

> *You can rest assured of*
> *We assure you of*

- As the goods are in stock, they will be shipped by the s/s "Arriving" leaving Busan around the 10th of May.

- Be assured that your instructions will be carefully followed.
- Our factory has been instructed to start manufacturing at once, and the goods will be shipped as near to the specified date as possible.
- As you requested, the order will be sent by June 10, and your specifications will be followed to the letter.
- We shall do our best to execute this order at the specified time.
- Please <u>let us have your instructions</u> regarding marks and numbers together with a letter of credit to cover.

> *let us have your instructions*
> *send us your instructions*
> *inform us of your instructions*

- Our factory has been instructed to start manufacturing at once, and the goods will be shipped within the date specified.

🗎 신용장개설요청

- We would appreciate knowing when you will open your letter of credit in our favor.
- Please open a Letter of Credit for US$ 200,000 upon receipt of which we will execute the order with our highest attention.
- The time of shipment is fast approaching, and we have to ask you to open a credit and send shipping instructions promptly.
- As this is going to be our first business transaction, we would like to ask you to arrange payment by opening an irrevocable credit in our favor through your bankers.
- The goods of your order are now ready for shipment, pending the arrival of your L/C.

🗎 맺음말

- We assure you of our most careful attention to this order.

■ We hope that this first transaction will be the beginning of a long and prosperous association. You may be sure that we shall <u>spare no efforts</u> to <u>satisfy</u> your <u>wishes</u>.

spare no efforts *do the utmost* *do our best*	*satisfy* *meet* *fulfill*	*wishes* *needs* *desires*

■ We thank you again for this order, which, we assure you, will have our prompt and careful attention.

■ We hope that this order will be the first of many and that we may enjoy many years of pleasant business relations together.

■ We wish to thank you for this order and await your further instructions.

■ We assure you that we will make every effort to meet your requirements.

■ We welcome you as a customer, and hope that this will lead to permanent business relations of mutual benefit.

⑧ 주문의 거절

📄 서 두

■ Regarding Item No. 3 on your Order No. 123, we regret that <u>we do not manufacture this item</u> in stainless steel.

we do not manufacture this item *this item is not available*

■ We <u>regret to inform you</u> that item No. 2 of your order is sold out at present and that we are unable to serve you at this time.

regret to inform you *are sorry to say*

- We regret very much to inform you that the goods you ordered are no longer in production. Therefore we would like to submit a quotation for a substitute.
- We are very sorry for being unable to accept your order, since the design of our product doesn't match your specifications.
- We are sorry we have to <u>decline</u> your order because our factory is fully occupied with other orders.

> decline
> turn down

- We appreciate your order No. 5 of August 10 for celluloid film, but regret that we are unable to accept it at the old price. Owing to the sudden rise in both material costs and wages, we had to revise all our prices.

📄 주문 수락을 못하는 이유

1. 가격문제

- Although we would like to do business with you, we are sorry that it is difficult for us to manufacture them at the price you <u>ask.</u>

> ask
> request

- We <u>would love to book your order,</u> but we regret that these goods cannot be bought today at your <u>limit</u> due to cost increases.

> would love to book your order
> would like to serve you
> sincerely appreciate your order

> limit
> price

- We have been compelled to raise our prices <u>due to</u> <u>increased labor costs.</u>

> due to
> owing to

> increased labor costs
> increased raw material costs
> the won appreciation

- We fear that we will have to revise our pricing considerably to produce the quantity you have in mind.

- The price is not attractive enough to induce us to take up the manufacturing of this item.

- We fear the quantity you require may not justify our expenses and the trouble involved in readjusting our manufacturing process.

- It would be difficult for us to supply the merchandise without raising the prices.

- We regret that we cannot accept it as the price you quoted is an old one which leaves us with no profit margin and is far lower than our competitors for goods of similar quality.

- Commodity prices are increasing sharply, so we are compelled to revise our prices to cover at least part of this increase.

- Because of the small quantity, we cannot accept your order at the price you mention. However, if you could double your order, we would reconsider.

2. 기술상 문제

- Supplies of raw materials are becoming increasingly difficult to obtain, threefore we <u>have to</u> decline your order.

> *have to*
> *are forced to*
> *cannot but*

- We may not supply exactly the same <u>articles</u> that you <u>want</u> as they are not in our line.

> | *articles* | *want* |
> | --- | --- |
> | *goods* | *need* |
> | *product* | *require* |
> | | *specify* |

- Owing to the technical difficulties we are facing in production, we may not be able to accept any further orders for some time.

- We have to retool our machines since your specifications of the product doesn't match our production line. The cost involved would be prohibitive unless you could place an order for more than 10,000 pieces.
- It has become very hard to get raw materials, therefore we have no alternative but to decline your order.

3. 상품의 확보, 인도시기 등의 문제

- We have many orders on hand for this article, and could not possibly effect shipment within the time you suggested.
- We shall have to decline this order because the earliest delivery we could promise at present would be next January.
- Unfortunately the recent rush of orders for our footwear has made it impossible to promise shipment earlier than July 31.
- Since you make delivery by June 10 a firm condition, we deeply regret that we cannot accept your order. Due to increased demand, we can ship this item no earlier than Aug. 1, 2021.

> *this item no earlier than Aug. 1, 2021*
> *these models Aug. 1, 2021 at the earliest*

- Since we are now fully occupied with orders, we are sorry to have to decline your order.
- We could not very well guarantee shipment within 3 weeks; we have on our waiting list a few dozen customers for this model.

4. 재고 문제

- They are out of stock, and we could not tell exactly when we might be able to lay in a large enough lot for you.
- We have accepted a rush of orders from European sources so that our stock is entirely cleared for the moment.

- The model you <u>asked for</u> is out of stock at present, and we no longer <u>produce</u> <u>it</u>. Although we have tried every source of supply we know, we have been unable to get the model.

asked for	*produce it*
requested	*carry this design*
wished for	*manufacture this item*

- Having been offered subject to prior sale, unfortunately the goods were sold out.

5. 기타 사정

- Although you asked us to ship your order on JS Lines, we must ship on a China flag vessel due to government regulation.
- Because of the acute shortage of shipping space available, we see no possibility of shipping the goods during June.
- We are now selling only to our sole agents, and refer you to SG company in your city, who we hope would be able to meet your needs.
- We have received your acceptance of our offer about 20 days after the expiry date. We are therefore unable to confirm your order.

📑 대체품 또는 대안의 권유

- We regret to inform you that this model is out of stock, and recommend <u>as a substitute Model No. 123</u>.

as a substitute Model No. 123
Model No. 123 as a substitute
Model No. 123 which is similar in all aspects
Model No. 123 which is an up−dated replacement
Model No. 123 which has replaced model No. 345
Model No. 123 at the same price and hope that you will agree
Model No. 123 as per the same quote and request your approval

- We can offer you a substitute which is the same price and of similar quality as the item ordered.
- As the article you ordered is temporarily out of stock, we ask you to choose another model from the enclosed samples.

> *to choose another model*
> *to select a suitable substitute*

- Our Model No. 123 is the nearest to the measurements you specified; however, it is only 32 in. deep instead of the 35 in. requested.

> *measurements you specified*
> *specification you requested*

- We can offer a very similar item FS No. 21 at US$ 1.20 instead. This chemical is available immediately from stock, and is perhaps even more suitable.
- We should appreciate your confirmation before supplying the goods of the nearest design.
- We are sorry for not being able to supply the exact goods as per your order. We recommend you buy the nearest ones as the enclosed sample.
- We strongly suggest you accept Item No. 3 in the catalog, as the item you selected is no longer obtainable.
- We are sorry for this and ask you, if possible, to consider extending the delivery date.

> *date*
> *terms*
> *time*

- We are eager to do business with you and we will be most happy to fulfill your order if you can consider extending the delivery date by 2 months.

| consider
accept | date
terms
time | by 2 months
to Aug. 1, 2021 |

📑 맺는말

- We will keep your letter in our file and will write to you again as soon as our suppliers resume production.
- You know how eager we are to assist you. In this case, however, it is really impossible to meet your wishes for the reasons given above.
- We shall be only too pleased to serve you as soon as conditions have improved.
- We are waiting for any further instructions you may give us.
- We sincerely regret that we are unable to serve you <u>at this time.</u>

| at this time
in this instance |

- Please inform us by return mail whether we may book your order at these prices.
- We hope that you will understand the circumstances which make us decline your order this time, and that you will allow us to help you in the future.
- Any further instructions that you may give us will receive our prompt attention.
- We look forward to your favorable reply.

CHAPTER
06

Standard
Trade
English

무역계약

1 무역계약의 의의

계약이란 일정한 권리관계의 발생을 목적으로 당사자간 의사의 합치에 의하여 성립하는 법률행위이다. 구두상의 합의를 포함한 어떠한 형태로의 합의로도 계약이 되지만 서면상의 계약은 월등한 증거능력을 갖는다. 그렇기 때문에 청약에 대한 승낙으로 의사는 합치되고 계약이 성립했지만 계약내용을 문서로서 명확히 함으로써 후일에 있을지 모를 분쟁을 방지하기 위하여 문서화하게 된다. 특히 국제무역에서는 국내거래에 비하여 지리적, 언어적 요인을 비롯한 여러 가지 요인으로 인하여 양 당사간에 의사소통이 원활하지 못하고, 계약의 합의시점에서 이행완료시점까지 상당한 시간이 소요되기 때문에 계약서를 작성해두는 것이 후일의 오해와 분쟁을 막아주는 대비책이 된다.

2 무역계약서의 형식

계약은 계약사항에 대한 당사자간 의사합치라는 실질적인 사항을 충족하면 되고 그 형식에 구애받지 않는다. 따라서 계약이라는 제목이 없거나 다른 말로 되어 있더라도 관계없다. Agreement, Contract 등의 제목하에 장문의 계약서도 계약이지만, 앞장에서 본대로 Sales Contract, Sales Note, Confirmation of Order, Purchase Contract, Purchase Note, Order Sheet 등도 양당사자가 서명함으로써 계약서가 된다. 본장에서는 장문계약을 중심으로 살펴보기로 한다.

3 일반거래조건협정(General Terms and Conditions)

일반거래조건협정은 거래에서 일반적이고 기초적인 사항에 대한 약정이다. 거래관계를 시작할 때 앞으로 계속될 거래관계에서 기본적으로 적용될 사항들에 대해서 사전적으로 합의하는 계약이다. 이러한 기본계약을 미리 교환해 두는 경우 이후의 개별계약에서는 기본계약에서 정하지 않은 사항만 합의하여 거래를 하면 되기 때문에 편리하다.

한편 개별거래에 사용되는 Sales Note나 Confirmation of Order 양식의 뒷면에 거래의 일반적이고도 기본적인 사항을 미리 인쇄해 두어 전면의 계약상에서 달리 명시하지 않는 한 그대로 적용토록 하는데 이도 일반무역조건협정이라 한다.

이러한 일반무역조건협정은 다음과 같은 사항들로 구성된다.

1. 계약의 본질에 관한 사항
2. 상품거래기초조건 : 품질결정기준, 가격표시기준, 수량과부족 허용범위, 인도일의 기준 및 인도방법, 상품검사 등
3. 계약의 성립에 관한 계약기초조건
4. 분쟁해결조항 및 준거법조항

4 무역계약의 종류

국제경제활동과 관련하여 다음과 같은 계약들이 있는데 무역에서는 물품매매계약이 가장 중요한 비중을 차지하고 있다.

1. 물품매매계약(Sales Agreement)
2. 판매점계약(Distributorship Agreement)
3. 대리점계약(Agency Agreement)
4. 기술제휴계약(License Agreement)
5. 위탁가공계약(Consignment Processing Agreement)
6. 합작투자계약(Joint Venture Agreement)

5 물품매매계약의 주요 조건

1) 품질조건(Quality)

(1) **품질의 결정방법** : 품질기준의 설정방법에 따라 ① 실견매매(Sale by Inspection), ② 견본매매(Sale by Sample), ③ 표준품매매(Sale by Standard), ④ 명세서매매(Sale by Specification / Description / Dimensions), ⑤ 규격매매(Sale

by Type / Grade), ⑥ 상표매매(Sale by Brand / Trade Mark) 등이 있다.

✓	표준품매매에서의 품질결정조건 용어

FAQ(fair average quality) Terms : 평균중등품질조건, 당해시기 당해장소 출하
　품의 평균 중등품을 기준으로 함. 농산물에 주로 사용
GMQ(good merchantable quality) Terms : 판매적격품질조건, 당해거래의 품질
　적격성을 기준으로 함. 목재, 냉동어류 등에 사용
USQ(usual standard quality) Terms : 보통품질조건, 미국 원면 거래에 사용

(2) **품질의 결정시기** : 어느 시점에서의 품질을 기준으로 하는가에 따라 선적
품질조건(shipped quality terms)과 양륙품질조건(landed quality terms)으로 나
뉜다.

✓	곡물류무역에서 사용되는 품질결정시기조건 용어

TQ(Tale Quale, Tel Quel) : 선적품질조건, 운송도중품질변화위험 매수인 부담,
　곡물거래에서 주로 사용
SD(Sea Damaged) : TQ와 동일하나 운송중 해수에 의한 품질변화위험은 매도
　인 부담
RT(Rye Terms) : 양륙품질조건, 운송도중품질변화위험 매도인 부담, 만주에서
　영국지역으로 수출되는 호밀(rye)거래에서 이 조건이 사용된 데서 유래

(3) **품질증명방법** : 검사기관, 검사방법 등을 정하게 된다.[1]

2) **수량조건(Quantity)**
(1) **수량의 단위** : 중량(weight), 용적(measurement), 개수(piece), 포장단위
(package), 길이(length), 넓이(width) 등의 단위기준을 정한다.
(2) **수량의 과부족** : 수량에 과부족이 발생할 경우 이에 대한 허용범위와 가격
산정방법 등을 정한다.

---

1) 감정기관을 surveyor라고 하고 품질감정보고서를 survey report라고 한다.
　[예] Lloyd's Surveyor, Societe Generale de Surveillance(SGS), Moody-Tottrup Int'l Co.

（3）**수량결정시기** : 선적수량조건(shipped weight terms, intaken quantity terms)과 양륙수량조건(landed weight terms, outturn quantity terms)이 있다.

（4）**수량증명방법** : 검량기관, 검량방법 등을 정한다.[2]

3) 가격조건(Price)

가격조건은 가격액수와 함께 거래통화를 정하고 정형거래조건상의 조건도 정하게 된다. 정형거래조건은 INCOTERMS로 대표되며 여기의 각 조건은 매도인과 매수인간에 소유권이전, 비용부담, 위험부담의 분계점과 양 당사자의 권리와 의무를 정하고 있다.

INCOTERMS의 각 조건은 매도인이 상품을 인도하는데 어디까지 부대 서비스를 제공하느냐를 나타내며, 이는 또한 해당상품의 가격에 포함되어지는 비용요소들의 범위를 나타내게 되는 것이다. 현행 INCOTERMS 2020의 각 조건의 주요내용은 아래의 표 및 그림과 같다.

INCOTERMS 2020

그 룹 별	약호	무역거래조건
모든 운송수단	EXW	Ex Works(현장인도조건)
	FCA	Free Carrier(운송인인도조건)
	CPT	Carriage Paid to(운송비지급조건)
	CIP	Carriage and Insurance Paid to(운송비보험료지급조건)
	DAP	Delivered At Place(도착지인도조건)
	DPU	Delivered at Place Unloaded(도착지양하인도조건)
	DDP	Delivered Duty Paid(관세지급반입인도조건)
해상운송	FAS	Free Alongside Ship(선측인도조건)
	FOB	Free on Board(본선인도조건)
	CFR	Cost and Freight(운임포함조건)
	CIF	Cost Insurance and Freight(운임보험료포함조건)

---

2) 검수 및 검량기관을 public weigher, official weigher, surveyor라고 하고, 발행하는 증명서를 certificate of weight, certificate of measurement라고 한다.

INCOTERMS 각 조건에서의 SELLER와 BUYER의 부담

모든 운송

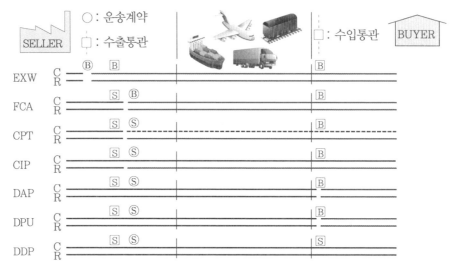

해상 운송

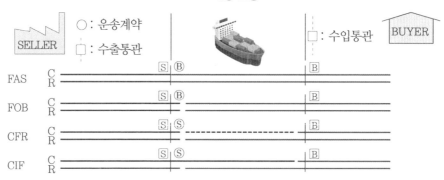

C : 비용부담   R : 위험부담

——— : SELLER의 부담(----- : 보험료 제외)   ——— : BUYER의 부담

S: SELLER의 통관   B: BUYER의 통관

Ⓢ : SELLER의 운송계약   Ⓑ : BUYER의 운송계약

4) 인도조건(Delivery)

선적시기, 선적일의 결정기준, 분할선적, 환적의 허용여부 등에 관하여 정한다.

5) 보험조건(Insurance)

CIF나 CIP의 경우와 같이 매도인이 매수인을 위해 보험에 드는 경우 보험종류, 보험금액, 화폐, 보험금지급장소 등에 대하여 정한다.

6) 대금결제조건(Payment)

신용장, D/P, D/A, T/T 등의 대금의 지급방법, 대금지급의 시기, 신용장에 의할 경우 신용장의 종류와 개설은행 및 개설시기, 연지급의 경우 어음기간 등을 정한다.

7) 포장조건(Packing)

포장의 종류 및 방법, 화인에 대하여 미리 약정하게 된다.[3]

8) 분쟁해결조건(Dispute Settlement)

클레임의 제기 방법 및 기한, 협의 및 중재 등의 분쟁해결방법 등에 대하여 정한다.

9) 기 타(Etc)

오퍼 및 주문의 조건 및 효력, 견본, 불가항력인정 사유와 처리, 재산권침해, 준거법 등에 관한 사항이 필요에 따라 포함된다.

---

[3] 국제거래에서는 국내거래에서 보다 포장의 중요성이 커진다. 상품이 장거리의 운송과정에서 손상될 가능성이 많고, 포장 잘못으로 인한 손실은 운송회사나 보험회사에서도 책임지지 않기 때문이다.

[F1] F1 일반거래조건 송부 서신

SM Company, Inc.

4501, 45th Floor, Trade Tower
511 Yeongdong-daero, Kangnam-gu, Seoul, Korea 06164

March 12, 2021

AMS Trading Company
908 Park Avenue
New York, NY 10017 U.S.A.

Gentlemen:

In reply to your letter of February 27 offering your business proposal, we are pleased to inform you that we are willing to serve you as our valued customer.

Before commencing any actual business, however, we wish to come to a complete agreement with you as to the general terms and conditions within which we should conduct our business activities. We propose that the terms and conditions specified in the enclosed memorandum be applied to all transactions between us unless otherwise prearranged.

Needless to say, the memorandum is submitted for your comment and is open to your suggestions. We hope, however, you will find the clauses acceptable as they stand, and if so, please sign and return the duplicate, keeping the original for yourself.

We are very pleased to have you as a business partner and trust this marks the beginning of an enduring and fruitful collaboration.

Very truly yours,

내용 SM사가 새로 거래관계를 갖게 된 AMS Trading사와 일반거래조건 약정을 교환하기 위하여 이를 송부하는 내용이다.

• 주요 용어 및 표현 •

- business proposal : 거래제의
- are willing to ~ : 기꺼이 ~한다.
- as our valued customer : 우리의 귀한 고객으로
- come to a complete agreement : 완전한 합의에 이르다(＝arrive at ~).
- general terms and conditions : 일반거래조건
- conduct business activities : 거래를 하다. 거래를 행하다.
- memorandum : 비망록, 각서. 여기서 양사가 교환하는 general terms and conditions를 말한다.
- unless otherwise prearranged : 사전에 달리 조정하지 않는 한, 사전에 달리 협의하지 않은 한
- needless to say : 당연히, 말할 필요도 없이
- be submitted for your comment : 당신의 논평을 받아들이겠다. 당신 의견을 따르겠다.
- is open to your suggestions : 당신의 제의에 대해서 개방되어 있다. 당신의 제의를 흔쾌히 받아들이겠다.
- find the clauses acceptable as they stand : 조건을 현재대로 받아들이다. 그대로의 조건에 만족하다.
- please sign and return the duplicate, keeping the original for yourself : 서명하여 원본은 당신이 보관하고 부본은 반송해주십시오. original과 duplicate은 효력상 동일하다.
- enduring : 영속적인(＝lasting)
- collaboration : 협조, 합작, 협동(＝cooperation)
- an enduring and fruitful collaboration은 같은 취지로 a prosperous business connection, a mutually profitable relationship 등으로 표현할 수 있다.

F2 일반무역거래조건

AGREEMENT ON
GENERAL TERMS AND CONDITIONS OF BUSINESS

This Agreement entered into between AMS Trading Company, New York, U.S.A.(hereinafter called the "Buyer") and SM Company, Inc., Seoul, Korea (hereinafter called the "Seller") witness as follows:

1. Business : Both Seller and Buyer shall act as principals on their own account and responsibility.
2. Goods : Goods in business, their unit to be quoted, and their mode of packing shall be stated in the attached list.
3. Prices : Unless otherwise specified in e-mail, facsimile, cable, telex, or letter, all prices submitted by either party shall be quoted in U.S Dollars on a CIF New York basis.
4. Firm Offers : All offers shall be considered "firm" subject to a reply reaching the Sellers within ten (10) days from and including the day dispatched. Sundays and all official Bank Holidays are excepted.
5. Orders : Any business closed by e-mail, facsimile, cable, or telex shall be confirmed in writing without delay, and orders thus confirmed shall not be cancelled unless by mutual consent.
6. Letter of Credit : An Irrevocable Letter of Credit shall be established in favor of the Seller immediately upon confirmation of sale. Credit shall be made available fourteen (14) days beyond the stipulated time of shipment in each contract.
7. Payment : Drafts shall be drawn under Letter of Credit at sight, documents attached, for the full invoice amount.
8. Shipment : All goods sold in accordance with this Agreement shall be shipped to the Buyers within the period stipulated. The date of the Bill of Lading shall be taken as a conclusive proof of the day of shipment. Unless expressly agreed upon, the port of shipment shall be at the Seller's option.
9. Marine Insurance : All shipment shall be covered per ICC(B) for a sum equal to the amount of the invoice plus ten (10) per cent, unless any other conditions are specifically agreed upon. All policies shall be made out in US Dollars and claims payable in Seoul.

• 주요 용어 및 표현 •

- hereinafter : 여기 이후로, 지금부터, 앞으로
- shall ~ : ~할 것이다. ~하기로 되어 있다. ~하기로 한다. ~하여야 한다. 여기 계약조항들에 나오는 shall은 당사자의 의무 의미를 담고 있다. 법규정이나 계약의 조항에서 이와 같은 shall이 많이 사용된다.
- act as principals : 본인의 자격으로 행한다.
- on their own account and responsibility : 그들 자신의 계산과 책임으로
- unit to be quoted : 가격산정되는 단위, 거래되는 단위
- mode of packing : 포장의 방식
- in the attached list : 첨부목록에
- within ten (10) days from and including the day dispatched : 발송일을 포함하여 발송 후 10일 이내
- in writing : 서면으로
- unless by mutual consent : 상호간의 합의에 의하지 않는 한
- in favor of the Seller : 매도인을 수취인으로 하여, 매도인을 위하여, 매도인에 지불되도록
- available fourteen (14) days beyond the stipulated time of shipment : 약정된 선적일자 이후 14일간까지 유효하도록
- documents attached : 서류를 첨부하여
- for the full invoice amount : 송장금액 전액에 대하여
- the date of the Bill of Lading shall be taken as a conclusive proof of the day of shipment : 선적일 기준을 B/L의 일자로 한다는 것
- unless expressly agreed upon : 달리 명시적으로 합의하지 않는 한
- be at the seller's option : 매도자의 선택이다. 매도자 임의로 한다.
- the amount of the invoice plus ten (10) per cent : 송장금액에 10%를 더한 금액, 즉 송장금액의 110%. 여기서 10%는 Buyer의 희망이익(expected profit)을 보호하기 위한 것이다.
- policy : 보험증권
- claims : 보험금

10. Quality : The Sellers shall guarantee all shipments to coincide with samples, types or descriptions, with regard to quality and condition.

11. Force Majeure : The Sellers shall not be responsible for any delay in shipment in any case of force majeure, including mobilization, war, riot, civil commotion, hostilities, blockade, requisition of vessels, prohibition of export, fires, floods, earthquakes, tempests, and any other contingencies, which prevent shipment within the period stipulated. In the event of any of the aforesaid causes arising, documents proving its occurrence or existence shall be sent by the Sellers to the Buyers without delay.

12. Delayed Shipment : In all cases of force majeure provided for in Article No. 11, the period of shipment stipulated shall be extended for a period of fourteen (14) days. In cases shipment within the extended period shall still be prevented by a continuance of the causes mentioned in the article or the consequences of any of them, it shall be at the Buyer's option either to allow the shipment of late goods or to cancel the order by giving the seller the notice of cancellation.

13. Claims and Arbitration : Claims, if any, shall be submitted by e-mail, facsimile, cable or telex within fourteen (14) days from the date of final discharge of the goods at destination. Certificates by recognized surveyors shall be sent by mail without delay. All claims which cannot be amicably settled between Sellers and Buyers shall be finally settled by arbitration in Seoul, Korea in accordance with the Commercial Arbitration Rules of the Korean Commercial Arbitration Board and under the Laws of Korea.

In witness whereof, the parties hereto have executed this Agreement as of the date hereunder written.

AMS Trading Company   SM Company, Inc.

_____   _____
                                       Dongjun Kim

_____   Dongjun Kim, President
                                       Seoul, Korea, March 3, 2021

• 주요 용어 및 표현 •

- guarantee : 보증하다. 담보하다.
- to coincide with : 일치하도록
- quality and condition : 품질과 상태
- force majeure「fɔ́ərs-maːʒə́ːr / fɔ́ːs-mǽ-」: 불가항력(=act of God)
- mobilization : 동원
- civil commotion : 내란
- hostilities : 교전상태, 적대행위
- blockade : 봉쇄조치
- requisition : 징발
- tempest : 대폭풍우, 대폭설
- any other contingencies : 다른 돌발사태, 어떠한 다른 우연사고
- in the event of any of ~ arising : 어떠한 것이든 상기 사유가 발생한 경우
- in cases shipment within the extended period shall still be prevented : 연장된 기간에도 선적을 못하게 될 경우에는
- by a continuance of ~ the consequences of any of them : 조항에 언급한 사유의 지속에 의해서나 사유의 결과에 의해서
- claim, if any : (발생하지 않겠지만) 만약 클레임이 발생한다면
- recognized surveyors : 공인 감정인
- the date of final discharge : 양륙 최종일
- amicably settled : 우호적으로 해결되다.
- be finally settled ~ Arbitration Board : 중재조항이다. 대한상사중재원의 상사중재규칙에 따라 한국 서울에서 중재로 최종 해결된다.
- under the Law of Korea : 준거법 조항이다. 대한민국 법에 따라
- in witness whereof : 이에 대한 증거로서, 이를 입증하면서
- execute : (계약서) 작성하다. (계약, 법) 이행하다. 실시하다.
- hereto : 여기에(=hereunto)
- as of the date hereunder written : 아래에 기재된 날짜에

☷ F3 계약서 송부 서신

SM Company, Inc.

4501, 45th Floor, Trade Tower
511 Yeongdong-daero, Kangnam-gu, Seoul, Korea 06164

April 5, 2021

AMS Trading Company
908 Park Avenue
New York, NY 10017 U.S.A.

Gentlemen: CONTRACT NO. K2203
                        ‾‾‾‾‾‾‾‾‾‾‾‾‾‾‾‾‾‾‾‾

We are pleased to send you the above contract, in duplicate, which has
been concluded through mail correspondence and telephone messages
exchanged between us.

Please sign the duplicate and send it to us as usual.

I am sure this will be the beginning of a long and pleasant business
relationship.

Very truly yours,

내용 SM사가 계약 상대회사인 AMS Trading Company에 계약서를 작성하여
보내면서 함께 동봉하는 편지이다.

• 주 요 용 어 및 표 현 •

- in duplicate : 2통, 2부, 한 쌍의
- sign the duplicate : 2통 중의 하나에 서명하다. 부본에 서명하다.
- as usual : 평소와 같이, 통상적인 방식으로

✓	부본과 사본

부본(duplicate)은 원본중의 하나 또는 원본과 동일한 효력을 갖는 문서이다. 반
면에 사본(copy)은 원본을 복사한 것으로서 법률적인 효력을 갖지 못하는 문서이다.

⊞ F4 무역계약서

SALES AGREEMENT

This Agreement made in Seoul, Korea this 5th day of April, 2021 by and between AMS Trading Company having its registered office at 908 Park Avenue, New York, NY 10017 U.S.A. (hereinafter called the "Buyer") and SM Company Inc., having its registered office at the 4501, 45th Floor, Trade Tower, 511 Yeongdong-daero, Kangnam-gu, Seoul, Korea 06164 (hereinafter called the "Seller")

WITNESSETH

WHEREAS, the Buyer desires to purchase from the Seller and the Seller desires to sell to the Buyer the Goods (as hereinafter defined),

Now, THEREFORE, in consideration of the mutual covenants herein contained, the parties hereto agree as follows:

Article 1. Sale of Goods
1.1 The Buyer shall purchase from the Seller and the Seller shall sell to the Buyer newly manufactured speaker systems (hereinafter called "Goods") subject to the terms and conditions herein provided.

Article 2. Quantity, Specification and Quality
2.1 For 3 years commencing May 1, 2021, the Buyer shall purchase from the Seller and the Seller shall sell to the Buyer ten thousand (10,000) sets of the Goods per year to make the total quantities of the sale of the Goods thirty thousand (30,000) sets from May 1, 2021 to April 30, 2024.
2.2 The specification of the Goods shall be prescribed and specified in the Specification attached hereto as Exhibit[I].

Article 3. Price
3.1 The agreed unit price of each Good (hereinafter called "Price") is One Hundred And Ten United States Dollars (US$ 110) on a C.I.F. New York basis.
3.2 The Price is fixed and effective up to shipments performed on or before the end of December, 2021 and thereafter the Price shall be readjusted every six months according to the Seller's request.

Article 4. Payment

4.1 Except otherwise agreed to by the parties, all the payments for the goods shall be made in United States Dollars by an irrevocable letter of credit in favor of the Seller. The letter of credit shall be established by the Buyer at least two months prior to each scheduled shipment date stipulated in Exhibit [Ⅱ] and to be negotiable at sight against draft and to be valid for no less than thirty (30) days after the latest date allowed for the shipment. The Buyer shall bear all banking expenses associated with establishing of the letter of credit. Partial shipment, transshipment and partial negotiations of the letter of credit shall be permitted and the letter of credit shall be worded accordingly.

4.2 Delay by the Buyer in establishing the letter of credit shall extend the time for performance of the Agreement by the Seller to such extent as may be necessary to enable it to make delivery in the exercise of reasonable diligence after such a letter of credit has been established. Should opening the letter of credit be delayed for causes for which the Buyer is liable, the Buyer shall pay the Seller an amount equal to two tenths of one percent (0.2%) of the amount of the relevant letter of credit per each full week as liquidated damages net cash or sight draft within three days from receipt of the relevant bill from the Seller. However, the total amount of liquidated damages shall not be more than one percent (1%) of the amount of the relevant letter of credit. Should opening of the letter of credit be delayed by more than five (5) full weeks, the Seller may terminate the Agreement without prejudice to the Seller's rights under the Agreement, including claims of said liquidated damages.

Article 5. Shipment of the Goods

5.1 The Goods shall be delivered by the Seller to the Buyer at any Korean port in accordance with the shipment schedule attached hereto as Exhibit [Ⅱ]

5.2 The Seller shall arrange a suitable vessel of any flag to transport the Goods to the destination, New York, U.S.A. or any other seaport designated by the Buyer on the relevant letter of credit provided that the C.I.F. price is not increased. The Seller shall notify by e-mail, facsimile, cable, or telex, the Buyer of the necessary information at least seven (7) days before each shipment so that the Buyer may make arrangements for receipt and inland transportation, if necessary, of the Goods.

Article 6. Late Delivery

6.1 In the event that the Seller delays shipment of the Goods in accordance with the shipment schedule for reasons solely attributable to the Seller, the Buyer shall grant the Seller seven days' grace, without liquidated damage on each specified delivery. After that seven days' grace period, the Buyer has the right to claim one percent (1%) of the contract price of the Goods of which shipment shall have been delayed, per each full week from seven days after the scheduled delivery date until the actual shipping date thereof. The total amount of the liquidated damage under the Agreement shall be limited to six percent (6%) of the contract price of the Goods delayed.

6.2 If the aforesaid delay of delivery exceeds six (6) full weeks, the Buyer has the right to cancel the Agreement, without prejudice to the Buyer's right under the Agreement, including claims of said liquidated damages.

6.3 In the event of Force Majeure, liquidated damages for late delivery shall not be applied.

Article 7. Packing and Marking

7.1 The Goods shall be packed and marked in a manner customary for exporting. In case special instructions are necessary, the Buyer shall furnish the Seller with such instructions in time for preparation or shipment of the goods.

Article 8. Insurance

8.1 The Seller shall effect marine insurance on all shipments against ICC (B) for 110% of the invoice amount.

Article 9. Warranty

9.1 Each good supplied by the Seller is hereby expressly warranted to be free from defects in material and workmanship under normal use and service.

9.2 This Warranty shall be limited to a period of 12 months after delivery thereof to the Buyer under storage in a roofed warehouse.

9.3 The above warranty shall not apply to any good, which is used for a purpose for which it was not designed or which has been subject to normal wear and tear, damage caused by accident, misuse, abuse, or damage occurred during shipment.

Article 10. Claims

10.1 Any claims by the Buyer of anything arising under this contract shall be made by e-mail, facsimile, cable, or telex within thirty (30) days after arrival of the goods at the destination specified in the bill of lading. Full particulars of such claims shall be made in writing, and forwarded by registered mail to the Seller within fifteen (15) days after advising by e-mail, facsimile, cable, or telex. The Buyer must submit sworn surveyor's reports when the quality or quantity of the goods delivered is in dispute.

Article 11. Force Majeure

11.1 Except for the payments due for the Goods delivered by the Seller, any party ('Affected Party') hereto shall not be responsible to the other party ("Non-Affected Party") for nonperformance, either in whole or in part, or delay in performance of the terms and conditions of the Agreement, due to war, warlike operation, riots, strikes or other labor disturbances, epidemics, floods, earthquakes, typhoon, inevitable accidents, embargoes, laws and regulations of government, or any other causes beyond the control of the parties. In case of any such event the terms of this Agreement relating to time and performance shall be suspended during the continuance of the event.

11.2 Within five (5) days from the date of commencement of the event, the Affected Party shall advise the Non-Affected Party by e-mail, facsimile, cable, or telex of the date when such delay in performance commenced, and the reasons therefor as enumerated in this Agreement; likewise, within five (5) days after the delays ends, the Affected Party shall advise the Non-Affected Party by e-mail, facsimile, cable, or telex of the date when such delay ended, and shall also specify the redetermined time by which the performance of the obligation hereunder is to be completed.

Article 12. Taxes/Duties, Contingent Charges

12.1 Any duties, tariffs for import and export, or other taxes or charges which are now assessed or imposed or which may hereafter be assessed or imposed by the U.S.A. Government or other competent authorities other than Korea in connection with the Goods and/or transactions thereof shall be borne and paid by the Buyer.

12.2 Increase in freight, insurance premiums, and/or surcharges, due to war, threat of war, warlike conditions, port congestion, or any other emergency or contingency unforeseen or not existent at the time of concluding the Agreement, shall be for the Buyer's account.

Article 13. After-sales Service

13.1 The Seller may, upon request of the Buyer and consent of the Seller, dispatch some experienced technicians to some places in the U.S.A. for the purpose of rendering effective after-service in connection with the Goods.

Article 14. Infringement

14.1 The Buyer shall be liable for and hold the Seller harmless from and against all losses and damages incurred and suits and claims brought by any third party due to possible infringement of any trademark, patent, copyright or other proprietary rights of the third party in connection with the Seller's manufacture and sale of the Goods according to the Specification attached here to as Exhibit[I].

Article 15. Termination

15.1 The Agreement may be terminated upon occurrence of any of the following events:

ⅰ) Agreement in writing of the parties;

ⅱ) by the non-defaulting party, upon default by the other party in the performance of any of its obligations under the Agreement, if not remedied within 30 days after receipt of written notice from the non-defaulting party;

ⅲ) By the other party, upon either party's (a) making an assignment for the benefit of creditors, being adjudged bankrupt, or becoming insolvent; (b) having a reasonable petition filed seeking its dissolution or liquidation not stayed or dismissed within sixty (60) days; or (c) ceasing to do business for any reason;

ⅳ) By the Seller, if the Buyer fails to open a relevant letter of credit by more than five (5) full weeks as stipulated in Article 4.2 hereof;

ⅴ) By either party, if a force majeure condition under Article 11 hereof makes it unreasonable to proceed with the Agreement in the foreseeable future.

15.2 Upon termination of the Agreement neither party shall be discharged from any antecedent obligations or liabilities to the other party under the Agreement unless otherwise agreed in writing by the parties.

15.3 Nothing in the Agreement shall prevent either party from enforcing the provisions thereof by such remedies as may be available in lieu of termination.

Article 16. Arbitration

16.1 All disputes, controversies, or differences which may arise between the parties, out of or in relation to or in connection with this contract or for the breach thereof, shall be finally settled by arbitration in Seoul, Korea in accordance with the Commercial Arbitration Rules of The Korean Commercial Arbitration Board and under the Laws of Korea. The award rendered by the arbitrator(s) shall be final and binding upon both parties concerned.

Article 17. Trade Terms and Governing Law

17.1 The Trade Terms under this agreement shall be governed and interpreted under the provisions of Incoterms, 2020.

17.2 This Agreement shall be governed by and construed in all respects under and by the laws of Korea.

17.3 In the event of a conflict between the laws of Korea and Incoterms, 2020, Incoterms, 2020 shall prevail and govern.

Article 18. Assignment

18.1 Either party shall not assign this Agreement to any other person without the other party's prior consent in writing. In the event of assignment with the written consent of the other, the one shall not be relieved from its obligations under this Agreement and shall be held responsible for its performance.

Article 19. Non-Waiver

19.1 No claim or right of either party under this Agreement shall be deemed to be waived or renounced in whole or in part unless the waiver or renunciation of such claim or right is acknowledged and confirmed in writing by such party.

Article 20. Notice

20.1 Unless otherwise agreed by the parties, all notices, invoices, and communications under the Agreement shall be sent to the Parties at their addresses set forth in the initial paragraph of the Agreement. All notices shall be sent by registered airmail and where circumstances require, notices may be sent by e-mail, facsimile, cable, or telex which shall be confirmed by registered air mail.

Article 21. Entire Agreement

21.1 This Agreement constitutes the entire agreement between the parties, all prior representations having been merged herein, and may not be modified except in writing and signed by duly authorized representatives of both parties.

Article 22. Effective Date and Term

22.1 This Agreement shall become effective upon signing of the duly authorized representatives of both parties and remain in full force and effect up to April 30, 2024 unless terminated earlier pursuant to Article 15.

IN WITNESS WHEREOF, the parties hereto have caused this Agreement to be signed by their duly authorized representatives in duplicate as of the date first above written.

Buyer
AMS Trading Company

Harry E. Porter

Harry E. Porter
President

Seller
SM Company Inc.

Dongjun Kim

Dongjun Kim
President

무역업무의 주요 내용

1 영문계약서의 구성

영문계약서는 대개 다음과 같이 구성된다.

구분	구 성 요 소	비고
제목	계약의 이름	
서문	1. 계약자체에 대한 사항 　① 계약장소, ② 계약일시, ③ 당사자 및 주소 2. 설명조항 3. 약인조항	
본문	1. 정의조항 2. 계약본질에 대한 조항 　매매계약의 경우 　① 품명, ② 품질, ③ 수량, ④ 가격, ⑤ 선적, ⑥ 보험, 　⑦ 대금결제, ⑧ 포장 등 3. 계약시행에 대한 조항 　① 계약기간, ② 계약의 해제와 종료, ③ 계약의 양도, 　④ 불가항력, ⑤ 분쟁해결, ⑥ 준거법 및 재판관할, 　⑦ 통지, ⑧ 계약의 수정 및 변경, ⑨ 완전합의	보통 조문 번호가 부 여된다.
결문	결미문언	
	서명	

2 서 문

이 계약에서 서문은 다음과 같은 형식으로 구성되어 있다.

문 장	구문	내용
This Agreement made in Seoul, Korea on the 15th day of April, 2021 by and between ~ and ~	주어	계약장소 계약일자 계약당사자
WITNESSETH	동사	
WHEREAS, the Buyer desires ~		설명조항
Now, THEREFORE, in consideration of ~		약인조항
the parties hereto agree as follows:	목적어	

- made : 작성된(=made and entered into : 작성되고 계약관계에 들어가는)
- by and between ~ : ~에 의해서 그리고 ~사이에(=by)
- registered office : 등록된 사무소, 등록된 회사 사옥
- hereinafter : 다음에, 아래에
- WITNESSETH : 증명하다. 증거가 되다.
- WHEREAS : ~하기 때문에
- THEREFORE : 그래서
- in consideration of the mutual covenants herein contained : 여기의 상호간의 약속을 약인으로 하여, 이 계약의 상호간의 약조를 상호대가교환으로 하여
- consideration : 약인(約因), 상호대가교환. 영미법상에서는 계약이 유효하게 성립하여 구속력을 가지려면 청약과 승낙에 의한 합의(mutual assent) 외에 약인(consideration)이 있어야 한다. 약인이란 계약당사간에 서로 주고 받는 (give and take) 상호간의 대가교환을 말한다. 여기서 교환되는 대가는 반드시 경제적으로 대등한 가치를 가질 것을 요구하는 것은 아니며 법적인 관점에서 적합(legally adequate)하면 계약은 유효하게 성립한다.

3 본 문

Article 1. Sale of Goods
◆ 당사자의 거래 대상에 대하여 명시하고 있는 조항이다.
- shall : 의무의 의미를 포함하는 shall이다. 이후의 조항에서도 동일하다.
- subject to ~ : ~에 따라, ~을 적용하여

Article 2. Quantity, Specification and Quality
◆ 상품의 수량과 규격, 그리고 품질에 대한 조항이다.
- specification : 명세, 명세서, 설명서
- attached hereto : 이 계약에 첨부된

Article 3. Price

◆ 상품의 가격과 가격설정에 대하여 정하고 있다.

- up to : ~까지
- on or before the end of December : 12월말을 포함하여 그 이전
- thereafter : 그 이후

Article 4. Payment

◆ 대금지급에 대하여 그 지급통화와 신용장 개설에 대하여 정하고 있다.

- except otherwise agreed to : 달리 합의되지 않는 한
- in favor of the Seller : 매도인을 수취인으로 하는, 매도인을 수익자로 하는
- valid : 유효한
- no less than ~ : ~ 이상, ~에 못지않게
- the latest date : 최종일
- partial negotiations : 분할매입, 부분네고
- worded : 표현되다. 명시되다.
- exercise : 실행, 이행
- reasonable diligence : 합리적인 노력, 온당한 성실성
- liquidated damages : 손해배상금, 손해변상금
- net cash : 현금
- sight draft : 일람출급어음
- relevant bill : 관련청구서
- terminate : 끝내다. 종식시키다.
- prejudice : 손상, 침해
- claims : (권리로서의) 요구, 청구

Article 5. Shipment of the Goods

◆ 선적의 일정과 선박에 관하여 정하고 있다.

- any Korean port : 한국의 어떤 항구라도
- in accordance with : ~에 따라, ~대로
- arrange : 수배하다. 준비하다.

- vessel of any flag : 어떤 국적선이라도
- designated : 지명한, 선정한
- provided that ~ : 만약 ~한다면(=if)
- at least : 적어도

Article 6. Late delivery

◆ 상품의 인도가 지연이 되는 경우의 처리방법을 정하고 있다.
- solely attributable to ~ : 전적으로 ~에 책임 있는, 전적으로 ~의 탓인
- seven days' grace : 7일간의 유예. grace는 은전을 베푸는 은혜기간(=grace period)의 뜻으로 유예기간, 또는 허용기간으로 사용된다.
- aforesaid : 앞에서 언급한, 전술한(=aforementioned)
- in the event of ~ : ~의 경우에
- force majeure「fɔərs-maːʒəːr / fɔːs-mæ-」: (F)불가항력(=superior force, Act of God)

Article 7. Packing and Marking

◆ 화물의 포장과 화인에 대하여 정하고 있다.
- in a manner customary : 통상적인 방법
- special instructions : 특별지시

Article 8. Insurance

◆ 매도자가 부보해야 할 해상적하보험에 대하여 정하고 있다.
- effect : 보험에 들다. 부보하다.
- marine insurance : 해상보험
- invoice amount : 송장금액

Article 9. Warranty

◆ 상품의 하자에 대한 보증사항을 정하고 있다.
- warranty : 담보, 보증
- hereby : 이로써

- free from defects : 결함이 없는
- material and workmanship : 재료와 기술, 자재와 제작기술
- normal use and service : 통상의 사용
- thereof : 그것에 대하여
- under storage : 저장되어, 보관상태로
- roofed warehouse : 지붕이 있는 창고, 옥내 보관소
- wear and tear : 마손, 닳고 찢어짐
- misuse : 오용
- abuse : 남용, 오용

Article 10. Claims
◆ 클레임 발생의 경우에 처리방법을 정하고 있다.
- particulars : 자세한 내용, 자초지종, 상세
- in writing : 서면으로, 글로 써서
- forward : 전송하다. 발송하다.
- registered mail : 등기우편
- sworn surveyor's reports : 공인 검정 보고서, 공인 검정인의 보고서
- in dispute : 논쟁중에, 분쟁중에

Article 11. Force Majeure
◆ 당사자가 불가항력에 의하여 의무를 이행하지 못하는 경우에 그 처리방법을 정하고 있다.
- be responsible for ~ : ~에 대해서 책임이 있는
- nonperformance : 불이행
- either in whole or in part : 전체이든 부분이든
- warlike operation : 군사작전
- riots : 폭동
- strikes or other labor disturbances : 파업이나 다른 노동소요
- epidemics : 전염병, 유행병
- floods : 홍수

- earthquakes : 지진
- typhoon : 태풍
- inevitable accidents : 불가피한 사고
- embargoes : 수출금지
- laws and regulations of government : 정부의 법규, 정부의 법과 규정
- beyond the control of the parties : 당사자가 통제할 수 없는
- be suspended : 연기되다. 연장되다.
- continuance of the event : 사건의 존속, 사건의 계속
- commencement : 시작, 개시(=beginning)
- affected party : 영향을 받은 당사자, 사고를 당한 당사자
- non-affected party : 영향을 받지 않은 당사자, 사고를 당하지 않은 당사자
- the reasons therefor : 그에 대한 이유
- enumerate : 열거하다.
- likewise : 마찬가지로, 같이
- redetermined : 다시 결정한, 재결정된
- the performance of the obligation hereunder : 이에 따른 의무의 이행

Article 12. Taxes/Duties, Contingent Charges

◆ 상품 수출입과 관련하여 세금 및 부대비용의 부담에 대하여 정하고 있다.
- tax : 세, 세금, 조세, 일반적인 의미의 세금
- duties : 세금, 관세, 주로 수출입과 관련한 세금
- tariff : 관세, 세율표
- contingent charges : 부수 비용
- competent authorities : 권한 있는 당국
- freight : 운임
- insurance premiums : 보험료
- surcharges : 특별요금, 할증금
- threat of war : 전쟁의 위협
- warlike conditions : 전쟁과 같은 상황, 전시 상황

- port congestion : 항만적체
- emergency : 비상사태
- contingency : 우발사고
- unforeseen or not existent : 예견할 수 없었거나 존재하지 않았던

Article 13. After-sales Service

◆ 상품판매 후의 사후수리 서비스에 대하여 정하고 있다.

- dispatch : 파견하다. 급파하다.
- experienced technicians : 경험 있는 기술자, 노련한 기술자
- in connection with ~ : ~와 관련하여

Article 14. Infringement

◆ 상품과 관련하여 권리침해문제가 수입국에서 발생하는 경우에 처리방법을 정
  하고 있다.

- infringement : 침해, 위반
- be liable for : 책임져야 할, 책임 있는
- hold the Seller harmless : 매도인이 해를 입지 않도록 책임지다.
- losses : 손실, 상실
- damages : 손해, 피해
- infringement : 침해, 위반
- trademark : 상표
- patent : 특허, 특허권
- copyright : 저작권, 판권
- proprietary rights : 소유권, 재산권

Article 15. Termination

◆ 계약의 해제사유와 해제 후의 당사자관계에 정하고 있다.

- terminate : 끝내다. 종결시키다.
- occurrence : 발생
- non-defaulting party : 의무 불이행을 하지 않은 당사자, 채무불이행을 하지

않은 당사자

- default : 채무불이행, 의무불이행
- remedied : 제거되다. 구제되다. 치유되다.
- written notice : 서면통지
- assignment : 양도, 이양
- for the benefit of ~ : ~를 위하여
- creditor : 채권자
- adjudged bankrupt : 파산 선고된, 파산판결을 받은
- insolvent : 지불불능의, 파산된
- petition : 소송, 소장, 탄원, 법적 신청
- filed : 제기되다. 신청되다. 제출되다.
- dissolution : (회사의) 해산
- liquidation : 청산, 정리
- stayed : 멈추다. 정지되다. 연기되다. 유예하다.
- dismissed : (소송사건) 각하되다. 취하되다.
- ceasing to do business : 영업의 정지, 업무의 정지
- unreasonable : 타당치 않은, 무모한, 부당한
- proceed with : 계속 진행하다. 속행하다. 나아가다.
- foreseeable future : 예지할 수 있는 미래, 가까운 장래
- discharged : 벗어나다. 면제되다.
- antecedent : 앞서는, 이전의, 전의, 선행의
- obligations or liabilities : 의무 또는 책임
- enforcing the provisions thereof : 이 계약의 조항을 시행하다. ~ 이행하다.
- remedies : 구제조치, 구제책, 교정
- in lieu of ~ : ~대신에(=instead of)

Article 16. Arbitration
◆ 분쟁발생시의 해결방법에 대하여 정하고 있다.
- arbitration : 중재, 중재재판, 재정

- disputes, controversies, or differences : 분쟁, 논쟁 또는 의견차이. 싸움, 논쟁, 또는 불화
- out of or in relation to or in connection with ~ : ~으로부터 발생하거나, 관한 것이거나, 또는 관련된
- finally settled : 최종적으로 해결된다. 최종적으로 결정된다.
- in accordance with ~ : ~에 따라
- award : 판정, 심판, 재정, 판정서
- arbitrator : 중재인, 중재자
- final : 최종적, 마지막의, 궁극적
- binding upon : 구속력을 갖는다. 구속한다.
- parties concerned : 관련 당사자

Article 17. Trade Terms and Governing Law
◆ 계약에 적용되는 무역조건 규정과 준거법에 대하여 정하고 있다.
- trade terms : 무역조건
- governing law : 준거법, 적용법
- governed : 적용되다.
- interpreted : 해석되다.
- construed : 해석되다.
- in the event of ~ : ~의 경우
- conflict : 상충, 마찰, 불일치
- prevail and govern : 우선되고 적용된다. 우선적으로 적용된다.

Article 18. Assignment
◆ 어느 일방당사자가 계약을 제3자에게 양도하는 문제에 대하여 정하고 있다.
- assign : 양도하다. 이양하다.
- prior consent : 사전 동의.
- be relieved from ~ : ~으로부터 벗어나다. ~으로부터 면제되다.
- be held responsible for ~ : ~의 책임을 지다.

Article 19. Non-waiver

◆ 당사자 권리의 행사와 포기에 대하여 정하고 있다. 즉 명확한 권리 포기의 의사 표시가 있어야만 권리포기가 됨을 규정하고 있다.

- non-waiver : 불포기
- deem : 간주하다. 생각하다.
- waive : 포기하다. 철회하다. 보류하다.
- renounce : 포기하다. 단념하다. 기권하다.
- acknowledged : 승인된, 인정된
- confirmed : 확인된, 확정된

Article 20. Notice

◆ 양당사자 상호간 의사전달을 위한 통지장소와 통지방법을 정하고 있다.

- notice : 통지, 통보
- invoices : 서류통지
- communications : 연락, 전달, 편지
- set forth : 보이다. 밝히다. 진열하다. 발표하다.
- initial paragraph : 첫 구절, 시작 단락

Article 21. Entire Agreement

◆ 이 계약이 당사자간 완전 합의 속에 이루어진 것이며, 계약 이전에 있었던 관련 합의사항은 이 계약에 흡수된다는 것을 표시하고 있다.

- entire agreement : 완전한 합의
- constitute : 구성하다.
- prior representations : 이전의 진술, 사전의 설명
- merged herein : 여기에 흡수된다. 여기에 병합된다.
- modified : 수정되다. 정정되다.
- duly authorized representative : 정식으로 권한 있는 대표자

Article 22. Effective Date and Term

◆ 계약의 효력발생시기와 계약의 효력기간을 정하고 있다.

- become effective : 효력을 갖다. 효력이 발생하다(＝come into force, come into effect, take effect).
- remain in full force and effect : 완전하게 시행되며 효력을 갖는다.
- pursuant to ~ : ~에 따라, ~에 의거하여

4 결 문

- IN WITNESS WHEREOF : 이를 입증하면서
- hereto : 여기에(＝hereunto)
- to be signed : 서명되다. to be executed(작성되다)도 사용된다.
- in duplicate : 2부로
- as of : ~일에, ~일 현재, ~부터(＝from, on or after)
- the date first above written : 서두에 기재된 일자

◆ 계약의 결미문언은 다음과 같이 표기하기도 한다.

IN WITNESS WHEREOF, the parties hereto have executed this Agreement as of the date first above written.

IN WITNESS WHEREOF, the parties hereto have executed this Agreement as of the day, month, and year first above written.

IN WITNESS WHEREOF, SM Company Inc. has hereunto set their hand on the 5th day of April, 2021, and AMS Trading Company has hereunto set their hand on the 15th day of April, 2021. This Agreement shall be valid on and from the 1st day of May, 2021, and any of the articles in the Agreement shall not be changed or modified unless by mutual consent.

매매계약서

미합중국 뉴욕주 뉴욕시 파크가 908번지에 등록 사무소를 둔 에이엠에스 무역회사(이하 "매수인"이라 한다)와 대한민국 서울특별시 강남구 영동대로 511 무역타워 45층 4501에 등록사무소를 둔 에스엠 주식회사(이하 "매도인"이라 한다)간에 2021년 4월 5일 대한민국 서울에서 체결된 이 계약은, 매수인은 매도인으로부터 상품(이후에 명시한다)을 구매하기를 원하고 매도인은 상품을 판매하기를 원하기 때문에, 지금 이 계약에 포함된 상호간의 약속을 약인으로 하여 양 당사자가 다음과 같이 합의함을 증명한다.

제1조 상품 매매
매수인과 매도인은 신제품 스피커 시스템(이하 "상품"이라 한다)을 이 계약에 규정한 조건에 따라 매수하고 매도한다.

제2조 수량, 규격, 품질
1. 2021년 5월 1일부터 2024년 4월 30일까지 매년 1만 세트씩 총 3만 세트의 상품을 매수인은 매도인으로 부터 매입하고 매도인은 매수인에게 판매한다.
2. 상품의 명세는 첨부된 표1의 명세서에 기재된 바와 같다.

제3조 가격
1. 합의된 상품의 단가(이하 "가격"이라 한다)는 운임 및 보험료 포함조건으로 미화 110달러이다.
2. 위의 가격은 2021년 12월말 이전에 선적된 상품에 적용되고 그 이후의 가격은 매도인의 요청에 의하여 매 6월마다 조정한다.

제4조 대금지급
1. 당사자간에 달리 합의하지 않는 한, 상품대금은 매도인을 수익자로 하는 취소불능신용장에 의하여 미달러화로 결제한다. 신용장은 표2에 기재한 선적예정일자보다 최소한 2개월 전에 개설되어야 하고, 환어음의 일람출급매입방식으

로 하며, 신용장의 효력은 선적가능 최종일 이후로부터 최소한 30일 이상 동안 유효하도록 하여야 한다. 매수인은 신용장 개설과 관련된 모든 은행비용을 부담한다. 분할선적, 환적, 신용장의 분할매입이 허용되며, 신용장에 이러한 사실을 명시하여야 한다.

2. 매수인의 신용장 개설에 지연이 있는 경우 매도인의 계약 이행기간은 신용장 개설 후 합리적인 노력으로 상품을 인도할 수 있는 기간만큼 연장된다. 매수인의 귀책사유로 신용장개설이 지연되는 경우에는 매수인은 지연되는 1주일마다 해당신용장 금액의 0.2%를 손해배상금으로서 매도인의 청구를 받은 후 3일 이내 현금이나 일람출급어음으로 매도인에게 지급하여야 한다. 그러나 손해배상금 총액이 해당 신용장금액의 1%를 초과할 수는 없다. 신용장의 개설이 5주 이상 지연되는 경우에는 매도인은 위 손해배상금의 청구를 포함하여 이 계약에 의한 매도인 권리의 손상 없이 이 계약을 해제할 수 있다.

제5조 선적

1. 표2에 첨부된 선적 일정에 따라, 매도인은 상품을 대한민국의 어느 항구에서라도 매수인에게 인도할 수 있다.

2. 매도인은 미국 뉴욕항이나 CIF가격이 증가하지 않는 범위 내에서 관련신용장에서 매수인이 지정한 다른 목적항으로 상품을 운송하기 위하여 그 국적에 관계없이 적합한 선박을 수배하여야 한다. 매도인은 매수인이 상품의 인수 및 내륙수송을 위한 필요한 조치를 취할 수 있도록 선적시마다 선적일 7일 이전에 이메일, 팩스, 전신, 또는 텔렉스로 매수인에게 관련정보를 통지하여야 한다.

제6조 인도지연

1. 매도인의 귀책사유로 선적일정에서 선적이 지연되는 경우에는 매수인은 예정된 인도에 관한 손해배상금 없이 7일간의 유예기간을 허용해야 한다. 7일간의 유예기간이 지난 이후에는 매수인은 인도예정일의 7일 이후부터 실제로 선적된 일자까지 매주마다 선적이 지연된 상품의 계약금액의 1%를 손해배상으로 청구할 권리를 가진다. 손해배상금의 총액은 지연된 상품의 계약금액의 6%를 초과하지 못한다.

2. 앞의 인도지연이 6주를 초과하는 경우 매수인은 위 손해배상금의 청구권을 포함하여 이 계약상의 매수인 권리의 손상 없이 계약을 해제할 권리를 가진다.
3. 불가항력의 경우 인도지연에 의한 손해배상금은 적용되지 아니한다.

제7조 포장과 하인
상품은 수출시의 관례적인 방법으로 포장되고 하인이 표시되어야 한다. 특별지시가 필요한 경우에는 매수인은 매도인에게 상품의 준비 또는 선적을 위한 적시에 해당 지시를 통지하여야 한다.

제8조 보험
매도인은 모든 선적화물에 대하여 송장금액의 110%를 협회적하약관 (B)조건으로 해상보험에 부보하여야 한다.

제9조 담보
1. 매도인이 인도한 모든 상품에 대하여 정상적인 사용을 조건으로 재료와 기술상의 하자가 없음을 명시적으로 담보한다.
2. 이 담보는 매수인의 창고에 입고된 후부터 12개월간 유효하다.
3. 상기 담보는 상품이 예정 외의 목적에 사용되거나, 통상의 마손, 사고에 의한 손상, 오용, 남용, 선적중의 손상 등의 경우에는 적용되지 않는다.

제10조 클레임
이 계약으로 인하여 발생하는 어떠한 종류의 매수인의 클레임도 상품이 선하증권에 기재된 목적지에 도착 후 30일 이내에 이메일, 팩스, 전신, 또는 텔렉스로 제기되어야 한다. 이메일, 팩스, 전신, 또는 텔렉스로 통보된 후 15일 이내에 동 클레임의 구체적인 내용이 서면으로 작성되어 등기우편으로 매도인에게 송부되어야 한다. 상품의 품질이나 수량이 문제가 되는 경우에는 매수인은 공인검정보고서를 제출하여야 한다.

제11조 불가항력

1. 매도인이 인도한 상품대금의 지급을 제외하고 어느 당사자도 전쟁, 군사작전, 폭동, 파업 또는 기타 노동소요, 전염병, 홍수, 지진, 폭풍, 불가피한 사고, 수출금지, 정부의 법규, 기타 당사자가 통제할 수 없는 사유로 인한 계약조건의 전부 혹은 일부의 불이행이나 이행지체의 경우에 상대방에 대하여 그로 인한 책임을 부담하지 않는다. 이러한 일이 발생하는 경우 이 계약에서 기간 및 이행에 대한 조건은 불가항력의 사유가 지속되는 동안만큼 연장된다.

2. 채무불이행 당사자는 불가항력 사유가 발생한 날로부터 5일 이내에 상대방에게 이메일, 팩스, 전신, 또는 텔렉스로 지연사유의 개시일자와 이 계약에 열거된 지연사유를 통보하여야 한다. 마찬가지로 채무불이행 당사자는 지연사유가 종료된 후 5일 이내에 상대방에게 이메일, 팩스, 전신, 또는 텔렉스로 지연사유의 종료일자와 계약의무의 이행을 완료할 수 있을 것으로 예상되는 일자를 통보하여야 한다.

제12조 세금, 관세, 비용

1. 상품 또는 이 거래와 관련하여 한국 이외의 미국정부 또는 기타 당국에 의하여 부과되거나 부과될 수 있는 수입과 수출에 대한 조세, 관세, 또는 기타 세금이나 경비 등은 매수인이 부담하고 매수인이 지급한다.

2. 계약체결 당시 예상할 수 없었거나 존재하지 않았던 전쟁이나 전쟁의 위협, 전쟁에 준하는 사태, 항만적체, 혹은 기타 긴급상황으로 인한 운임인상, 보험료 인상, 그리고 혹은 추가경비 등은 매수인의 부담으로 한다.

제13조 판매사후 서비스

매수인의 요청과 매도인의 동의에 따라 매도인은 상품과 관련하여 효율적인 사후서비스를 위하여 미국 내 어느 지역에 유능한 기술자를 파견한다.

제14조 권리침해

표1로서 첨부된 명세서에 따라 제조된 상품과 관련하여 매수인은 상표, 특허, 저작권, 또는 기타 제3자의 재산권 침해로 인하여 제3자가 제기한 손해 및 손실 그

리고 소송이나 클레임에 대하여 책임을 지며 매도인은 면책이 된다.

제15조 계약 종료

1. 이 계약은 다음의 경우에 종료한다.
  1) 서면에 의한 당사자의 합의에 의하여,
  2) 계약의무불이행이 있고 이에 따른 채무불이행당사자가 상대방의 서면에 의한 이행최고 후 30일 이내 구제 조치를 하지 않을 때, 그 상대방에 의하여,
  3) 일방이 (a) 채권자를 위해서 재산을 위탁하거나, 파산 선고를 받거나, 지급불능인 사태가 되는 경우, (b) 해산 또는 청산을 구하는 소가 60일 이내 정지되지 않거나 기각되지 않은 경우, (c) 기타이유로 영업을 중단한 경우, 그 상대방에 의하여,
  4) 이 계약 제4조 2항에 규정된 바와 같이 매수인이 5주 이상 관련 신용장을 개설하지 않은 경우, 매도인에 의하여,
  5) 이 계약 제11조의 불가항력 상황으로 인하여 예측할 수 있는 미래에 계약을 지속하는 것이 불합리한 경우에 어느 당사자에 의하여,
2. 이 계약이 종료되는 경우, 어느 당사자도 종료 이전의 상대방에 대한 이 계약상 책임과 의무에서 면제되지 않는다. 다만, 당사자들이 서면으로 이와 다른 약정을 한 경우에는 그러하지 아니하다.
3. 이 계약의 어느 조항도 어느 일방이 계약종료를 대신하여 이용가능한 구제조치로서 이 계약의 조항이 이행되도록 하는 것을 막지 못한다.

제16조 중재

이 계약으로부터, 이 계약에 관하여, 이 계약과 관련하여, 또는 이 계약의 불이행으로 말미암아 발생하는 당사자간의 모든 분쟁 논쟁, 또는 의견불일치는 대한민국법에 따라 중재에 의하여 최종적으로 해결한다. 중재인들에 의하여 내려지는 판정은 최종적인 것으로 하며 당사자 쌍방에 대하여 구속력을 가진다.

제17조 무역조건의 해석 기준 및 준거법

1. 이 계약에 의한 무역조건은 Incoterms, 2020에 의하여 준거되고 해석된다.

2. 이 계약은 한국법에 의하여 준거되고 해석된다.

3. Incoterms, 2020과 한국법이 상치되는 경우에는 Incoterms, 2020이 우선적으로 적용된다.

제18조 계약의 양도

어느 일방 당사자도 서면에 의한 사전동의 없이는 이 계약을 제3자에게 양도하지 못한다. 상대방의 서면 동의에 의하여 계약을 양도하는 경우에도 양도한 당사자는 이 계약에 의한 의무를 면하지 못하며 계약이행에 대하여 책임을 진다.

제19조 권리 불포기

이 계약에 따른 당사자의 클레임이나 권리의 전부 또는 일부는 그러한 클레임이나 권리의 포기를 서면으로 승인하거나 확인하지 않는 한 포기한 것으로 간주되지 않는다.

제20조 통지

당사자간에 달리 합의되지 않는 한, 이 계약에 의한 모든 통지, 서류통보, 통신 등은 이 계약의 서두에 기재된 주소로 송부되어야 한다. 모든 통지는 등기우편으로 이루어져야 하며 상황에 따라 이메일, 팩스, 전신, 또는 텔렉스로 통지하는 경우에는 항공등기우편으로 확인하여야 한다.

제21조 완전 합의

이 계약은 이전의 모든 의사표시는 이 계약에 흡수되어 당사자간에 완전한 합의로서 이루어져 있다. 양당사자간의 정당한 권한 있는 대표의 서명이 있는 서면에 의하지 아니하고는 변경할 수 없다.

제22조 효력일 및 기간

이 계약은 정당한 권한을 가진 양당사자의 대표가 서명한 즉시 효력을 발생하며 2024년 4월 30일까지 유효하다. 다만 제15조에 따라 계약이 조기에 종료하는 경우에는 그러하지 아니하다.

이를 증거하면서, 여기 당사자들은 그들의 정당한 권한을 가진 대표자들로 하여금 첫머리에 기재된 일자에 본계약서 2부를 서명하게 하였다.

매수인
에이엠에스 무역회사

Harry E. Porter

해 리 이 포 터
사　　장

매도인
에스엠 주식회사

Dongjun Kim

김 동 준
사　　장

Useful Expressions

📑 계약서 내용 검토

- The draft is submitted for your comment and is open to your suggestions.
- We would like to insert a clause on the extension of this contract.
- We are in agreement in principle, but there are a few details to be ironed out. Please allow us enough time to examine it.
- As we are in agreement on all points, let's put in writing and sign it.

> *put in writing*
> *make out the contract*

- If there are any discrepancies, errors, or omissions, please let us know.

📑 계약서 서명

- Please sign the duplicate and sent it to us as usual.
- If you find the clauses acceptable as they stand, please sign and return the duplicate, keeping the original for yourself.
- Please return one set of agreement to us with your signature.
- The contract is all drawn up and ready to sign.
- If you are completely satisfied with the terms of contract, please put your signature.

> *are completely satisfied with the terms of contract*
> *find everything in order*

📑 계약서 송부

- We are pleased to send you the agreement which has been concluded between us.
- We have enclosed a draft of the agreement.
- We are sending 2 copies of the Sales Contract for your review and signature.

📑 계약서 서신 맺음말

- I am sure this will be the beginning of a long and pleasant business relationship.
- We are very pleased to serve you as our valued customer.
- We trust that this marks the beginning of an enduring and fruitful collaboration.
- We hope this agreement will be the beginning of a long and prosperous association.

Standard
Trade
English

신용장

무역업무의 주요 내용

① 신용장의 의의

신용장은 수입상의 거래은행이 수입상의 요청에 따라 수출상 앞으로 개설하여 수출상이 제시하는 환어음과 무역서류가 신용장상 조건에 부합하기만 하면 반드시 인수하거나 지급하겠다는 약정이다.

국제무역거래의 양당사자는 상대방에 대한 신용위험을 갖게 되는데 이러한 문제를 해결하는 하나의 방법이 신용장이다. 즉 수입자 측의 은행이 신용장을 발행하여 수출자가 신용장상에 명시한 조건에 맞게 상품을 선적하면 신용장발행은행이 수출자에게 대금을 지급하기로 약속하고 이에 따라 대금을 지급함으로써, 상대방의 신용에 관계없이, 수출자는 대금회수에 있어서 수입자는 상품인수에 있어서, 안심하고 거래를 할 수 있게 하는 제도이다.

② 신용장의 거래절차

먼저 수입자가 자신의 거래은행에 신용장의 개설을 신청하게 되면 개설은행은 신용장을 수출자 지역의 거래은행을 통하여 수출자에게 보내게 된다. 신용장을 받은 수출자는 상품을 선적하고 신용장에서 요구하는 무역서류를 자신의 거래은행에 매도한다. 서류를 매입한 수출자 거래은행은 신용장개설은행에 무역서류를 송부하고 대금을 받게 된다(52 page 무역거래 연관도 참조).

③ 신용장의 당사자

신용장거래의 당사자는 ① 개설의뢰인(applicant, opener), ② 개설은행(opening bank, issuing bank, credit writing bank, grantor), ③ 수익자(수출자 : beneficiary)이다. 신용장의 취소나 수정변경은 이 세 주체의 합의가 있어야 가능하다.

신용장은 앞의 세 당사자간에 이루어지는 독특한 하나의 거래로서, 상품매매계약과 독립된 별도의 계약이 된다. 신용장의 이러한 성격을 신용장의 독립성이라 하고, 무역서류의 문면만을 중심으로 거래한다는 면에서 신용장의 추상성이라 하며, 이 둘을 합하여 신용장의 독립·추상성이라 한다.

1 신용장의 내용

화환신용장에 일반적으로 기재되는 사항은 ① 신용장의 개설은행, 수익자, 개설의뢰인, 금액 등의 신용장 자체에 관한 사항, ② 환어음에 관한 사항, ③ 상품과 그 선적에 관한 사항, ④ 무역서류에 관한 사항, ⑤ 기타 필요사항 등이다.

2 신용장의 개설통지

수입상이 신용장의 개설을 신청한 후 이에 대한 사실을 수출자에게 통지하게 된다. 이 통지에는 관련 계약 또는 주문, 신용장 개설은행, 통지은행, 신용장 도착예정일 등에 대한 내용이 포함된다.

3 신용장의 개설독촉 통지

만약 신용장 개설이 지체되는 경우에 수출자는 수입자에게 신용장을 빨리 개설해 줄 것을 내용으로 하는 독촉통지를 하게 된다.

4 신용장 조건변경 요청 서한

개설한 측의 업무상의 착오나 잘못으로 인하여 신용장의 내용을 정정해야 하는 경우는 이에 대한 사실을 알리는 형식으로 된다. 반면에 수출자 자신의 사정으로 인하여 신용장조건 변경을 요청하는 서신을 낼 때는 구체적이고 합리적인 이유로서 상대방을 설득해야 한다. 그리고 변경 전의 조건과 변경을 희망하는 조건을 함께 열거함으로써 이해하기 쉽고 일하기도 쉽도록 해주는 것이 좋다.

5 신용장 조건변경 요청에 대한 답신

신용장 조건변경의 요청에 대해서 수입자가 회신하게 된다. 개설은행에 조건변경 신청하는 경우 이에 대한 사실을 수출자에게 회신하게 되고, 개설은행은 신용장 개설 때와 같은 경로로 수출자에게 변경내용을 통지하게 된다.

⊞ G1 신용장개설통지

AMS Trading Company

908 Park Avenue
New York, NY 10017 U.S.A.

May 20, 2021

SM Company, Inc.
4501, 45th Floor, Trade Tower
511 Youngdong-daero,
Kangnam-gu, Seoul, Korea

Dear Mr. Smith:

We are pleased to have received your Sales Note No. 1223 of May 5, 2021. Having found it correct, we signed it and sent the duplicate by express mail on May 17.

We have already instructed CBA Bank, New York to establish an irrevocable letter of credit at sight in your favor for the amount of US$ 125,000.⁻ The advising bank, Korea Best Bank in Seoul, will transmit it to you within a few days.

We believe that you will execute our order in accordance to the instructions specified in the L/C. As the products are urgently required, we would like to ask you to ship the goods by the earliest possible vessel.

We hope you will do everything possible to expedite the shipment.

Yours very truly,

내용 수입자인 AMS Trading사가 수출자인 SM사에 서명한 계약서 부본의 송부와 동시에 신용장개설 사실을 통보하고 있다.

• 주요 용어 및 표현 •

- having found it correct : 틀림없음을 확인하고
- duplicate duly signed by us : 우리측이 정식으로 서명한 부본, 우리에 의해서 틀림없이 서명된 부본
- establish : 개설하다.
- an irrevocable letter of credit at sight : 일람출급취소불능신용장
- in your favor : 당신이 수취하도록, 당신에게 지불되도록
- advising bank : 통지은행
- transmit : 전하다. 전달하다(=advise, notify).
- within a few days : 수 일 이내. a few days는 보통 3, 4일에서 10일 정도의 기간을 의미한다.
- execute : 이행하다(=carry out).
- by the earliest possible vessel : 가능한 가장 이른 선편으로
- expedite : 진척시키다. 신속히 처리하다(=dispatch).

✓	수출자와 수입자의 상황에 따른 명칭		
수 출 자		수 입 자	
exporter	수출자	importer	수입자
seller	매도자	buyer	구매자
beneficiary, user	신용장 수익자	applicant, opener	신용장개설의뢰인
addressee	신용장 수령인	accountee	수입대금결제인
accreditee	대금의 수취인	payer	대금지급인
shipper	수출화물선적인	consignee	수입화물수하인
drawer	환어음발행인	drawee	환어음지급인

G2 신용장개설독촉

KSK ELECTRONICS

11 Myongdong-gil, Jung-gu
Seoul, Korea 04534

May 30, 2021

ABBA Co., Inc.
1156 5th Avenue
New York, NY 10017 U.S.A.

Gentlemen:

Thank you very much for your order with No. 3311 of May 3, 2021 for our color television units.

However, we would like to bring to your attention the fact that we have not received the Letter of Credit covering your order.

Since we have a very limited amount of time to ship the goods during the month of June we must urge our producers to expedite an early delivery of the goods. However, we are not able to proceed because we have not received your L/C yet. I am afraid that we can not secure on time delivery if we do not receive it by June 20.

Therefore, we need you to open your L/C immediately. We are ready to make the arrangements for your order as soon as we receive your L/C.

Very truly yours,

내용 KSK ELECTRONICS사가 수입자인 ABBA사에 신용장이 아직 내도하지 않고 있음을 알리고 신용장을 빠른 시일 내에 개설해 줄 것을 요청하는 내용이다.

• 주요 용어 및 표현 •

- television unit : 텔레비전 세트, 텔레비전
- bring to your attention : 당신이 관심을 가져줄 것을 부탁하다(=draw your attention).
- the Letter of Credit covering your order : 당신의 주문에 대한 신용장
- limited amount of time : 제한된 시간
- urge : 재촉하다. 설득하다.
- expedite : 진척시키다. 신속히 이행하다.
- proceed : 계속하다. 속행하다. 진척시키다.
- secure : 확보하다. 보장하다.
- on time : 정시에, 정해진 기일에
- need you to ~ : ~ 당신이 ~해줄 필요가 있다.
- arrangements : 준비, 마련

✓	무역영어에서 주로 사용되는 cover의 의미

① ~에 대한 : the shipment covering your order No. 1234
② ~을 맡을, 담당하는 : open a branch to cover the East Asian region
③ 충당하는 : the price barely covers the cost of production
④ 포함하는 : freight is not covered by this quotation
⑤ 보상하는 : to cover losses
⑥ ~에 대한 대금조로 : to cover this shipment, we draw a draft
⑦ ~을 망라한 : catalog covering all our goods
⑧ 보험에 들다 : please cover the shipment against War Risk
⑨ 봉투, 표지 : under separate cover

🗂 G3 신용장 1

CBA BANK
1 WALL STREET
NEW YORK 15, NY U.S.A.

Date : May 20, 2021

Irrevocable Documentary Credit No. AN211123

SM Company, Inc.
511 Yeongdong-daero, Kangnam-gu,
Seoul, Korea 06164

Gentlemen:

We hereby authorize you to draw on CBA Bank, New York, NY, for account of AMS Trading Company, New York, NY up to the aggregate amount of US$ 125,000(One Hundred Twenty-Five Thousand US Dollars) available by your draft at sight for full invoice value accompanied by the following documents:
- Commercial Invoice in triplicate
- Customs Invoice in triplicate
- Full set of clean on board Bills of Lading made out to the order of CBA Bank, New York, marked "Freight Prepaid" and "Notify : AMS Trading Company New York"
- Marine Insurance Policy in duplicate endorsed in blank for 110% of the invoice value covering All Risks
- Packing List in triplicate
Evidencing shipment from Busan to New York not later than June 30, 2021 of SM MP3 Player NP-101, as per Sales Note No. 1223 of April 5, 2021.

Partial shipments are allowed.
Transhipments are prohibited.

All drafts must be marked "Drawn under the letter of credit of CBA Bank No. AN211123 dated May 20, 2021" and the amount negotiated endorsed on the reverse hereof by the negotiating bank.

Unless otherwise expressly stated, this credit is subject to the "Uniform Customs and Practice for Commercial Documentary Credits" (2007 Revision), International Chamber of Commerce, Publication No. 600.

We hereby agree with the drawers, endorsers, and bona-fide holders of drafts drawn under and in compliance with the terms of this credit that such drafts will be duly honored upon presentation to the drawee bank.

Yours very truly,

CBA Bank

John E. Baker

• 주요 용어 및 표현 •

- hereby authorize you : 이와 같이 당신에게 권한을 부여합니다.
- draw on ~ : ~ 앞으로 어음을 발행하다. ~에 대금을 청구하다(=value on).
- for account of ~ : ~의 계정으로, ~의 계산과 책임으로
- up to the aggregate amount of ~ : 총액 ~의 한도까지
- available by your draft : 어음의 발행으로 이용가능한
- draft at sight : 일람출급어음
- for full invoice value : 송장금액 전액에 대해서
- accompanied by the following documents : 다음의 서류를 첨부하여
- Commercial Invoice : 상업송장
- triplicate : 3부
- Customs Invoice : 세관송장
- full set : 전 부수, 전통, 전체 세트
- clean on board Bills of Lading : 무고장 선적선하증권
- made out : 작성되다. 씌어지다.
- to the order of CBA Bank : CBA 은행지시의 지시식으로. 즉 지시식 선하증권(Order B/L)으로 할 것을 지시하고 있다.
- marked "Freight Prepaid" and "Notify : AMS Trading Company New York" : 운임지급필로 기재되고 착화통보처는 AMS사로 기재된, 즉 선하증권상의 운임란과 착화통보처(Notify)란에 기재되어야 할 사항에 대한 지시이다.

- Marine Insurance Policy : 해상보험증권
- duplicate : 2부
- endorsed in blank : 백지식 배서된. 양도방법에서 기명식이 아닌 백지식 배서를 지시하고 있는 문언이다.
- 110% of the invoice value : 송장금액의 110%
- covering All Risks : 전위험담보 조건으로 부보된
- evidencing shipment from Busan to New York not later than June 30 of ~ : ~이 부산에서 뉴욕행으로 6월 30일 이전에 선적되었음을 입증하는
- drafts must be marked "~" : 어음상에 "~"을 명시할 것을 지시하는 문언
- drawn under ~ : ~에 따라 발급되었음.
- the amount negotiated endorsed on the reverse hereof : 매입(네고)된 금액은 이 신용장의 뒷면에 이서되어야 한다. 매입은행에서 매입할 때마다 매입된 금액을 신용장 뒷면에 기재하게 된다. 이는 이중으로 매입하거나 신용장 금액 내에서 여러 번 나누어서 매입할 때 신용장 금액을 초과하여 매입되는 것을 방지하기 위해서다.
- unless otherwise expressly stated : 달리 명시되지 않은 한
- this credit is subject to ~ : 신용장 통일규칙 적용 문언이다.
- we hereby agree with ~ that ~ : 우리는 ~와 that 이하를 약속한다.
- drawers : 발행인
- endorsers : 양도인, 이서인, 배서인
- bona-fide holder : 선의의 소지자. 선의의 소지자는 어음이 문제가 생겼을 때 이러한 사실을 모르고 소지하고 있는 사람을 말한다. 이에 대응하는 말은 악의의 소지자(mala-fide holder)로서 이러한 사실을 알고 있는 사람을 말한다. 예를 들어 어음의 유통과정에서 어느 사람이 어음을 훔쳐서 다른 사람에게 팔았다면 그 어음을 산 사람이 절도사실을 모르고 샀다면 선의의 소지자로서 어음대금을 받을 수 있지만, 만약 이를 알고 샀다면 불의에 협조한 사람이기 때문에 대금지급의 보호를 받지 못하게 되는 것이다.
- drafts drawn under and in compliance with the terms of this credit : 이 신용장에 의하여, 그리고 이 신용장의 조건에 일치하게 발행된 어음
- duly honored : 정히 존중(지급, 인수)될 것이다.(=duly paid or accepted)
- upon presentation to the drawee bank : 지급은행에 제시되면(될 때)

⑥ SWIFT 전신 신용장

현재 신용장은 대부분 SWIFT망을 통하여 교환되고 있다. SWIFT(Society for Worldwide Interbank Financial Telecommunication)는 전 세계 은행들이 외국환거래와 관련된 각종 메시지를 교환하는 통신망으로 1973년 15개국 239개 은행에 의하여 창립되었고 우리나라는 1992년 3월부터 이용하고 있다.

SWIFT 신용장의 각 항목은 숫자와 알파벳으로 된 코드가 정해져 있다. SWIFT 신용장은 전신신용장으로서 그 독특한 형식을 갖고 있을 뿐 기본적으로 서면형식의 신용장의 내용과 크게 다르지 않다. 은행에 따라 필수기재사항에는 *표를 붙이기도 하며, 은행마다 출력형식에 조금씩 차이가 있다.

<표 7-1> SWIFT 전신신용장의 코드명

코드	이 름	내 용
20	documentary credit number	개설은행의 L/C 번호
21	receiver's reference	통지은행 등의 전문번호
27	sequence of total	L/C전송 페이지를 표시
30	date of amendment	amend한 날짜
31C	date of issue	L/C 개설일자
31D	date and place of expiry	L/C 유효기일 및 기준 지역 표시
32B	currency code amount	L/C 금액 및 통화표기
39B	maximum credit amount	최대허용금액
40A	form of documentary credit no.	L/C 종류 및 번호
41A	available with/by-swift addr	L/C 통지은행 표시
41D	available with/by name/address	Nego은행, 인수은행, 지급은행
42A	drawee-	환어음의 지급인
42C	draft at	환어음의 종류, 즉, At sight
42D	drawee name/address	환어음의 지급인, 수취인, 상환은행
42P	deferred payment	연지급
43P	partial shipment	분할선적 여부
43T	transshipment	환적 가능여부
44A	on board/disp/taking charge	수출 선적항
44B	for transportation to	운송지, 도착항
44C	latest date of shipment	최종 선적일
45A	descript of goods and/or services	수출상품의 내역
46A	documents required	요구서류
47A	additional conditions	부가요구사항
48	period for presentation	서류 제시기간
49	confirmation instructions	확인은행의 확인여부
50	applicant	L/C 개설의뢰인
51D	applicant bank name/address	개설은행
53A	reimbursing bank	상환은행을 표시함
59	beneficiary	수출업자, L/C 수익자
71B	charges	서류관련 수수료
72	sender to receiver information	통지은행에 대한 지시, 은행간 서류
78	instructions to pay/acc/neg bk	지급, 인수, 네고은행에 대한 지시사항
79	narrative	중요한 변동사항

⊞ G4 신용장 2

Korea Best Bank

Head office : 66 Ulchi-ro, Chung-gu, Seoul, 04538, KOREA
(CPO BOX 2924. CABLE : KOBBANK. YLX NO : 23141-5)

* Advice Br. : KEB EULCHI
  Advice of
  Issue of Documentary Credit
* Beneficiary :
  SM COMPANY, INC.
  511 Yeongdong-daero, Kangnam-gu
  Seoul, Korea 06164
* Amount : USD 10,000.
* Expiry Date : 2021. 07. 30
* Receipt NO. : 2102032
* Sender's bank : 110970934

* Advice Date : 2021. 06. 07
* Advice No : A-10012-1002
* Credit No : 014/110/4030
* Applicant :
  AMS TRADING COMPANY

* Issuing Bank :
  CBA BANK, NEW YORK
  401 WEST 42ND ST
  NEW YORK NY, 10036 U.S.A.

Gentlemen :
At the request of the issuing bank, and without any engagement or responsibility
on our part, we are pleased to inform you that we have received the following
AUTHENTICATED teletransmission dated 2021. 06. 07.

```
:  : 700 ISSUE OF A DOCUMENTARY CREDIT
:27    Sequence of Total                  : 1/1
:40A   Form of Documentary Credit         : IRREVOCABLE
:20    Documentary Credit Number          : M111224499
:31C   Date of Issue                      : 210607
:31D   Date and Place of Expiry           : 210730 IN KOREA
:50    Applicant                          : AMS TRADING COMPANY
                                            908 PARK AVENUE
                                            NEW YORK, NY 10017 U.S.A.
:59    Beneficiary                        : SM COMPANY, INC.
                                            511 Yeongdong-daero, Kangnam-gu
                                            Seoul, Korea 06164
:32B   Currency Code. Amount              : USD 10,000.
:41D   Available With . . . By . . .      : ANY BANK
                                            : By NEGOTIATION
:42C   Drafts At . . .                    : AT SIGHT FOR 100 PCT OF
                                            THE INVOICE VALUE
```

```
:42D  Drawee                          : CBA BANK, NEW YORK
:43P  Partial Shipment                : ALLOWED
:43T  Transshipment                   : ALLOWED
:44A  Loading/Dispatch/Taking Charge  : KOREAN PORT
      at from
:44B  For Transportation to . . .     : NEW YORK
:44C  Latest Date of Shipment         : 210715
:45A  Description of Goods and/or Services :
      SM MP3 PLAYER NP-101
      6GB MEMORY, MP3, WAV
      DIMENSION 5"×1"×5"(WxDxH)
:46A  Documents Required              :
      1. MANUALLY SIGNED COMMERCIAL INVOICE IN 5 COPIES.
      2. FULL SET(INCLUDE 3 ORIGINALS AND NON-NEGOTIABLE COPIES) OF
      CLEAN ON BOARD "FREIGHT COLLECT" OCEAN BILLS OF LADING MADE
      OUT TO ORDER AND BLANK ENDORSED. MARKED "NOTIFYING APPLICANT."
      3. PACKING LIST IN 5 COPIES.
:47A  Additional Conditions           :
      A DISCREPANCY FEE OF USD 54.00 WILL BE DEDUCTED FROM THE
      PROCEEDS IF DOCUMENT ARE PRESENTED WITH DISCREPANCY(IES).
:71B  Charges                         :
      BANKING  CHARGES  OUTSIDE  THE  OPENING  BANK  ARE  FOR
      BENEFICIARY'S ACCOUNT.
:48   Period for Presentaion          :
      DOCUMENT MUST BE PRESENTED FOR NEGOTIATION WITHIN 15 DAYS
      AFTER BILL OF LADING DATE, BUT WITHIN THE VALIDITY OF THIS L/C.
:49   Confirmation Instructions       : WITHOUT
:78   Inst to the Pay/Accept/Negotiate Bank  :
      1. ALL DOCUMENTS ARE TO BE FORWARDED TO CBA BANK, NEW YORK
      401 WEST 42ND ST, NEW YORK, NY, 10036 U.S.A. IN ONE LOT.
      2. UPON RECEIPT OF ALL DOCUMENTS IN ORDER WE WILL DULY honor
      / ACCEPT THE DRAFTS AND EFFECT THE PAYMENT AS INSTRUCTED AT
      MATURITY.
:72   Sender to Receiver Information
      THIS IS SUBJECT TO UCP(2007 REV.) I. C. C. PUB. 600.
```

Please note that we reserve the right to make such corrections to this advice as may be necessary upon receipt of the cable confirmation and assume no responsibility for any errors and/or omissions in the transmission and/or translation of the teletransmission and for any forgery and/or alteration on the credit.

• 주요 용어 및 표현 •

- CBA Bank 뉴욕지점이 개설하고 KEB 을지지점이 통지하는 신용장이다.
- AUTHENTICATED teletransmission : 진본 전송, 진본 전송문
- 2021. 06. 07 : 2021년 6월 7일(연월일 순)
- Available With ANY BANK : 어떤 은행에 매입해도 좋다는 뜻
- By NEGOTIATION : 매입신용장을 의미
- KOREAN PORT : 한국의 어떤 항구도 가능하다는 의미
- MANUALLY SIGNED : 손으로 서명한
- NON-NEGOTIABLE COPIES : 비유통성 사본
- FREIGHT COLLECT : 도착불운임, 후불운임
- BLANK ENDORSED : 백지식으로 배서된
- NOTIFYING APPLICANT : 개설의뢰인(수입자)을 착화통보처로 하여
- DISCREPANCY FEE : 하자(서류가 신용장조건과 불일치할 때)수수료
- DEDUCTED FROM THE PROCEEDS : 금액계산에서 차감된다.
- BANKING CHARGES : 은행수수료
- FOR BENEFICIARY'S ACCOUNT : 수익자(수출자)의 부담
- Period for Presentaion : 제시기간
- VALIDITY : 유효기일
- Confirmation Instructions : 확인 지시, 확인은행여부를 명시하는 난
- BE FORWARDED TO ~ : ~에 송부되어야 한다.
- honor / ACCEPT : 지급 또는 인수하다.
- EFFECT THE PAYMENT : 지급하다.
- AT MATURITY : 만기에
- UCP ~ 600 : ICC 발간물 600호인 신용장 통일규칙 및 관례(2007 개정판)
- Please note that ~ confirmation : 통지은행이 부가한 내용으로 전신확인수령시 필요에 따라 이 통지가 정정될 수 있음을 알리는 내용이다.
- assume no ~ on the credit : 전송 및 전송중계상의 착오, 누락 또는 신용장의 위조 및 변조에 대한 면책을 명시하고 있다.

G5 신용장 3

```
2021NOV16 18:32:18
                                              Logical Terminal SWAF01P1
MT S700              Issue of a Documentary Credit
                                                        Page 00001
                                                        Func BRNPRO
MSGACK { 1 : F21CZBKRSEAXXX4531895095} 4 :
{177:0111161832}{451:0}{108:F011116S7
Basic Header                      F 01 CZNBKRSEAXXX 4531 895095
Application Header                 L 700.‾MIDLSESXAXXX N
                                  *HSBC BANK PLC
                                  *STOCKHOLM
User Header                       Service Code 103:
                                  Bank Priority 113:
                                  Msg User Ref. 108 : F01116S70050217
Sequence of Total   *27   : 1 / 1
From of Doc. Credit     *40 A   : IRREVOCABLE
Doc. Credit Number      *20     : MO748111NU200783
Date of Issue        31 C : 211116
Expiry              *31 D : Date 211221 Place AT THE NEGO BANK
Applicant           *50   : ASIA TRADING COMPANY
                            212 Yoi-daero, Youngdeungpo-gu
                            Seoul, Korea 07325
Beneficiary         *59   : HOGANAS AB(PUBL)
                            S-263 83 HOGANAS SWEDEN
Amount              *32 B : CURRENCY USD AMOUNT 35,911.
Available with/by   *41 A : MLDLSESX
                            *HSBC BANK PLC
                            *STOCKHOLM
                            BY NEGOTIATION
Drafts at . . .      42 C : AT 20 DAYS AFTER SIGHT
Drawee               42 A : KOOKMIN BANK, YOIDO BR.
                            215 Yoi-daerp.Youngdeungpo-gu
                            SEOUL, KOREA 07323
Partial Shipments    43 P : ALLOWED
Transhipment         43 T : ALLOWED
Loading in Charge    44 A : EUROPEAN PORT
```

For Transport to   44B   : Busan PORT
Latest Date of Ship 44C   : 211221
Descript. of goods   45 A :
                     MATERIALS AS PURCHASING ORDER NO. DSAC 211010.
Documents required 46 A :
    FULL SET OF CLEAN ON BOARD OCEAN BILLS OF LADING MADE OUT TO
    THE ORDER OF KOOKMIN BANK SEOUL, KOREA MARKED FREIGHT
    PREPAID AND NOTIFY ACCOUNTEE.

    SIGNED COMMERCIAL INVOICE IN THREE FOLD.

    PACKING LIST IN TWO FOLD.

    FULL SET OF INSURANCE POLICY OR CERTIFICATE, ENDORSED IN
    BLANK FOR 110 PERCENT OF THE INVOICE COST. INSURANCE POLICIES
    OR CERTIFICATES MUST EXPRESSLY STIPULATE THAT CLAIMS ARE
    PAYABLE IN THE CURRENCY OF THE DRAFT AND MUST ALSO INDICATE
    A CLAIMS SETTLING AGENT IN KOREA : I.C.C.(A) CLAUSES.
Additional Cond.   47 A :
    A FEE OF USD 50 OR EQUIVALENT IS TO BE DEDUCTED FROM EACH
    DRAWING FOR THE ACCOUNT OF BENEFICIARY, IF DOCUMENTS ARE
    PRESENTED WITH DISCREPANCY(IES).
    T/T REIMBURSEMENT ALLOWED.
Details of Charges   71 B :
    ALL BANKING CHARGES COMM. INCLUDING REIM CHARGE OUTSIDE
    KOREA FOR ACCOUNT OF BENEFICIARY.
Presentation Period 48   :
    WITHIN 10 DAYS AFTER THE DATE OF SHIPMENT BUT WITHIN THE
    VALIDITY OF THE CREDIT.
Confirmation   *49   : CONFIRM
Instructions   78   :
    1. THE AMOUNT OF EACH DRAWING MUST BE ENDORSED ON THE
               REVERSE HEREOF.
    2. ALL DOCS MUST BE MAILED TO KOOKMIN BANK, YOIDO BR. 215
    Yoi-daero, Youngdeungpo-go Seoul, Korea 07323 BY COURIER IN ONE
    LOT.
Send. to Rec. Info. 72   :
    THIS CREDIT IS SUBJECT TO UCP(2007 REV.) I.C.C. PUB 600.

• 주요 용어 및 표현 •

- 국민은행이 Sweden 수출자에게 발행하는 수입신용장이다.
- EUROPEAN PORT : 유럽항구, 유럽의 어느 항구라도 가능
- Available with HSBC Bank : 선적서류 매입은행을 HSBC 은행으로 지정
- MATERIAL : 물질, 물품
- FREIGHT PREPAID : 운임선지급, 운임선불
- NOTIFY ACCOUNTEE : 착화통보처는 수입자
- ENDORSED IN BLANK : 백지 배서
- INSURANCE POLICY OR CERTIFICATE : 보험증권 또는 보험증명서
- EXPRESSLY STIPULATED : 명시되다.
- INDICATE : 나타내다. 보이다. 가리키다.
- CLAIMS : 보험금
- CURRENCY OF THE DRAFT : 환어음상의 통화
- CLAIMS SETTLING AGENT IN KOREA : 한국의 대리점에서 지급되도록
- USD 50 OR EQUIVALENT : 50달러나 이에 상응하는 금액
- BE DEDUCTED : 뺀다. 차감된다.
- DOCS MUST BE MAILED TO ~ : 모든 서류는 ~로 송부되어야 한다.
- COURIER : 서류배달서비스
- IN ONE LOT : 하나의 묶음으로, 전체 하나로

✓	지시식

    지시식이란 증권에서 특정인명을 기재하지 않고 지시문구를 기재하는 형식을 말한다. 지시식 선하증권(order B/L)의 경우 화물수취인란에 "order" 또는 "to the order of CBA Bank"와 같이 기재하며, 지시식 환어음(Order B/E)의 경우는 피지급인란에 이와 같이 기재하게 된다. 이에 대하여 기명식은 특정인명을 기재하게 된다.

✓	백지식 배서

    백지식 배서(Blank Endorsement)는 증권을 양도할 때 피배서인의 이름은 기재하지 않고 배서인만 기명날인하는 것을 말하며 이를 무기명 배서, 백지 배서, 약식 배서라고도 한다. 이에 대해서 기명식 배서(정식 배서)는 피배서인의 명칭, 배서문구, 배서인의 기명날인이 들어가게 된다.

⊞ G6 신용장 정정 요청

SM Company, Inc.

4501, 45th Floor, Trade Tower
511 Yeongdong-daero, Kangnam-gu, Seoul, Korea 06164

June 2, 2021

ANC Co., Ltd
32 Walker Street, North Sydney,
N.S.W. 2060 Australia

Gentlemen:

We received with thanks your letter of credit No. AT-8938 covering your order No. 2467 for multimedia speakers.

Upon checking it, however, we found it stipulated that transshipment is prohibited. Owing to the fact that no direct vessel to Sydney is available from here, transshipment at Kobe is necessary.

We, therefore, request that transshipment be allowed and send us an amendment notice for the letter of credit replacing the clause, "transshipment is prohibited" with the clause, "transshipment is allowed".

Please note that the amendment notice should reach us by the end of this month at the latest in order for the shipment to be made on time.

Your prompt attention to this matter will be much appreciated.

Very truly yours,

내용 SM사가 수입자인 AMS Trading사에 대해서 신용장의 환적조항을 불허에서 허용으로 정정해 줄 것을 요청하는 내용이다.

• 주요 용어 및 표현 •

- covering ~ : ~에 대한, ~에 해당하는
- upon checking it : 신용장을 점검하자 곧, 신용장을 점검하는 중
- stipulated : 명시된, 조건으로 된, 규정된
- transshipment : 환적(=transhipment)
- be prohibited : 금지되다.
- direct vessel : 직항 선박, 바로 가는 선박
- available : 이용할 수 있는, 가능한
- be allowed : 허용되다.
- amendment notice : 정정통지
- clause : 조목, 조항
- please note that ~ : ~을 유의하십시오.
- by the end of this month : 이 달 말까지
- at the latest : 늦어도
- on time : 정시에, 정해진 기일에

✓	신용장 관계은행
advising bank, notifying bank, transmitting bank	통지은행 : 신용장을 통보하는 은행
negotiating bank	매입은행 : 화환어음을 매입하는 은행
confirming bank	확인은행 : 개설은행이 환어음을 매입하지 못할 경우 자신이 매입할 것을 확약하는 은행
paying bank	지급은행 : 신용장상에서 대금을 특정은행이 지급하기로 되어 있는 경우의 그 은행
accepting bank	인수은행 : 기한부 환어음의 경우 환어음을 인수하는 은행
settling bank	결제은행 : 매입은행과 개설은행 중간에서 결제하는 은행
reimbursing bank	상환은행 : 매입은행과 개설은행 중간에서 상환하는 은행
renegotiating bank	재매입은행 : 매입은행으로부터 다시 서류를 매입하는 은행

G7 신용장 기간연장 요청

SM Company, Inc.

4501, 45th Floor, Trade Tower
511 Yeongdong-daero, Kangnam-gu, Seoul, Korea 06164

June 17, 2021

AMS Trading Company
908 Park Avenue
New York, NY 10017 U.S.A.

Gentlemen:

We regret to inform you that there will be a delay in the shipping of our Sales Note No. 1223 due to circumstances beyond our control.

Our supplier has informed us that the work has been suspended for two weeks because of temporary labor strikes and so he was not able to meet the delivery date as previously arranged.

The strike ended yesterday and the supplier had assured us that he would give a special priority to deliver the goods as soon as possible. However, a delay in shipment seems inevitable. We estimate that the delivery to us will be delayed by about two weeks and the shipping date will pass the scheduled shipping date of June 30.

Under these circumstances, we would like to ask you to extend the shipping date and expiry date of the L/C as follows:

Shipping date : July 15, 2021
Expiry date : July 25, 2021

We ask your cooperation in this matter and hope this doesn't cause you too much inconvenience.

Very truly yours,

내용 SM사가 수입자인 AMS Trading 회사에 대해서 선적일자와 신용장 유효
기간을 연장해 줄 것을 요청하는 내용이다.

· 주요 용어 및 표현 ·

- due to ~ : ~로 기인한, ~로 인하여
- circumstances beyond our control : 우리가 통제할 수 없는 사정, 불가항력적인 상황
- be suspended for two weeks : 2주 연기되었다.
- temporary labor strikes : 일시적 노동파업
- meet the delivery date : 인도일(＝shipping date)에 맞추다.
- as previously arranged : 이전에 합의한 대로
- strike ended : 파업은 끝났다.
- special priority : 특별 우선권, 특별 선취권
- assured us that ~ : 우리에게 확실히 ~라고 말하다(＝tell confidently).
- the date will be past the scheduled shipping date : 그 일자는 예정된 선적일을 지나서일 것이다.
- under these circumstances : 이러한 상황에서
- extend : 연장하다.
- shipping date : 선적일
- expiry date : 유효기일
- cause you inconvenience : 불편을 주다. 폐를 끼치다(＝inconvenience you, cause inconvenience to you, give you unconvenience).

✓	공 장
	① factory : 제품이 주로 기계로 대량 생산되는 공장 ② mill : 주로 제분, 제재, 제지, 방적 등의 공장 ③ plant : 공장, 제조공장, 기계장치, 공장설비 ④ works : 공장, 제작소

✄ G8 신용장 정정조치 통보

AMS Trading Company

908 Park Avenue
New York, NY 10017 U.S.A.

June 30, 2021

SM Company, Inc.
4501, 45th Floor, Trade Tower
511 Youngdong-daero,
Kangnam-gu, Seoul, Korea

Gentlemen:

In compliance with your letter of June 17 requesting to amend the letter of credit No. AN211123 we are glad to inform you that we have arranged the amendment as you requested.

We have instructed the issuing bank, CBA Bank, New York to extend the latest shipping date and the expiry date of the L/C to the 15th of July and the 25th of July, respectively. You will be able to receive the amendment within a week by the issuing bank.

We hope our arrangement will be helpful to you.

Very truly yours,

내용 AMS Trading사가 수출자인 SM사의 요청에 따라 신용장 기간연장 조치를 취하였음을 통보하는 내용이다.

• 주요 용어 및 표현 •

- arranged the amendment : 신용장 정정을 조치하다. 신용장을 정정토록 하다.
- instruct : 지시하다.
- latest shipping date : 최종선적일
- expiry date : 유효기일
- respectively : 각각

✓	신용장의 종류	
1	irrevocable L/C revocable L/C	취소불능신용장 취소가능신용장
2	confirmed L/C unconfirmed L/C	확인신용장 미확인신용장
3	with recourse L/C without recourse L/C	상환청구가능신용장 상환청구불능신용장
4	negotiation L/C straight L/C	매입신용장 지급신용장
5	general/ open/ negotiation L/C special L/C, restricted L/C	보통신용장 특정신용장
6	documentary L/C clean L/C	화환신용장 무담보신용장
7	sight L/C usance L/C	일람출급신용장 기한부신용장
8	transferable L/C non-transferable L/C	양도가능신용장 양도불능신용장
9	revolving L/C	회전신용장
10	red clause L/C, packing L/C	전대신용장
11	extended L/C	연장신용장
12	back to back L/C	동시개설신용장
13	escrow L/C	기탁신용장
14	stand-by L/C	보증신용장
15	domestic L/C	내국신용장

Useful Expressions

① 신용장 개설

📄 신용장방식의 대금결제

수출자

- For payment, please arrange for an irrevocable letter of credit in our favor <u>for the amount of</u> US$ 10,000 covering your order No. 123.

  > *for the amount of*
  > *to the amount of*

- We would like to ask you to pay by either T/T or opening an Irrevocable Letter of Credit in our favor.

- We thank you very much for your L/C and shipping instructions covering your trial order.

수입자

- We will open an Irrevocable Letter of Credit against our order upon the receipt of your confirmation of order.

- In order to cover this business, we shall instruct our bankers to open an Irrevocable Letter of Credit for the amount of this transaction in your favor.

- We do not open a letter of credit for any order of less than US$ 5,000 because our bank's fees are too high.

📄 신용장개설 통지

- We advise you that we have <u>established</u> an irrevocable letter of credit No. NS13-104NN-12345 <u>with</u> the Korea Best Bank, in your <u>favor for US$ 100,000</u>.

  > | *established* | | |
  > | *opened* | *with* | *in your favor* |
  > | *issued* | *through* | *in favor of you* |

- An irrevocable letter of credit, covering your Sales Note No. 456, for US$ 50,000 was established in your favor available until August 31.
- We are pleased to inform you that we have instructed the Korea Best Bank, Seoul, to open an irrevocable letter of credit US$ 70,000 in your favor covering your order No. 123 for car audios.
- We have instructed our bankers to open an irrevocable transferable credit so that you can ship the goods before the end of this month.
- We have instructed our bankers, CBA Bank in Seoul, to open an L/C and you may be advised the said L/C very soon.

instructed asked requested	advised notified

- The L/C in question having already been established, you may have been advised of it by this time.

신용장발행 독촉

- We request you to open an L/C in our favor with the Bank of Tokyo to the amount of US$ 100,000 covering your order as soon as possible.
- We are pleased to inform you that your order No. 345 is now ready for shipment. Therefore we would very much like to receive your L/C as soon as possible.
- The letter of credit to cover our contract has not yet reached us, although the shipment is to be made by the end of this month. We would appreciate it if you establish an L/C immediately.
- Please open a Letter of Credit for US$ 2,000 upon receipt of which we will execute the order with our best attention.
- We ask you to open an L/C for your order No. 10 without further delay.
- Despite the fact that you placed an order with us for a printing machine with the special instruction of prompt shipment, your letter of credit has not yet

reached us.

- We regret to say that we have received no banker's advice yet in spite of hearing the advice of the letter of credit from you.

🗎 신용장 내에 사용되는 문구

- We hereby establish our Irrevocable Letter of Credit in your favor available by your draft at 60 days after sight.
- Full set of clean on board B/L made out to the order of ABC Bank, Seoul, marked "Freight Prepaid" and "Notify ABC Company," evidencing shipment from Busan to London not later than May 10, 2021.
- All banking charges including postage outside Korea are to the account of the beneficiary.
- Shipment should be effected by Korean flag vessel only.
- All negotiable sets of B/L made out to order must be endorsed by the shipper.
- Transshipments are permitted. Partial shipments are prohibited.

permitted	prohibited
allowed	not allowed

- Drafts and documents as specified in this L/C must be forwarded to our issuing office directly by the negotiating bank by two successive, registered airmails.

forwarded	successive
sent	consecutive

- The amount of each draft drawn under this credit and the date of negotiation must be endorsed on the reverse hereof by the negotiating bank.

- All drafts drawn hereunder must indicate the number, date of issue, and name of the issuing bank of this credit.
- We hereby engage with the drawers, endorsers, and bona-fide holders of

drafts drawn under and in compliance with the terms of this credit that such drafts will be duly honored upon presentation to the drawee bank.

engage agree	drawee bank drawee

2 신용장 조건변경

1. 일반적 조건변경, 착오정정 등

- Please amend L/C No. 1234 as follows :
  a. Amount to be increased to US$ 10,000.
  b. Validity to be extended to August 31.
  c. The words "XYZ" are to be deleted.
  d. "ABC" are to be replaced by "DEF."
  All other conditions remain unchanged.
- We thank you for your credit No. 1234, but there are a typo in the amount. Please correct the amount to reflect US$ 50,000.
- The name of the merchandise is incorrectly described in the letter of credit. As our bankers do not overlook the slightest discrepancy, we ask you to amend the credit as soon as possible.
- Please increase the credit amount by US$ 200 from US$ 1,800 to US$ 2,000 to pay for an additional 10 cases.
- In connection with L/C No. 1234, we request you to delete the clause "American Flag Ship."

2. 유효기일연장 요청

■ We would like to ask you to extend the validity and shipping dates of the credit No. 456 to June 30 and confirm the changes to us by e-mail.

■ As your L/C expires on August 9, 2021, would you please extend the date on your L/C to December 10, 2021?

expires on	extend the date of your L/C to
is valid until	extend the expiry date of your L/C to
is available until	allow an extension of credit until
is in force until	extend the validity of your L/C till

■ We regret to inform you that we shall not be able to ship your order No. 12 under your credit No. 1234 within the stipulated date due to a strike at our factory and we ask you to extend the credit for one month.

stipulated date	for one month
expiry date	by one month

■ The vessel you arranged has not yet arrived at Busan. Therefore, we wish to ask you to extend the validity of the L/C by two weeks, until May 15.

■ We ask you to extend your Letter of Credit, to enable us to complete the shipment.

3. 신용장조건 변경요청에 대한 회신

■ As requested, we have immediately arranged with our bankers to extend the expiry date of our L/C No. 1234 for two weeks up to the 15th of October, 2021.

■ In accordance with your letter of May 7 requesting an amendment to the L/C, we have instructed CBA Bank, Tokyo to comply.

■ We are glad to inform you that the L/C was amended by our bank, and it will be delivered by ABC Bank, Seoul in a couple of days.

Standard
Trade
English

운송 및 보험

무역업무의 주요 내용

1 물품의 인도와 선적

무역은 원거리의 거래이므로 무역에서 상품의 인도는 직접 인도하는 것이 아니고 수출자가 운송인에 상품을 맡기면 운송인이 수입자에게 전달하는 것이 일반적이다. 수출자가 운송인에게 상품을 맡길 때 운송인은 선하증권을 발급하게 되는데 이 증권으로 수출자가 계약상의 상품을 제대로 선적했는지의 여부가 확인되며, 또 수출자는 이 증권을 수입자에 인도함으로써 상품을 인도하게 된다.

2 운송관련 비용과 책임, 그리고 운송계약

운송과 관련된 비용이나 책임문제는 계약조건, 특히 가격조건에 따라 달라지게 된다. 예를 들어 현장인도조건(EXW)의 경우는 매수인이 모든 책임과 비용을 다 부담하는 반면, 관세지급필 인도조건(DDP)의 경우는 매도인이 모든 비용과 책임을 다 부담하게 된다. FOB의 경우는 수출자가 선적항에서 본선까지 부담하고 그 이후는 수입자가 부담하며, CIF 경우는 수출자가 위험은 선적항에서 본선까지 부담하되 비용은 본선이 목적항에 도착할 때까지 부담하게 되는 것이다. 따라서 계약상의 각 조건에 따라 운송비 부담이나 운송계약을 누가 해야 하는가가 달라지게 된다.

3 운송서류

수출자 또는 수입자는 상품의 성격, 수량, 운항일정, 운임 등을 고려하여 운송회사와 운송계약을 체결하게 된다. 이 후 제반 검사·검량 및 통관 절차를 거쳐 물품이 선적되면 선하증권(B/L)을 발급 받게 된다. 선적된 물품은 선하증권을 통해서만 수령할 수 있고, 선하증권상의 권리자가 물품의 권리자이기 때문에 수출자는 이 선하증권의 양도와 함께 수입자로부터 물품대금을 받게 된다.

무역영문통신의 주요 사항

1 선적관련통신

수출자와 수입자는 선적과 관련하여 선박의 지정이나 선적지시, 운송계약의 요청, 선적의 독촉, 운송과 관련한 상품의 이상유무 확인 등 여러 업무과정에서 수입자와 수출자간에 긴밀한 연락관계를 취하지 않으면 안 된다.

2 선적통지

선적을 하게 되면 수출자는 즉시 수입자에게 이 사실을 통보하여야 한다. 이는 수입상이 상품의 수령, 보관, 처분, 보험, 대금결제 등을 대비할 수 있도록 하기 위해서다. 선적통지는 대개 다음과 같은 사항이 주요 내용으로 된다.

1. 해당상품 : 품목 및 수량, 주문 또는 신용장의 표시
2. 선적 정보 : 선박명, 출항일, 도착예정일
3. 포장, 화인, 컨테이너 번호, B/L번호 등에 관한 사항
4. 운송서류의 송부 및 서류매입에 관한 사항
5. 상품의 안전한 도착 희망 및 다음 주문의 기대 등 맺음말

3 선적독촉통지

선적이 약정된 기일 내에 이루어지지 않고 있을 때 수입자는 수출자에게 빨리 선적해 줄 것을 독촉하게 된다. 선적 독촉통지는 대개 다음과 같은 내용이 포함된다.

1. 해당상품 : 상품의 품목 및 수량, 주문 또는 신용장의 표시
2. 선적이 지연되고 있는 사실과 이로 인한 문제사항
3. 선적을 빨리 해줄 것을 요청, 또는 선적되어야 할 최종기일 제시

4 선적지연통지

선적의 통지와 마찬가지로 지연의 경우에도 즉시 통지를 하여야 한다. 선적지연의 통지는 대개 다음과 같은 사항이 포함된다.

1. 해당상품 : 품목 및 수량, 주문 또는 신용장의 표시 2. 선적지연의 사정
3. 예상되는 지연기간 및 선적가능일 4. 양해의 요청

무역업무의 주요 내용

1 적하보험

운송도중에 발생할 수 있는 물품의 멸실 및 손상 위험은 무역의 가장 큰 위험 중의 하나이다. 이에 대한 보험이 적하보험이다. 적하보험은 가장 오랜 역사를 가진 보험으로서 긴 시간에 걸쳐 발전되어 오늘날에는 무역의 중요한 한 부분이 되고 있다.

2 적하보험계약

적하보험은 계약 및 Incoterms의 각 거래조건에 따라 운송과정에 위험을 부담하는 측이 자신의 위험에 대해서 자신의 비용으로 들게 된다.

다만 CIF와 CIP의 경우는 수입자의 위험에 대해서 수출자가 보험에 들어주게 되는데, 이 때 수출자는 다른 무역서류와 함께 보험증권을 수입자에게 인도하게 된다. 또 어떠한 보험에 얼마의 보험금액으로 들어주어야 하는가는 계약에서 정하게 되며, 이에 대한 합의가 없는 경우 Incoterms에서는 송장금액의 110% 이상, 보험조건은 ICC(C) 또는 FPA 이상으로 하는 것으로 명시하고 있다.

무역영문통신의 주요 사항

1 보험관련통신

적하보험의 가입, 보험서류, 보험사고의 처리와 보상금 등과 관련하여 당사자 간에 정보를 교환하게 된다. 때에 따라서는 FOB나 CFR과 같이 수입자가 보험에 부보해야 하는 경우에도 수입자가 수출자에게 보험부보를 대신 해줄 것을 요청하기도 하고 수출자는 이에 대한 결과를 통보하기도 한다.

적하보험에 대한 통신에서 주로 다루게 되는 내용은 대개 다음과 같다.

1. 부보대상 물품에 관한 사항(품명, 수량, 금액 등)
2. 운송에 관한 사항(선편, 선적항, 목적항, 출항일 등)
3. 보험조건에 관한 사항(부보조건, 보험금액 등)
4. 물품의 거래관련사항(신용장번호, 송장번호 등)
5. 보험증권 및 보험료에 관한 사항

✓	보험조건
구 약 관	A/R(All Risks) : 전위험담보 WA(With Average) : 분손담보 FPA(Free From Particular Average) : 분손부담보 TLO(Total Loss Only) : 전손담보
신 약 관	ICC(A)(Institutes Cargo Clauses(A)) : 협회적화약관 A약관 ICC(B)(Institutes Cargo Clauses(B)) : 협회적화약관 B약관 ICC(C)(Institutes Cargo Clauses(C)) : 협회적화약관 C약관
부 가 조 건 담 보 손 해	1. TPND(Theft, Pilferage and Non-Delivery) : 도난, 발하, 불착 손해 2. RFWD(Rain and/or Fresh Water Damage) : 빗물, 해수에 의한 손해 3. COOC(Contact with Oil and/or Other Cargo) : 유류 및 타물체 접촉손 4. WOB(Washing Overboard) : 갑판유실 손해 5. Hook and Hole : 갈고리에 의한 손해 6. Breakage : 파손 7. Leakage and/or Shortage : 누손, 부족손 8. SH(Sweat and/or Heating) : 습기와 열에 의한 손해 9. Denting and Bending : 곡손(曲損) 손해 10. Contamination : 오염 손해 11. Spontaneous Combustion : 자연발화 손해 12. Mildew and Mould : 곰팡이 손해 13. Rust : 녹 손해 14. Rat and/or Vermin : 쥐, 벌레 손해 15. War : 전쟁 손해 16. Strike : 동맹파업 손해

⊞ H1 선박의 수배

ABBA Co., Inc.
1156 5th Avenue
New York, NY 10017 U.S.A.

June 23, 2021

TWC Shipping Co.
1124 Third Avenue
New York, NY 10015

Dear Sir:

We have 500 sets of color televisions weighing about 1,000 kgs and measuring about 500 cubic meters for shipment from Busan to New York.

Would you please give us a sailing schedule and quote us the lowest rate of freight inclusive of basic rate, additional charge, surcharge, lighterage, landing charges, dock dues, and all other expenses and charges for them?

Your prompt reply will be highly appreciated.

Sincerely yours,

내용 ABBA사가 TWC 해운회사에 선박의 운항일정과 운임에 대하여 문의하는 내용이다.

• 주요 용어 및 표현 •

- cubic meter : 입방미터
- sailing schedule : 운항 시간표, 출항 일정표, 운항스케줄
- rate of freight : 화물운송요금, 화물운임
- inclusive of ~ : ~를 포함하여
- lighterage : 부선료
- landing charges : 양륙비(=landing rates)
- dock dues : 부두 수수료, 부두 사용료
- expenses : 비용, 소요경비
- charges : 요금, 비용

✓	해상운송관련용어
운송선박	liner : 정기선 tramp : 부정기선
항해	ETA(Expected Time of Arrival) : 입항예정일 ETD(Expected Time of Departure) : 출항예정일 shipping gazette : 운항일정회보
운임단위	measurement cargo : 용적화물 weight cargo : 중량화물 ad valorem rate cargo : 종가화물
운임	prepaid freight, freight in advance : 선불운임 freight collect, freight payable at destination : 후불운임
	〈정기선 선적절차〉
	shipping date(선적일자) 결정 → sailing schedule(배선표) 확인 → S/R(shipping request : 선복요청서) 제출 → booking note(인수확약서) 교부 → S/O(shipping order : 선적지시서) 교부 → shipment(선적) → M/R(mate's receipt : 본선수취증) 발급 → B/L(bill of lading : 선하증권) 발급

⊞ H2 선박안내

TWC Shipping Co.

1124 Third Avenue
New York, NY 10015 U.S.A.

July 2, 2021

ABBA Co., Inc.
1156 5th Avenue
New York, NY 10017 U.S.A.

Dear Mr. Park:

Thank you for your inquiry of June 23. We are pleased to inform you of our sailing schedule and freight rate for your cargo.

The nearest departure is the Silver Star which is due to sail on the 24th of this month. The second vessel available is scheduled to sail on the 4th of next month. The goods should have reached us by the 21st of this month for the first vessel, or the 1st of next month for the second vessel.

The freight from Busan to New York is US$ 24.⁻ per cubic meter, which is the lowest rate we can quote.

Please find enclosed our shipping request form, complete it, and return it to us as soon as possible.

Very truly yours,

내용 ABBA사의 운임 및 운항일정 등의 문의에 대하여 TWC 해운회사가 회신
하는 내용이다.

• 주요 용어 및 표현 •

- freight rate : 운임률, 운임
- The nearest departure : 가장 일찍 출항하는 배편
- be due to sail : 출항예정인(=be scheduled to sail)
- the second vessel available : 둘째 배편, 가능한 두번째의 배
- please find enclosed ~ : ~을 동봉합니다. ~을 보내드립니다.
- shipping request form : 선적요청서 양식
- as soon as possible : 최대한 빨리, 가능한 빨리(=ASAP)

✓	해상운송 운임의 기본료, 부과료, 할증료
basic rate	basic rate(기본요금)
charge / additional charge (부과료)	1. transshipment charge(환적료) 2. optional charge(양륙항선택료) 3. diversion charge(양륙항변경료) 4. minimum charge(최저운임)
surcharge (할증료)	1. heavy lift surcharge(중량할증료) 2. bulky surcharge(용적할증료) 3. long length surcharge(장척할증료) 4. outport surcharge(외항할증료) 5. bunker surcharge(BAF : 유류할증료) 6. port congestion surcharge(체화활증료) 7. war risk surcharge(전쟁위험할증료) 8. government surcharge(정부징수금할증료) 9. currency surcharge(CAF : 통화할증료)

H3 선적통지

KSK ELECTRONICS

11 Myongdong-gil, Jung-gu
Seoul, Korea 04534

July 20, 2021

ABBA Co., Inc.
1156 5th Avenue
New York, NY 10017 U.S.A.

Dear Mr. Smith:

Thank you for giving us shipping instructions on your order No. 3311 for color televisions.

As instructed, we shipped the goods yesterday via the S/S "KL 505" sailing from Busan on July 24, scheduled to arrive at New York on or about August 20.

We are sending you a copy of all relative shipping documents while the original documents with our bill of exchange at 90 days after sight were forwarded by our negotiating bank to the L/C issuing CBA Bank.

We are glad to have completed our service to you, and are looking forward to continued business.

Yours very truly,

내용 KSK ELECTRONICS사가 수출물품의 선적 후 수입자인 ABBA사에 보내는 선적통지이다.

• **주 요 용 어 및 표 현** •

- shipping instructions : 선적지시
- via ~ : ~편으로(=by ~, per ~)
- S/S : 기선, 기계선박, 대형상선(=steam ship, M/V(motor vessel), M/S (motor ship))
- scheduled to arrive : 도착예정인(=due to arrive)
- arrive at New York : =arrive in New York
- on or about August 20 : 8월 20일을 전후해서
- original document : 서류 원본, 원본서류
- bill of exchange at 90 days after sight : 90일 기한부 환어음
- were forwarded : 발송되었다. 전송되었다.
- negotiating bank : 네고은행, 매입은행

✓	용선계약관련용어
용선계약	charter party : 용선계약 chargerage : 용선계약, 용선료 charterer : 용선자 chartering broker : 용선중개인 chartering agent : 용선대리점
용선계약 종류	partial charter : 일부용선계약 whole charter : 전체용선계약 time charter : 정기용선계약 voyage charter : 항해용선계약 bare boat charter : 선박임대계약
계약절차	offer : 신청서 fixture note : 성약각서 charter party(C/P) : 용선계약서

⊞ H4 선적통지

SM Company, Inc.
4501, 45th Floor, Trade Tower
511 Yeongdong-daero, Kangnam-gu, Seoul, Korea 06164

July 12, 2021

AMS Trading Company
908 Park Avenue
New York, NY 10017 U.S.A.

Dear Mr. Smith:

We are pleased to inform you that we have shipped our Sales Note No. 1223 of May 5, 2021 as per the details given below:
Commodity : SM MP3 Player, NP-101
            32GB MEMORY, MP3, WAV
            Dimensions 5"×1"×5"(W×D×H)
Shipment : By M/V "Asia" of Koreana Line, sailing from Busan on July 12, and scheduled to arrive in New York on August 10, 2021.
Packing : 50 cases, 20 MP3 Players to a case.
Marking : A diamond with "SM" inscribed in capital letters as shown below.

New York

Against this shipment, we have drawn a draft on CBA Bank, New York at sight for US$ 125,000⁻ under the terms of the L/C through the Korea Best Bank, Seoul. We are sending you a copy of the complete set of shipping documents.

We trust the goods will reach you in perfect condition and give you complete satisfaction.

Yours very truly,

내용 SM사가 선적 후 수입자인 AMS Trading 회사에 선적에 대한 내용을 알리는 선적통지이다.

· 주요 용어 및 표현 ·

- as per ~ : ~와 같이, ~에 따라
- details given below : 아래의 명세, 아래의 상세한 기술
- sailing from ~ : ~을 출항하는
- A diamond with "SM" inscribed in capital letters : 안에 대문자의 "SM"을 적은 다이아몬드(◇) 표시
- a draft on CBA Bank : CBA Bank를 지급인으로 하는 어음
- under the terms of the L/C : 신용장의 조건에 따라
- through the Korea Best Bank : Korea Best Bank를 통하여
- complete set of shipping documents : 선적서류전체(=full set of ~)
- in perfect condition : 완전한 상태로, 조금도 이상이 없는 상태로

✓	**shipping marks, cargo marks(화인)**

shipping marks는 화물의 식별과 취급을 용이하게 하기 위하여 외장에 하는 표시이다. 이러한 표시는 선하증권, 송장 등의 서류상에도 동일하게 기재한다.
① main mark(주화인) : 화물의 식별을 위해서 기호, 문자, 숫자 등으로 표시
   ◇, □, ○, △, ☆
② counter mark(부화인) : 주화인을 보조하여 표시
③ weight mark(중량표시)
④ port mark(목적항표시)
⑤ case number mark(번호표시)
⑥ country of origin mark(원산지표시)
⑦ caution mark/ care mark(주의표시)
   NO HOOK, KEEP DRY, FRAGILE, HANDLE WITH CARE, EXPLOSIVE
⑧ 기타 취급상 편의를 위한 일정한 표시

H5 선적기간연장요청

SM Company, Inc.

4501, 45th Floor, Trade Tower
511 Yeongdong-daero, Kangnam-gu, Seoul, Korea 06164

July 11, 2021

AMS Trading Company
908 Park Avenue
New York, NY 10017 U.S.A.

Dear Mr. Smith:

We are sorry to inform you that it has become impossible to complete the shipment of our Sales Note No. 1223 within the stipulated date on account of a typhoon.

We had already completed everything for your order and all of the goods were ready for shipment. However, a typhoon struck the southern part of the Korean peninsula on the 8th of July and the S/S "Asia", the vessel chosen for your goods, suffered serious damage and her July 13th departure was cancelled indefinitely.

Moreover, because of this disaster, a considerable amount of cargo has been congested and it has become quite difficult to secure any shipping space.

Under these circumstances, a shipment delay of about half a month is unavoidable. However please rest assured that we will do everything possible to forward the goods as soon as possible.

In the meantime, we hope you will agree to extend the shipping date until the 30th of July.

Though the delay is beyond our control, we are none the less sorry for the inconvenience this must be causing you.

Thank you for your patience in this matter and we look forward to your cooperation.

Yours very truly,

내용 SM사가 수입자인 AMS Trading 회사에 태풍으로 인하여 선적이 지연됨을 알리고 선적기간을 연장해 줄 것을 요청하는 내용이다.

• 주요 용어 및 표현 •

- stipulated date : 약정일자
- on account of ～ : ～때문에, ～을 이유로
- are ready for shipment : 선적 준비가 된
- the southern part of the Korean peninsula : 한반도 남부
- suffered serious damage : 심각한 피해를 입다.
- indefinitely : 무기한으로
- disaster : 천재, 재앙, 불행
- a considerable amount of cargo : 적잖은 물량의 화물
- congested : 체증된, 정체한
- shipping space : 선복, 선박의 화물적재 창고
- under these circumstances : 이러한 상황에서
- unavoidable : 피할 수 없는
- please rest assured : 안심하십시오.
- do everything possible : 가능한 모든 방법을 다하다.
- in the meantime : 그 동안에
- beyond our control : 불가항력의, 우리로서는 어쩔 도리가 없는
- none the less : 그래도, 역시, 그럼에도 불구하고(＝nonetheless)

✓ 하역비 부담 조건		
하역비 조건	선적비용부담자	양륙비용부담자
① Berth Terms	선주	선주
② F.I.(Free In)	하주	선주
③ F.O.(Free Out)	선주	하주
④ F.I.O.(Free In and Out)	하주	하주

⊞ H6 선적 독촉

ABBA Co., Inc.
1156 5th Avenue
New York, NY 10017 U.S.A.

September 4, 2021

KSK ELECTRONICS
11 Myongdong-gil, Jung-gu
Seoul, Korea 04534

Dear Mr. Smith:

We would like to draw your attention to our order No. 3311 of May 3 for color televisions. The delivery is now two weeks overdue and the delay is causing difficulties for us.

Would you kindly confirm the current situation of the order, and when we might expect delivery?

We are receiving numerous complaints from our customers due to the delay and this will certainly cause us serious problems. We definitely need the goods by the end of September if the order is not to be cancelled.

We look forward to hearing from you promptly.

Yours very truly,

내용 ABBA사가 수출자인 KSK ELECTRONICS사에 주문품의 인도가 지연되고 있는 것에 대하여 조속한 인도를 요청하는 내용이다.

· 주요 용어 및 표현 ·

- draw your attention : 관심을 부탁하다. 배려를 요청하다.
- two weeks overdue : 2주일이 지난, 2주일을 지연하고 있는
- kindly confirm : 확인하다.
- current situation : 현 상황, 현재 상태(=current status)
- when we might expect delivery? : 언제쯤 도착할 것으로 생각해야 하는가?
- numerous : 수많은(=many)
- complaints : 불평, 불만
- cause us serious problems : 우리에게 심각한 문제를 야기시키고 있다.
  =incur upon us serious consequences
- definitely need the goods by ~ : 물품이 ~까지는 꼭 필요하다.
- if the order is not to be cancelled : 주문이 취소되지 않으려고 한다면

✓	Laydays, laytime(정박기간) 조건 및 용어	
laytime 조건	CQD (Customary Quick Dispatch)	관습적 조속하역. 해당항의 관습적 하역방법과 능력에 따라 가능한 조속하게 하역. 불가항력에 의한 하역불능은 하역일에서 제외
	Running Laydays	경과일수. 하역개시일에서 완료일까지의 경과일수를 계산. 불가항력, 일요일, 공휴일은 특약이 없는 한 삽입
	WWD (Weather Working Days)	하역가능일. 하역이 가능한 날씨의 일수만 정박기간으로 계산
	WWD SHEX(Sundays and Holidays Excepted even if used)	일요일, 공휴일은 작업을 하였어도 제외
	WWD(SHEX unless used)	일요일, 공휴일은 제외하나 작업을 한 경우에는 기간에 삽입
laytime 관련용어	demurrage dispatch money laydays statement	체선료 : 계약기간을 초과하면 부담 조출료 : 계약기간 이전 완료시 환급 정박기간 계산서

H7 선적지연양해요청

KSK ELECTRONICS

11 Myongdong-gil, Jung-gu
Seoul, Korea 04534

September 7, 2021

ABBA Co., Inc.
1156 5th Avenue
New York, NY 10017 U.S.A.

Dear Mr. Smith:

We are very sorry to inform you that your order No. 3311 was not shipped by the end of August on account of being out of stock.

Our inventory is running low due to a recent rush of orders which has overloaded our capacity and made it impossible to meet production demand.

However we are making every effort to produce the goods in order to deliver as soon as possible. We would like you to know that your order has been given special priority and we will do our best to ship the goods by September 20. We would be very grateful if you could wait an additional week.

Please accept our deepest apologies for the inconvenience the delay has caused you.

We await your reply with great anticipation.

Very truly yours,

내용 KSK ELECTRONICS사가 주문폭주로 인하여 물품인도가 지연되고 있음을 수입자인 ABBA사에 대하여 알리고 양해를 구하는 내용이다.

• 주요 용어 및 표현 •

- out of stock : 재고부족(＝inventory shortage)
- inventory : 재고(＝stock)
- running low : 재고가 줄어, 재고부족으로(＝run short, out of stock)
- due to ~ : ~로 인하여(＝owing to ~)
- rush of orders : 주문의 쇄도
- overloaded : 과도하게 부담지우다.
- make every effort : 모든 노력을 다하다.
- do our best : 최선을 다하다.
- an additional week : 한 주 더
- please accept our deepest apologies : 심심한 사과를 드린다.
- anticipation : 기대, 예상

✓	해운동맹 용어
conference liner / member liner	동맹선
non-conference liner / outsider	맹외선
freight conference	운임동맹
navigation conference	항로동맹
open conference	미국식 공개적 동맹
closed conference	영국식 폐쇄적 동맹
fighting ship	경쟁억압선
contract rate system	계약운임제도
dual rate system	이중운임제도
triple rate system	삼중운임제도
rebate system	환급제도
fidelity rebate system	충실보상제도
VIP	특별고객우대제도

H8 선적연기에 대한 허락

ABBA Co., Inc.
1156 5th Avenue
New York, NY 10017 U.S.A.

September 11, 2021

KSK ELECTRONICS
11 Myongdong-gil, Jung-gu
Seoul, Korea 04534

Dear Mr. Park:

Thank you for your letter of September 7 notifying us that there will be a delay in delivering our order No. 3311 dated May 3 due to an inventory shortage.

We can confirm that we are prepared to accept a delayed delivery on the understanding that the goods will be to us not later than October 15.

If we have not received them by that date, we are afraid to say that we shall have to cancel the order and take our customers elsewhere on this occasion.

Yours very truly,

내용 수입자인 ABBA사가 수출자 KSK ELECTRONICS사의 물품인도가 지연에 대한 양해요청에 대하여 지연을 허가하는 내용이다.

• 주요 용어 및 표현 •

- inventory shortage : 재고부족(＝stock shortage, out of stock)
- be prepared to ~ : ~할 준비가 되어있는, ~할 각오가 되어 있는
- delayed delivery : 지연된 인도
- on the understanding that ~ : ~한다는 조건으로, ~한다는 양해하에
- the goods will be with us : 우리에게 상품을 보낸다는
- not later than : 이전에(＝before, by, sooner than, prior to, no later than)
- we are afraid to say that ~ : 유감이지만 ~이다.
- shall have ~ : ~할 수밖에 없다(＝will be forced ~).
- take our customers elsewhere : 우리의 고객을 다른 곳으로 모시겠다. 우리 고객에게 다른 상품을 선택하도록 하겠다.
- on this occasion : 이 경우에

✓	Container 운송 용어
LCL : less than container load cargo(컨테이너 단위미만화물) FCL : full container load cargo(컨테이너 단위화물) CFS : container freight station(컨테이너 화물집하소) CY : container yard(컨테이너 야적장)	

✓	국제복합운송관련 용어
multimodal transport operator(MTO) : 복합운송인 multimodal transport B/L : 복합운송선하증권 SLB : Siberia Land Bridge(시베리아 횡단 운송경로) ALB : America Land Bridge(미대륙 횡단 운송경로) MLB : Mini Land Bridge(북미 횡단 운송경로) piggyback : 철도복합운송 fishyback : 선박복합운송 birdyback : 항공복합운송	

H9 선적지연에 대한 주문취소

ABBA Co., Inc.

1156 5th Avenue
New York, NY 10017 U.S.A.

October 17, 2021

KSK ELECTRONICS
11 Myongdong-gil, Jung-gu
Seoul, Korea 04534

Dear Mr. Park:

We regret to inform you that we must cancel our order No. 3311 of May 3 for color televisions.

We did inform you in a letter dated September 11 that these goods were required by October 15. As they have not arrived, we did not have an alternative but to purchase them elsewhere.

We trust that any future orders will be given your prompt attention.

Yours very truly,

내용 수입자 ABBA사가 인도가 지연되고 있는 물품에 대하여 주문 취소를 수출자 KSK ELECTRONICS사에 통보하는 내용이다.

• 주요 용어 및 표현 •

- did inform : informed가 아니고 did inform으로 한 것은 강조한 것
- as they ~ : =since they ~
- did not have an alternative but to purchase them elsewhere : 다른 데서 구매할 수밖에 없었다. 다른 데서 구매하는 것 외에 다른 대안이 없었다.
- purchase them elsewhere : =make other arrangement
- prompt attention : 신속한 처리, 신속한 관심, 신속한 배려

✓	선하증권의 종류
1) shipped / on board B/L	선적 선하증권
2) received for shipment B/L	수령 / 수취 선하증권
3) foul / dirty / remarked B/L	고장 / 사고 / 유보 / 불완전 선하증권
4) clean B/L	무고장 / 완전 선하증권
5) stale B/L	기한경과 선하증권
6) straight B/L	기명식 선하증권
7) order B/L	지시식 선하증권
8) ocean B/L	해양 선하증권
9) local B/L	국내선 선하증권
10) multimodal transport B/L	복합운송 선하증권
11) short form B/L	약식 선하증권
12) negotiable B/L	유통 선하증권
13) non-negotiable B/L	비유통 선하증권
14) red B/L	적색 선하증권

☐ H10 보험가입 요청

ABBA Co., Inc.
1156 5th Avenue
New York, NY 10017 U.S.A.

July 10, 2021

LLD Insurance Co.
1173 Broad Street
Red Bank, NJ 07701 U.S.A.

Dear Sir:

We are writing this letter to request that you insure the shipment against All Risks, including War Risks, to the value of US$ 100,000 for 500 sets of color televisions at the rate of 1.12% as you quoted us by telephone on the 30th of June.

The goods will be loaded on the S/S "KL 505" sailing from Busan to New York on the 24th of July.

Enclosed please find a copy of the commercial invoice. We will remit payment to your bank account for the premium upon receipt of your bill.

Please be good enough to insure our cargo immediately and send us the policy as soon as possible.

Very truly yours,

내용 ABBA사가 수입하는 텔레비전에 대한 해상적하보험의 부보를 LLD 보험 회사에 신청하는 내용이다.

• 주요 용어 및 표현 •

- insure against All Risks, including War Risks : 전쟁위험담보조건과 함께 전위험담보조건의 보험에 들다.
- insure : 보험에 들다(= cover, assure, under-write).
- All Risks : 전위험 담보
- War Risks : 전쟁위험담보
- to the value of ~ : ~의 가액에 대해서, 여기서는 ~의 보험금액에 대해서
- at the rate of ~ : ~의 보험요율로
- will be loaded on ~ : ~에 적재될 예정이다(=are to be loaded on ~).
- enclosed please find~ : ~을 동봉합니다. ~을 보내 드립니다.
- will remit payment to your bank account : 당신의 은행계좌로 입금시키겠다.
- premium : 보험료
- upon receipt of your bill : 당신의 청구서를 받는대로
- policy : 보험증권

✓	해상보험관련 용어
insurer, assurer(보험회사)	insured, assured(보험가입자)
insurance policy(보험증권)	insurable value(보험가액)
insured amount(보험금액)	insurance money, claim paid(보험금)
premium(보험료)	insurable interest(피보험이익)

✓	marine peril(해상위험)	
해상고유의 위험 (perils of the sea)	shipwreck(파선), sinking(침몰), stranding(좌초) grounding(교사), collision(충돌), heavy weather(악천후)	
해상위험 (perils on the sea)	fire(화재), barratry of mariners(선원의 악행), jettison(투하), pirates(해적), rovers(절도), thieves(강도)	
선박외부의 위험	war(전쟁), warlike operation(변란), arrest(강류) detainment(억류), strike(파업)	

⊞ H11 적하보험 부보사실 통지

LLD Insurance Co.

1173 Broad Street
Red Bank, NJ 07701 U.S.A.

July 13, 2021

ABBA Co., Inc.
1156 5th Avenue
New York, NY 10017 U.S.A.

Dear Mr. Park:

Thank you for your letter of July 10. As you requested, we are pleased to inform you that we have insured against All Risks, including War Risks at the rate of 1.12% to the value of US$ 100,000 for 500 sets of color televisions to be shipped from Busan to New York via the S/S "KL 505" sailing on the 24th of July.

Enclosed is a copy of the pertinent insurance policy. Please check to see if everything is to your satisfaction.

Also enclosed is the invoice totaling US$ 765 and our bank account information. Please transfer the appropriate amount for the premium to our account.

Thank you very much; it is always a great pleasure for us to serve you.

Very truly yours,

내용 LLD 보험회사가 해상적하보험을 신청한 ABBA사에게 부보되었음을 알리는 내용이다.

• 주요 용어 및 표현 •

- insure : 보험을 인수하다(=assure, under-write, subscribe).
- at the rate of ~ : ~의 요율로
- pertinent insurance policy : 관련 보험증권
- check to see : 보고 확인하다(=review to be sure).
- if everything is to your satisfaction : 모든 것이 만족스러운지
- totaling ~ : ~ 총액의, 총액이 ~인
- bank account : 은행계좌
- transfer : 송금하다. 금액을 이전시키다.
- to our account : 우리 계좌로

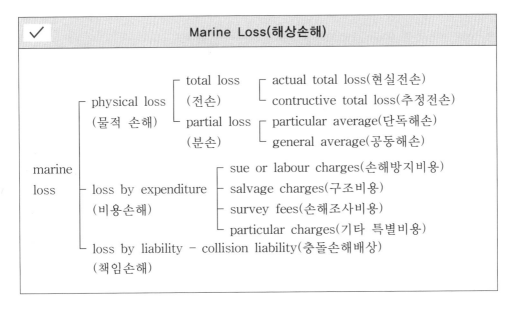

✓	Marine Loss(해상손해)

marine loss
- physical loss (물적 손해)
  - total loss (전손)
    - actual total loss(현실전손)
    - contructive total loss(추정전손)
  - partial loss (분손)
    - particular average(단독해손)
    - general average(공동해손)
- loss by expenditure (비용손해)
  - sue or labour charges(손해방지비용)
  - salvage charges(구조비용)
  - survey fees(손해조사비용)
  - particular charges(기타 특별비용)
- loss by liability - collision liability(충돌손해배상) (책임손해)

Useful Expressions

① 운 송

▣ 운송요청 및 문의

- Please book the shipping space for our cargo of 100 tons on your ship "Arirang" scheduled to sail on the 15th of this month.
- How many direct sailings are there in a month from Incheon to Sydney.
- We would like to know the port of call of S/S Venus.
- Please let us know your lowest rate of freight for 100 cases of silk goods to be shipped during October from Inchon to Houston via the Panama Canal.
- The cargo is composed of 50 cartons of leather handbags and 100 cartons of clothing, weighing 220 kgs and measuring 25 cubic meters.

▣ 선적계획

- We are now under negotiation for booking space on a vessel. We will be able to inform you of the name of the vessel within a few days before completion of loading.
- When do you think you will be able to make shipment?

> *you will be able to make shipment?*
> *the goods will be arriving?*

- We figure the shipment would be made on or about May 20.
- As soon as the shipment is finished, we will immediately inform you of the name of the vessel, which is now intended to be the m/s "Arirang" sailing on April 5.
- You will receive our advice very shortly since the shipment is scheduled to be made via m/s "Arirang" during the 1st week of June.

선적지시

1. 포장, 화인 등에 관한 사항

■ We wish to draw your attention to the following shipping instructions and require that you <u>implement</u> our order <u>in strict accordance with</u> them.

implement fulfill ship	in strict accordance with in compliance with agreeably to

■ Packing in tough wooden cases is essential. Cases must be nailed, and secured by overall metal strapping.

■ If cartons are used, please pack each article in strong polyethylene bags to make certain they are protected against dampness.

■ Carton boxes must have an interior lining of stout, moisture-resistant paper.

■ Please limit the weight of each carton to 10 lbs and metal strap it crosswise.

■ Please use normal export containers unless you receive special instructions from us.

■ As the goods will be checked at customs, the cases must be of a type that can be easily opened and refastened at once after checking.

■ Please stencil our shipping marks in 3 inches high letters, and indicate gross and net weight on each case.

■ All boxes must be marked in the same manner as before, but please number them consecutively starting from No. 1.

■ Please mark a triangle with "SKS" inscribed in capital letters on all cases and send to our forwarding agent's warehouse in Incheon.

2. 서류에 관한 사항

■ All shipments of live animals must be accompanied by a quarantine certificate issued by relevant authorities.

- You are requested to send us a copy of the inspection certificate signed by the authorized surveyor.
- Please send us one copy of the Bill of Lading as soon as you ship the goods stipulated.
- Please send us a certificate of origin issued by the Chamber of Commerce in your area with other shipping documents.

선적통지

1. 선적사실

- We are pleased to <u>inform</u> you that we have <u>shipped</u> your order No. 112 of May 30 for Wireless Headphoness <u>by</u> the <u>S/S</u> "DONGHAE" which <u>sails</u> from Busan to Hong Kong today.

inform *advise*	*shipped* *forwarded* *dispatched*	*by* *via* *per*	*S/S(s.s.)* *M/V(m.v.)* *M/S(m.s.)*	*sails* *leaves* *is scheduled to sail*

- Please be advised that the 1,000 pieces of leather handbags have been shipped by the S.S. "President Wilson," which is scheduled to sail from Busan to Kobe this afternoon.
- Today, we have forwarded to you by KE-007, twenty cartons containing the wool sweaters which you ordered on June 5.
- In reference to your order No. 123, we are dispatching the goods to you by the M.S. "Red Sun" sailing on June 10, 2021.
- Your order No. 1002 has been forwarded by the "Arirang" which leaves this port today and arrives at your port on June 20.
- We have already instructed our shipping agents to load the goods by the m/v "Arirang" sailing on June 10.
- We have the pleasure of informing you that your goods will be shipped by the M.V. "Arirang," leaving Busan for Manila on the 2nd of April.

- We hope that you will understand our <u>position</u> that the <u>substitution</u> of the vessel by the S.S. "Silver Star V" was <u>the only practical option</u> we had.

| position | substitution | the only practical option |
| situation | replacement | the only possible way |

2. 포장, 화인 및 선적지시 이행

- As requested, we have carried out perfectly the marking and numbering of the cases.
- We are pleased to inform you that your packing and marking instructions have been carried out accurately by our shipping agent in Busan.
- Your brass tubes will be sent in 50 bundles, firmly clamped by wires.
- The goods are shipped in wooden barrels of 30 gallons in capacity.
- Soy oil is contained in rust-proof drums of 10 gallons.
- Styrofoam boxes are used to reduce weight, and they are easy to carry.
- After collecting all items of your order at our factory, we packed them into suitable sizes for delivery.
- The goods ordered are shipped in 25kg canvas boxes, wrapped and sealed in polyethylene bags.

📋 선적통지의 맺는 말

- We hope the goods will reach you <u>in good condition</u> and <u>give you complete satisfaction</u>.

| in good condition
in good order
in safety
safely | give you satisfaction
render you satisfaction
open up to your satisfaction
meet your expectations | complete
full |

- We thank you for this order and trust <u>the goods</u> will reach you <u>promptly</u> and in good order.

the goods the shipment the cargo	promptly soon in due time

- Should the contents of the parcel not be in perfect condition when it reaches you, please let us know at once.
- We trust this purchase will bring you a good profit and result in your further orders.
- If we can be of any further service to you, please let us know.
- We trust the high quality of our articles will prove to be an inducement to further business.
- We hope the shipment will reach you safely, and we look forward to your further orders.
- We trust the shipment will reach you in due time, and hope that you will honor our draft upon presentation.
- We are looking forward to the continuation of our pleasant business relations.
- We have been very happy to serve you and look forward to receiving your future orders.
- We thank you for this order and trust the goods will reach you promptly and in good order.

📖 선적지연 통지

- We regret to inform you that the shipment against our Sales Note No.15 has been delayed as the result of recent typhoons.

as the result of due to because of	typhoons / floods fires / waterfront strikes

- We regret to inform you that the sailing of the s/s "SEA STAR," by which your order No. 10 was to be shipped, has suddenly been cancelled.

- The factory strike prevents us from shipping your order No. 345 by the due time. We shall keep in touch with the manufacturers and make every effort to prevent further delay.

- All Korean dock workers have been on strike for the past one week and there is no sign of the strike letting up. We hope you will understand that these circumstances are beyond our control as indicated in the enclosed certificate.

- Owing to the dock workers' strike, the sailing of s.s "Wilson," scheduled to leave on July 31, has been cancelled. We ask you, therefore, to extend the date of shipment to August 31.

🗐 선적독촉

- Would you please check on the shipment of our order immediately?

- Although 2 months have passed since we placed an order, we have not received the goods yet.

- When we sent you our order, we pointed out that early delivery <u>was essential</u>.

> *was essential*
> *was extremely important*
> *was required.*

- We are afraid that we have no choice but to cancel our order if the goods do not arrive here by May 20.

- Please try to <u>speed up</u> your shipment as soon as possible.

> *speed up*
> *hurry up*

- As the goods are urgently required, we must ask you to dispatch them without further delay.

② 적하보험

▤ 보험회사에 부보 문의 및 신청

- Please quote us the insurance rate against All Risks on general merchandise for US$ 10,000 from Incheon to Singapore during March.
- Please cover US$ 150,000 on 5,000 pieces of leather handbags against ICC(C).
- Please insure for US$ 100,000 on stuffed toys on ICC(B) from Busan, Korea to New York, U.S.A., and let us have the insurance policy as soon as possible.
- Please quote your lowest ICC(C) rates on 1,000 sets of car stereos for US$ 30,000 per M/S "Donghae Ho" from Kobe, Japan to Busan, Korea.
- Kindly let us have the Marine Cargo Insurance Policy for this insurance today.
- We would like to you insure against All Risks for US$ 10,000 value of 50 cartons of clothes per M/S "Namhae Ho" from Busan to Hong Kong.
- We have received your notice that you will insure at 0.25%. As we are satisfied with the rate quoted, please insure and send us the insurance policy at once.

▤ 보험회사의 부보 문의 및 신청에 대한 회신

- We are pleased to advise you that we have insured for US$ 100,000 on the 50 cartons of clothes.
- We have the pleasure to establish for you a policy of insurance for US$ 510,000 effected by us on the goods by the s.s "SEA STAR 7," from Hong Kong to Busan.
- We have insured for ¥51,000,000 on rice at 0.30 percent as you requested.

▤ 수출자에게 부보 의뢰

- Please cover insurance for the goods against all risks.
- Please take out insurance for the shipping cargo with 10% expected profit.

take out insurance for get insurance for cover	expected profit imaginary profit

- We leave the insurance arrangements to you, but we wish to have the goods covered against All Risks <u>to the value of</u> US$ 5,000 on 10 cases of wine glasses, from Seoul to Manila by the m/v "SEA STAR 7."

to the value of to the extent of

- Please cover 110% of the invoice value for 900 sets of car radios on Institute Cargo Clauses (B) including TPND.
- We request that you do your best to take out the cargo insurance at the best possible terms.

수입자에 부보사실 통지

- As <u>instructed,</u> we have gotten insurance with ABC Insurance Company on W.A. terms including War Risk.

instructed directed, requested desired

- We have covered the goods against ICC(A) on 110% of the invoice value for US$ 11,000 at 0.15 percent.
- We enclose the covering note for US$ 20,000 on rice by the steamer "Pan-Asia" from Los Angeles to Busan.
- The rate of 0.25 percent is a fine one ; it includes Inland Transit Extension for inland transportation.

Standard
Trade
English

무역서류

무역서류(Transport Documents)란 수출자가 수입자에게 제공하는 서류를 말한다. 무역서류는 어느 경우나 항상 제공되는 기본서류와 수출자와 수입자의 합의로 필요에 따라 제공되는 부속서류로 나뉜다.

1 필수서류

1) 운송서류

대표적으로 해상운송에서의 선하증권(B/L)이다. 운송방법에 따라 항공화물수령증(Airway Bill), 복합운송서류(Multimodal Transport Document), 철도운송서류(Railroad B/L), 우편소포수령증(Post Receipt) 등이 사용되기도 한다.

선하증권은 무역서류 중에서 가장 중요한 서류로서 운송인이 자기 선박에 운송화물을 적재한 것을 증명하고, 도착항에서 그 선하증권과 상환하여 인도할 것을 약정하는 증서이며, 화물을 대표하는 유가증권이다.

2) 송 장

송장(Invoice)이란 수출자가 수입자에게 보내는 선적상품의 명세서이다. 이는 동시에 계산서와 대금청구서의 역할을 한다. 송장은 그 용도에 따라 상업송장(Commercial Invoice)과 공용송장(Official Invoice)이 있는데, 상업송장에는 상품의 선적시에 사용되는 선적송장(Shipping Invoice), 견적을 낼 때 사용되는 견적송장(Pro-forma Invoice)이 있고, 공용송장으로는 통관목적의 세관송장(Customs Invoice)과 거래내용입증을 위한 영사송장(Consular Invoice)이 있다.

2 부속서류

1) 보험증권

보험증권(Insurance Policy)은 보험계약의 내용 및 조건을 기재한 증서이다. 무역서류에 보험증권이 반드시 포함되어야 하는 경우는 CIF와 CIP조건일 때이다. 보험증권 외에 포괄보험 계약 체결시에는 보험증명서(Insurance Certificate)도 사용된다.

2) 원산지증명서

원산지증명서(Certificate of Origin)는 상품이 특정국가에서 생산되었음을 증명하는 문서이다. 원산지 증명서는 ① 특정국가에서의 수입 통제나 금지를 위한 목적, ② 특정국가에 대한 쿼터관리를 위한 목적, ③ 소비자에 원산지 정보 제공 목적, ④ 국별 수입통계 목적, ⑤ 개발도상국에 대한 일반특혜관세의 부여 등의 목적으로 사용된다.

원산지 증명서는 일반 원산지증명서와 일반특혜관세 적용목적의 일반특혜관세 원산지증명서(GSP C/O)가 있다.

3) 포장명세서

포장명세서(Packing List)는 포장된 화물의 내용물에 대한 명세서이다. 포장명세서는 송장을 보충하여 화물의 포장, 포장단위별 총중량 및 순중량, 일련번호, 화인 등을 명시함으로써 운송과 통관을 용이하게 한다.

4) 중량 및 용적증명서

중량 및 용적증명서(Certificate of Quantity / Certificate of Measurement)는 상품의 중량 및 용적을 확인하는 증명서이다.

5) 검사증명서

검사증명서(Certificate of Inspection)는 상품의 품질을 확인하는 증명서이다. 품질증명서(Certificate of Quality), 분석증명서(Certificate of Analysis) 등이 여기에 해당된다.

6) 위생 및 검역증명서

위생 및 검역증명서(Certificate of Health / Certificate of Quarantine)는 동식물, 식품, 의약품 등의 무역에서 수입국의 보건 및 위생상의 안전을 위해서 사용되는 보건 및 검역의 확인을 위한 증명서이다.

⊞ I1 무역서류송부

SM Company, Inc.
4501, 45th Floor, Trade Tower
511 Yeongdong-daero, Kangnam-gu, Seoul, Korea 06164

July 25, 2021

AMS Trading Company
908 Park Avenue
New York, NY 10017 U.S.A.

Dear Mr. Smith:

We are pleased to inform you that we have shipped your order of 1,000 units of the "SM MP3 Player, NP-101" via the S/S "Koreana" scheduled to depart Inchon on July 30th.

Enclosed are copies of the Commercial Invoice, Ocean Bill of Lading, Packing List, Certificate of Origin, Certificate of Inspection.

For the amount of the invoice, we have drawn a draft at sight and negotiated it through the Korea Best Bank under the L/C issued by CBA Bank, New York.

We have been happy to serve you and look forward to receiving your further orders.

Yours very truly,

내용 SM사가 선적 후 수입자인 AMS Trading 회사에 선적에 대한 내용을 알리는 선적통지이다.

• 주 요 용 어 및 표 현 •

- via ~ : ~편으로(=by ~, per ~)
- depart : 출발하다. 출항하다(=leave).
- Commercial Invoice : 상업송장
- Ocean Bill of Lading : 해양 선하증권, 대양 해상운송의 선하증권
- Packing List : 포장명세서
- Certificate of Origin : 원산지 증명서
- Certificate of Inspection : 검사 증명서
- negotiated it through the Korea Best Bank : 환어음을 한국최고은행에 매입 의뢰(네고)하다. 환어음을 한국최고은행을 통하여 유통시키다.

✓	무역서류명	
B/E	Bill of Exchange(Draft)	환어음
B/L	Bill of Lading	선하증권
C/O	Certificate of Origin	원산지증명서
D/O	Delivery Order	화물인도지시서
E/D	Export Declaration	수출신고(서)
E/L	Export Licence	수출승인(서)
E/R	Export Report	수출보고서
I/D	Import Declaration	수입신고(서)
I/L	Import Licence	수입승인(서)
I/P	Insurance Policy	보험증권
I/V	Invoice	송장
L/C	Letter of Credit	신용장
L/G	Letter of Guarantee	보증서
L/G	Letter of Guarantee	화물선취보증서
L/I	Letter of Indemnity	파손화물보상장
P/L	Packing List	포장명세서
S/O	Shipping Order	선적지시서

⌈↲⌉ I2 무역서류 송부요청

HK Trading Inc.

12/Floor, St. John's Building
33 Garden Road, Central, Hong Kong

August 10, 2021

SM Company, Inc.
4501, 45th Floor, Trade Tower
511 Yeongdong-daero, Kangnam-gu
Seoul, Korea 06164

Dear Mr. Park:

We have received shipping documents via CBA Bank, Hong Kong against our order No.1332.

However, we have found that the customs invoice form was an outdated one. From July 1 of this year, the new certified customs invoice form 64A is required by the Hong Kong Customs Administration Office and the old forms are no longer acceptable.

Therefore, please send us immediately a customs invoice using the new form 64A by express mail. Unless your documents are accompanied by the correct customs invoice, we cannot pass customs clearance and cannot protect your draft.

We would appreciate it if you give prompt attention to this matter.

Very truly yours,

내용 수입자 HK사가 수출자 SM사에게 통관에 필요한 새로운 양식에 의한 세관송장을 급히 보내줄 것을 요청하는 내용이다.

· 주요 용어 및 표현 ·

- shipping documents : 선적서류(＝transport documents)
- customs invoice : 세관 송장
- outdated : 구식의
- certified customs invoice form : 공식 세관송장 양식
- Customs Administration Office : 세관당국
- by express mail : 속달 우편으로
- pass customs clearance : 통관을 하다. 세관 통관절차를 통과하다.
- protect draft : 어음을 받아들이다. 인수 또는 결제하다(＝honor draft).

✓	서류의 수	
한　　부	original	original
두　　부	two-fold	duplicate
세　　부	three-fold	triplicate
네　　부	four-fold	quadruplicate
다섯 부	five-fold	quintuplicate
여섯 부	six-fold	sextuplicate
일곱 부	seven-fold	septuplicate
여덟 부	eight-fold	octuplicate
아홉 부	nine-fold	nonuplicate
열　　부	ten-fold	decuplicate

1. original은 원본, 정본의 의미
2. duplicate는 정본과 부본 2통, 2통 중의 하나, 부본 등의 의미이다.
3. 일반적으로 오른쪽의 라틴계통의 말보다는 two-fold 또는 two copies 등과 같이 사용하며, 특히 다섯 이상에서는 sextuplicate와 같은 표현은 거의 사용하지 않는다.

I3 무역서류 송부요청

JAN Trading Co.

414-11, Marunouchi, 3-Chome,
Chiyoda-Ku, Tokyo, Japan

September 15, 2021

SM Company, Inc.
4501, 45th Floor, Trade Tower
511 Yeongdong-daero, Kangnam-gu
Seoul, Korea 06164

Dear Mr. Park:

We have just received an arrival notice from the shipping company urging us to take delivery of the goods which are now in customs. However, we cannot take possession of the goods as we have not yet received the shipping documents.

Under these circumstances, we can take possession of the goods if we tender a Letter of Guarantee signed by our bank with copies of the shipping documents. Therefore we are asking you to send us one set of copies of the shipping documents without delay.

Your prompt attention to this matter would be highly appreciated.

Yours very truly,

내용 JAN Trading사가 SM사에게 수입화물선취보증서 발급을 위한 무역서류 한 세트를 급히 보내줄 것을 요청하는 내용이다.

• 주요 용어 및 표현 •

- shipping company : 해운회사
- arrival notice : 도착통지, 도착 통보
- take delivery of the goods : 물품을 인수하다.
- take possession of the goods : 물건을 손에 넣다. 물건을 점유하다.
- under these circumstances : 이러한 상황에서
- tender : 제출하다. 제공하다.
- Letter of Guarantee : 수입화물 선취보증서

  letter of guarantee(L/G)란 일반적인 의미로 보증서란 말이다. 무역에서 L/G 는 두 가지의 의미로 사용된다. 하나는 수입화물 선취보증서로서 화물은 도착했으나 무역서류가 도착되지 않은 경우에 화물을 수령하기 위해서 선박회사에 제출하는 수입상과 신용장 개설은행의 연대보증서이다.

  또 다른 하나는 수출 후 네고시에 무역서류상 하자가 있는 경우 매입은행은 문제발생시 수출자가 책임을 지도록 하는 보증서를 받는데 이를 L/G라 하고, 이 매입을 L/G 네고(negotiation)라 한다.

✓	무역영어에서 많이 사용되는 복수형 명사		
accounts(계산, 계정)	arrangements(준비)	assets(자산)	bankers(은행)
circumstances(상황)	conditions(조건, 상황)	contents(내용물)	customs(세관)
details(명세)	documents(서류)	dues(부과금)	earnings(수입)
exports(수출품)	funds(기금)	gains(이득)	goods(상품)
greetings(인사장)	headquarters(본사)	imports(수입품)	instructions(지시)
liabilities(부채)	means(수단, 재력)	necessities(필수품)	papers(서류)
particulars(명세)	proceeds(수익)	proceedings(소송)	regards(안부)
relations(관계)	resources(자원)	revenues(총수입)	sales(판매업무)
securities(유가증권)	specifications(명세서)	sundries(잡화)	terms(조건)
thanks(감사)	wages(임금)	wishes(기원)	works(공장)

상 업 송 장
(COMMERCIAL INVOICE)

① Shipper/Exporter SM COMPANY, INC. 4501, 45th Floor, Trade Tower 511 Yeongdong-daero, Kangnam-gu Seoul, Korea 06164	⑧ No. & date of invoice NO. 0008-01 JULY 10, 2021
	⑨ No. & date of L/C NO. AN 211123
② For account & risk of Messrs. TO ORDER	⑩ L/C issuing bank CBA BANK, NEW YORK
	⑪ Remarks :
③ Notify party AMS TRADING COMPANY 908 PARK AVENUE NEW YORK, NY 10017 U.S.A.	

④ Port of loading Busan, KOREA	⑤ Final destination NEW YORK U.S.A.
⑥ Carrier DONGHAEHO	⑦ Sailing on or about JULY 12, 2021

⑫ Marks & numbers of Pkgs.	⑬ Description of Goods	⑭ Quantity/Unit	⑮ Unit Price	⑯ Amount
No. 2543-81-01	SM MP3 PLAYER NP-101 6GB MEMORY, MP3, WAV DIMENSIONS 5"×1"× 5"(W×D×H)	1,000 sets	US$ 125 CIF New York	US$ 125,000

⑰ P.O. Box   :
   Cable address :
   Telex code   :
   Telephone No. :

SM COMPANY, INC

⑱ *C. H. JANG*

C. H. JANG,   MANAGER

선 하 증 권
(BILL OF LADING)

Shipper/Exporter SM Company, Inc. 4501, 45th Floor, Trade Tower 511 Yeongdong-daero, Kangnam-gu Seoul, Korea 06164	Document No. 0003-01
	Export references NO. 569321-EX01
Consignee TO ORDER OF CBA BANK, NEW YORK	Forwarding Agent References NO. HJ93215-63
	Point and Country of Origin REPUBLIC OF KOREA
Notify Party AMS TRADING COMPANY 908 PARK AVENUE NEW YORK, NY 10017 U.S.A.	Domestic Routing/Export Instructions

Precarriage by	Place of receipt Busan KOREA	Onward Inland Routing
Ocean Vessel ASIANA	Port of loading Busan, KOREA	For Transshipment to
Port of Discharge NEW YORK U.S.A.	Place of delivery NEW YORK U.S.A.	Final Destination for the Merchants' Only

Particulars Furnished by Shipper

Marks and Numbers	No. of Cont. or Other PKGS.	Description of Packages and Goods	Gross Weight (KGS)	Measurement (CBM)
No. 2543-81-01	C/T No. 1-01	SM MP3 PLAYER NP-101 6GB MEMORY, MP3, WAV DIMENSIONS 5"×1"× 5"(WxDxH)	645 KGS	13.50CBM

Freight and Charges Revenue Tons Rate Per	Prepaid	Collect	
FREIGHT US$ 1,750 CHARGE US$ 190 TOTAL US$ 1,940	US$ 1,940		IN ACCEPTING THIS BILL OF LADING, the shipper, owner and consignee of the goods, and the holder of the bill of lading expressly accept and agree to all its stipulations, exceptions and conditions, whether written, stamped or printed as fully as if signed by such shipper, owner, consignee and/or holder. No agent is authorized to waive any of the provisions of the within clauses. IN WITNESS WHEREOF, the master or agent of the said ship has affirmed to THREE(3) bills of lading, all of this tenor and date, ONE of which being accomplished, the others to stand void.

B/L NO. BS-0006	Dated at SEOUL, KOREA, JULY 11, 2021

KOREANA LINE Co. Ltd.

BY *CHANJOO KIM*

CHANJOO KIM, MANAGER

MARINE CARGO INSURANCE POLICY

Assured(s),etc SM COMPANY, INC.		
Policy No 01HG21035		Ref. No. L/C No. AN211123 INV. No. 0008-01
Claim if any payable at/in ILM CO., LTD NEW YORK, U.S.A. USD CURRENCY		
		Amount insured hereunder US$ 137,500 (US$ 125,000.⁻ ×110%)
Survey should be approved by SAME AS ABOVE		
Local Vessel or conveyance	From (interior port or place of loading)	Conditions and Warranties
Ship or Vessel ASIA	Sailing on or about JULY 12, 2021	INSTITUTE CARGO CLAUSES (A) INSTITUTE WAR CLAUSES (CARGO)
at and from Busan, KOREA	transhipped at	
arrived at NEW YORK, U.S.A.		

Subject-matter Insured
1,000 PCS/50 CASES of SM MP3 PLAYER NP-101 6GB MEMORY, MP3, WAV, DIMENSIONS 5"×1"×5"(WxDxH)
Mark and Number as Invoice No. specified above

Place and Date signed in SEOUL, KOREA JULY 5, 2021	Number of Policies issued THREE

IMPORTANT

PROCEDURE IN THE EVENT OF LOSS OR DAMAGE FOR WHICH UNDERWRITERS MAY BE LIABLE

LIABILITY OF CARRIERS, BAILEES OR OTHER THIRD PARTIES

It is the duty of the Assured and their Agents, in all cases, to take such measures as may be reasonable for the purpose of averting or minimising a loss and to ensure that all rights against Carriers, Bailees or other third parties are properly preserved and exercised. In particular, the Assured or their Agents are Required :
1. To claim immediately on the Carriers, Port Authorities or other Bailees for any missing packages.
2. In no circumstances, except under written protest, to give clean receipts where goods are in doubtful condition.
3. When delivery is made by container, to ensure that the Container and its seals are examined immediately by their responsible official.
If the Container is Delivered Damaged or with seal broken or missing or with seals other than as started in the shipping documents, to clause the delivery receipt accordingly and retain all defective or irregular seals for subsequent identification.
4. To apply immediately for survey by Carrier's or other Bailees' Representatives if any loss or damage be apparent and claim on the Carriers or other Bailees for any actual loss or damage found at such survey.
5. To give notice in writing to the Carriers or other Bailees within 3 days of delivery if the loss or damage was not apparent at the time of taking delivery.
NOTE : The Consignees or their Agents are recommended to make themselves familiar with the Regulations of the Port Authorities at the port of discharge.

INSTRUCTIONS FOR SURVEY

In the event of loss or damage which may involve a claim under this insurance, immediate notice of such loss or damage should be given to and a Survey Report obtained from this Company's Office or Agents specified in this Policy or Certificate.

DOCUMENTATION OF CLAIMS

To enable claims to be dealt with promptly, the Assured or their Agents are advised to submit all available supporting documents without delay, including when applicable :
1. Original policy or certificate of insurance.
2. Original or certified copy of shipping invoices, together with shipping specification and/or weight notes.
3. Original or certified copy of Bill of Lading and/or other contract of carriage.
4. Survey report of other documentary evidence to show the extent of the loss or damage.
5. Landing account and weight notes at port of discharge and final destination.
6. Correspondence exchanged with the Carriers and other Parties regarding their liability for the loss or damage.

☞ In the event of loss or damage arising under the Policy, no claims will be admitted unless a survey has been held with the approval of this Company's office or Agents specified in this policy.

CONDITIONS

Notwithstanding anything contained herein or attached hereto to the contrary, this insurance is understood and agreed to be subject to English law and practice only as to liability for and settlement of all claims.

This insurance does not cover any loss or damage to the property which at the time of the happening of such loss or damage is insured by or would but for the existence of this Policy be insured by any fire or other insurance policy or policies except in respect of any excess beyond the amount which would have been payable under the fire or other insurance policy or policies had this insurance not been effected.

We, hereby agree, in consideration of the payment to us by or on behalf of the Assured of the premium as arranged, to insure against loss damage liability or expense to the extent and in the manner herein provided.

In witness whereof, I the Undersigned of LLD INSURANCE CO., LTD. on behalf of the said Company have subscribed My Name in the place specified as above to the policies, the issued numbers thereof being specified as above, of the same tenor and date, one of which being accomplished, the others to be void, as of the date specified as above.

For LLD INSURANCE CO., LTD.

By *Lee Dong-Suna*

포 장 명 세 서
(PACKING LIST)

① Shipper/Exporter SM COMPANY, INC. 4501, 45th Floor, Trade Tower 511 Yeongdong-daero, Kangnam-gu Seoul, Korea 06164	⑧ No. & date of invoice No. 0008-01 & July 10, 2021
② For account & risk of Messrs. TO ORDER	⑨ Remarks : L/C NO. : 013-I0-980052
③ Notify party AMS TRADING COMPANY 908 PARK AVENUE NEW YORK, NY 10017 U.S.A.	

④ Port of loading Busan, KOREA	⑤ Final destination NEW YORK, U.S.A.
⑥ Carrier ASIA	⑦ Sailing on or about JULY 12, 2021

⑩ Marks & numbers of PKGS.	⑪ Description of goods	⑫ Quantity	⑬ Net weight	⑭ Gross weight	⑮ Measurement
No. 2543-81-01	SM MP3 PLAYER NP-101 6GB MEMORY, MP3, WAV DIMENSIONS 5"x1"x5"(WxDxH)	1,000	556 KGS	645 KGS	13.50 CBM

⬦ SM

NEW YORK

Q'TY : 50 IN BOX:
MADE IN KOREA
BOTH SIDE
HANDLE WITH CARE

⑯ P.O. Box:
Cable address:
Telex code:
Telephone No.:

SM COMPANY, INC.

⑰ *C. H. JANG*

C. H. JANG,   MANAGER

Useful Expressions

🗎 무역서류의 매입

- In order to cover this shipment, we have drawn a draft on you at sight for the invoice amount under L/C No. 1234 issued by the Bank of America, Manila, and negotiated through our bankers, the ABC Bank, Seoul, and ask you to honor it upon presentation.

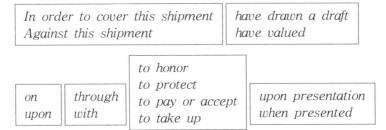

In order to cover this shipment	*have drawn a draft*
Against this shipment	*have valued*

on *upon*	*through* *with*	*to honor* *to protect* *to pay or accept* *to take up*	*upon presentation* *when presented*

- We have negotiated the Bill of Exchange through the ABC Bank.
- A clean, shipped on board B/L in complete set, together with the Commercial Invoice and Insurance Certificate, both in triplicate, have been handed to the Korea Best Bank, Tokyo Branch at sight draft for US$ 65,000 in accordance with the terms of the letter of credit.

🗎 무역서류의 송부

- We are waiting for on board ocean Bills of Lading from the ACL Line which will be airmailed to you with the Commercial Invoice and Insurance Policy.
- We are sending you two copies of the Commercial Invoice, Packing List, and Bill of Lading.
- As requested, two copies of the non-negotiable B/L and three copies of the Commercial Invoice are enclosed.
- Three copies of the B/L will be sent you by express mail.
- We are pleased to send you the Invoice with the Bill of Lading and the Insurance Policy covering shipment of order No. 1212.
- We are enclosing a copy of the C/O which you have requested in connection

with our last shipment.

📄 서류 및 통관

- We need customs invoice in order to declare import in customs.
- It usually does not take a long time <u>to get cleared through customs</u>.

> *to get cleared through customs*
> *for customs clearance*

- The invoice and packing list were not <u>in accord</u> with the description of item.

> *in accord*
> *agree*

- Please send us a pro-forma invoice for customs purposes.

Standard
Trade
English

대금결제

무역대금의 결제는 결제방식 및 지급시기에 따라 다양하게 나뉘어진다.

1 대금결제방식

1) 신용장 방식

신용장이 개설된 경우에는 수출자는 선적을 하고 개설은행을 지급인으로 하는 환어음과 함께 무역서류를 수출자 거래은행에 매입신청하게 된다. 매입은행은 수출대금을 수출자에게 지급하고 신용장 발행은행에 환어음과 무역서류를 보내게 된다. 서류를 송달받은 개설은행은 신용장에 명시한 대로의 선적 여부를 확인하고 매입은행에 수출대금을 입금하게 된다. 수입자는 개설은행에 수입대금을 지급하고 무역서류를 받아 상품을 찾게 된다(52 page 그림 참조).

2) 신용장 외 방식

신용장 이외의 방식의 경우에는 지급도조건(Documents against Payment : D/P), 인수도조건(Documents against Acceptance : D/A), 전신송금(Telegraphic Transfer : T/T) 등 다양한 방식이 있다.

D/P, D/A에서는 수출자가 수입자를 지급인으로 하는 환어음과 함께 무역서류를 수출자 거래은행을 통하여 수입자에게 보내게 되는데, D/P는 무역서류인도 시에 대금을 지급받게 되고, D/A는 무역서류는 먼저 인도하고 일정기간 후에 대금을 지급받게 된다.

그리고, T/T는 수입자가 수출자 앞으로 전신으로 송금하는 방법이다.

2 대금결제시기

대금지급방식과는 별도로 대금 지급시기를 언제 하느냐에 따라 선지급, 즉시불, 후지급으로 나누어진다. 금액을 나누어 여러 번에 걸쳐 지급하는 할부급이 있으며, 계속거래시 매거래마다 결제하지 않고 일정기간 동안 누적된 거래에서의 서로간의 대차관계를 상계하여 결제하는 상호계산 등이 있다.

1 대금의 결제

무역거래의 대금은 송장을 비롯한 무역서류와 환어음으로 청구 및 결제가 되는 것이 일반적이다. 그러나 commission, claim 대금과 같이 대금만 별도로 청구하는 경우나 D/A와 같은 외상거래에서 대금회수를 위하여 대금지급을 청구하거나 독촉해야 하는 경우도 발생한다.

1) 청구서 발송

편지에 청구 및 계산서 양식을 첨부하여 보내는 것이 일반적이다. 이 때의 편지는 주문에 대한 감사 표시와 청구서를 동봉하니 지불을 부탁한다는 내용 등이 포함된다.

2) 지불통지 및 영수통지

송금수표나 전신환 등으로 송금을 하는 경우 송금통지를 하게 된다. 이 때는 해당 청구서 표시, 금액, 송금일자, 송금수표번호 및 서류번호 등에 대한 사항을 포함하게 된다. 한편 송금을 받는 쪽에서는 송금을 수령하는 즉시 수령사실을 통지하게 된다.

3) 독촉장

독촉장에서의 목표는 첫째는, 어떻게 하면 돈을 받느냐 이고, 둘째는, 어떻게 하면 상대방과의 관계를 손상하지 않느냐 이다. 독촉장은 단계별로 처음에는 정중하게 대금지연사실을 알리고, 그 다음부터 부드러운 톤으로 설득하기 시작해서 점점 강한 톤으로 나가게 된다. 처음부터 감정적 혹은 위협적인 태도를 보이지 말고 의연한 태도를 보이는 것이 필요하다.

강제적인 법적 절차를 밟을 수도 있지만 이는 어디까지나 최후의 수단이다. 그리고 이러한 경우에도 양 당사자가 국가를 달리하는 경우에 사법적 절차로서 채권을 받아낸다는 것은 매우 어렵다는 것을 염두에 두어야 한다.

⌨ J1 수출대금 환어음 발행 통지 1

SM Company, Inc.

4501, 45th Floor, Trade Tower
511 Yeongdong-daero, Kangnam-gu, Seoul, Korea 06164

July 12, 2021

AMS Trading Company
908 Park Avenue
New York, NY 10017 U.S.A.

Dear Mr. Smith:

We are glad to inform you that we have shipped 1,000 sets of our "SM MP3 Player, NP-101" via the S/S "DOKDOHO" sailing from Busan on July 12.

To cover the shipment, we have drawn our draft on Bank of America, New York, at sight for the invoice amount of US$ 125,000.⁻ under L/C No. AN211123 and negotiated it with ABC Bank, Seoul. We kindly ask you to protect the draft by the L/C issuing bank upon presentation.

All shipping documents are being forwarded to Bank of America, New York, through our negotiating bank, and we are enclosing a copy of the shipping documents as requested.

We hope that the shipment will reach you in complete satisfaction so that you will favor us with further orders.

Yours very truly,

내용 SM사가 선적 후 수출대금에 대하여 환어음을 발행하여 네고하였음을 수입자인 AMS사에 통지하는 내용이다.

• 주요 용어 및 표현 •

- to cover the shipment : 선적에 대해서, 선적대금조로
- draw our draft on Bank of America : Bank of America 앞으로 우리의 어음을 발행하다. Bank of America를 지급인으로 하여 우리 어음을 발행하다.
- at sight : 일람출급으로
  draw our draft on BOA, New York at sight는 draw our draft at sight on BOA, New York이나 draw our sight draft on BOA, New York으로도 쓴다.
- under the L/C : 신용장에 의거하여, 신용장에 따라
- for the invoice amount of ~ : ~의 송장금액에 대해서
- negotiated it with the ABC Bank : 서울은행에 어음을 매입의뢰(네고)하였다.
- protect the draft : 어음을 받아들이다. 여기서 protect란 결제 또는 인수를 한다는 의미이다(＝honor, pay or accept).
- upon presentation : 제시되면, 제시될 때
- forward : 발송하다. 전송하다.
- through our negotiating bank : 매입은행을 통하여
- we are enclosing ~ : ~을 동봉합니다. ~을 보내드립니다.
- complete satisfaction : 완전한 만족, 매우 큰 만족
- further orders : 뒤따르는 주문(＝subsequent orders)

J2 환어음 대금 지급

AMS Trading Company

908 Park Avenue
New York, NY 10017 U.S.A.

July 22, 2021

SM Company, Inc.
4501, 45th Floor, Trade Tower
511 Yeongdong-daero, Kangnam-gu
Seoul, Korea 06164

Dear Mr. Park:

Thank you for your shipment of 1,000 sets of the "SM MP3 Player, NP-101" against our order No. 1244.

We have received the shipping documents on the 21st of July and your draft was duly honored by the L/C issuing bank.

We wish to express our gratitude for your prompt shipment and we hope the goods will arrive soon and in good condition.

Yours very truly,

내용 AMS사가 수출자인 SM사에 선적서류의 인수와 무역대금의 결제 사실을 통보하는 내용이다.

• 주요 용어 및 표현 •

- against our order : 주문에 대해서(=as per our order)
- shipping documents : 선적서류, 무역서류(=transport documents)
- duly honored : 정히 받아 들여지다. 정식으로 결제 또는 인수되었다.
- express our gratitude : 감사를 표하다. 감사드린다(=express our thanks).
- prompt shipment : 조속한 선적
- in good condition : 좋은 상태로, 양호한 상태로(=in good order)

✓	대금결제방법에 대한 용어	
지급시기에 따라	advance payment (선지급)	CWO(cash with order) : 주문불 CBD(cash before delivery) : 인도전지불 Red-Clause L/C : 전대신용장
	spot payment (즉시불)	COD(cash on delivery) : 현물상환도지불 CAD(cash against document) : 서류상환도지급 Sight L/C : 일람출급신용장 D/P : 지급도조건
	deferred payment (후지급)	Sale on Credit : 외상 Usance L/C : 기한부신용장 D/A : 인수도조건
기 타		progressive payment, installment, rate payment : 할부급 down payment, initial payment : 선불보증금 open account, current account, running account : 상호계산

② 환어음

1) 의 의

환어음은 어음발행인이 지급인에게 일정한 금액을 일정한 일자와 장소에서 대금 수령인에게 지급할 것을 요청하는 지급요구서이다. 환어음은 돈과 같이 지급수단으로 유통되기 때문에 그 형식을 반드시 구비해야 하는 엄격한 요식증권이다. 따라서 필수기재사항은 반드시 기재되어야 법적 효력을 갖는다.

2) 필수 기재사항

① 환어음의 표시(Bill of Exchange), ② 금액(Amount), ③ 지급위탁의 문구(Pay to), ④ 지급인(Payer/Drawee), ⑤ 지급지(Payment Place), ⑥ 지급일(Payment Date), ⑦ 수령인(Payee), ⑧ 발행일자 및 발행지(Issuing Date and Place), ⑨ 발행인 서명(Drawer)

3) 부수적 기재사항

부수적 기재사항은 필요에 따라서 기재되는 것으로 환어음의 효력에는 영향이 없다. 무역결제에 사용되는 환어음에서는 어음번호와 신용장과 관련된 신용장의 발행은행, 번호, 발행일자 등이 부수적 기재사항으로 된다.

4) 환어음의 주요사항

■ **금액** : 숫자표기금액과 문자표기금액이 다를 경우 문자금액을 금액으로 한다. 문자금액표기에서 금액 앞에는 "SAY"를, 뒤에는 "ONLY"를 붙인다.

■ **지급만기일** : 어음은 지급 만기일표시방법에 따라 다음의 네 가지의 방식이 있는데 앞의 두 가지가 주로 사용된다.

① 일람출급 : 환어음이 지급인에 제시되는 날이 만기일로 된다. 보다 정확하게는 제시되는 날로부터 2영업일 이내에 지급해야 한다. 어음상에서 AT와 SIGHT 사이의 여백에 XXX 표시를 한다. 이 때 이 난을 빈 공간으로 두었을 때에도 일람출급으로 간주한다.

② 일람후정기출급 : 환어음이 지급인에 제시되는 날로부터 일정기간이 지난 날이 만기일이 된다. AT와 SIGHT 사이에 "○○ Days After"를 기재한다.

③ 발행일자후정기출급 : 발행된 날로부터 일정기간이 지난 날을 만기일로 한다.

④ 확정일출급 : 만기일을 어음상에 표시한다.

■ **수취인** : 지급을 받는 사람을 정하는 방법으로 다음 네 가지가 있는데 앞의 두 가지가 주로 사용된다.

① 기명식 : "pay to ABC"　② 지시식 : "pay to ABC or order"

③ 소지인식 : "pay to bearer"　④ 선택소지인식 : "pay to ABC or bearer"

여기서 지시식은 수취인으로 지정된 사람이나 그가 지명하는 사람에게 지급하라는 의미이다. 이는 어음을 배서하여 유통시키기 위해서이다.

✓　　　　　　　　　**환어음이란 무엇인가?**

환어음의 기원에 대하여 여러 가지의 설이 있는데 그 중 하나인 다음의 이야기는 환어음과 그 유통체계의 이해에 도움을 준다.

중세기 한때 유럽 각지에서 유태인에 대한 박해가 있었다. 프랑스 지역의 일부 유태인들은 멀리 이탈리아 지역에 피신하게 되었다. 급히 피신하느라 재산을 이웃에 맡기고 피신한 사람들이 많았다. 시간이 지나도 고향에 돌아갈 수 없게 된 유태인들은 프랑스를 왕래하는 이탈리아 상인편으로 자신의 옛 재산을 찾아오는 방법을 생각하게 되었다. 즉 프랑스로 가는 상인이 자기 재산을 맡고 있는 이웃을 만나 자신이 쓴 서찰을 보여주고 돈을 받아오도록 하는 것이었다.

이 때 써준 그 서찰의 줄거리는 대개 다음과 같은 것이었다.

"친애하는 블랑(Blanc)씨, 내가 당신으로부터 받아야 할 돈을 이 편지를 전하는 까를로스(Carlos)씨에게 지급하시오. 아담(Adam)(서명)"

환어음의 체계는 이와 같은 것이다. B로부터 돈을 받을 것이 있는 A가 자신이 받을 돈을 C가 대신 받도록 하도록 하는 문서이다. 따라서 환어음의 문구 내용을 보면 다음과 같음을 알 수 있다.

At sight of this bill pay to C the sum of $

To : B　　　　　　　　　　　A(signature)

「B귀하, 이 어음을 보고 금액 얼마를 C에게 지급하시오. A(서명)」

어음 문구의 주요 사항

① BILL OF EXCHANGE

NO. _____   ⑧ _____

FOR   ②

AT____⑥____ SIGHT OF THIS FIRST BILL OF EXCHANGE(SECOND OF THE SAME TENOR
AND DATE BEING UNPAID) ③PAY TO ⑦THE KOREA BEST BANK OR ORDER THE SUM OF

②

VALUE RECEIVED AND CHARGE THE SAME TO ACCOUNT OF _____

DRAWN UNDER _____
L/C NO. _____   DATED _____

TO ④ _____

⑤ _____   ⑨

- AT XXX SIGHT OF THIS BILL : 이 어음을 본 시점에
  AT 60 DAYS AFTER SIGHT OF : 이 어음을 본 후 60일 되는 시점에
- SECOND OF THE SAME TENOR AND DATE BEING UNPAID : 환어음은 통상
  안전을 위하여 2부의 set로 발행된다. 2부를 시간상으로 전후로 나누어 지급인에
  보내게 되는데 어느 것이든 먼저 도착하는 것이 효력을 갖는다. 첫 장인 이 어음
  에서는 둘째 장이 먼저 도착하여 지급되지 않았으면 이 어음에 따라 지급하라는
  내용이다. 반대로 둘째 장 어음에서는 첫 장에 의하여 지급되지 않았으면 이 어
  음에 따라 지급하라는 내용이다. 이렇게 하여 먼저 도착한 것에 의하여 대금이
  지급되면 나중의 것은 자동적으로 효력을 상실하게 된다.
- PAY TO ～ : ～ 에게 지급하시오.
- THE SUM OF ～ : 합계 ～를
- VALUE RECEIVED : 어음 발행인이 어음의 대가는 수령하였음.
- CHARGE THE SAME TO ACCOUNT OF ～ : ～의 계정에서 같은 금액을 청구하
  시오.

BILL OF EXCHANGE

NO. 123456   DATE   JULY 12, 2021   SEOUL, KOREA

FOR   US$ 125,000

AT 60 DAYS AFTER SIGHT OF THIS FIRST BILL OF EXCHANGE(SECOND OF THE SAME TENOR AND DATE BEING UNPAID) PAY TO THE KOREA BEST BANK OR ORDER THE SUM OF

US DOLLARS SAY ONE HUNDRED TWENTY-FIVE THOUSAND ONLY.

VALUE RECEIVED AND CHARGE THE SAME TO ACCOUNT OF   AMS TRADING COMPANY

DRAWN UNDER   CBA BANK, NEW YORK

L/C NO.   AN211123   DATED   MAY 20, 2021

TO   CBA BANK, NEW YORK   SM COMPANY, INC.

    401 WEST 42ND ST

    NEW YORK NY, 10036 U.S.A.   *Dongjin Jang*

                                DONGJIN JANG, MANAGER

BILL OF EXCHANGE

NO. 123456   DATE   JULY 12, 2021   SEOUL, KOREA

FOR   US$ 125,000

AT 60 DAYS AFTER SIGHT OF THIS SECOND BILL OF EXCHANGE(FIRST OF THE SAME TENOR AND DATE BEING UNPAID) PAY TO THE KOREA BEST BANK OR ORDER THE SUM OF

US DOLLARS SAY ONE HUNDRED TWENTY-FIVE THOUSAND ONLY.

VALUE RECEIVED AND CHARGE THE SAME TO ACCOUNT OF   AMS TRADING COMPANY

DRAWN UNDER   CBA BANK, NEW YORK

L/C NO.   AN211123   DATED   MAY 20, 2021

TO   CBA BANK, NEW YORK   SM COMPANY, INC.

    401 WEST 42ND ST

    NEW YORK NY, 10036 U.S.A.   *Dongjin Jang*

                                DONGJIN JANG, MANAGER

J3 대금지급 통지

AMS Trading Company

908 Park Avenue
New York, NY 10017 U.S.A.

August 17, 2021

SM Company, Inc.
511 Yeongdong-daero, Kangnam-gu
Seoul, Korea 06164

Dear Mr. Park:

We are pleased to inform you that we have received with satisfaction the 1,000 sets of the SM MP3 Player, NP-101 that you shipped via the S/S "DOKDO" on July 12.

We credited the amount of US$ 125,000.⁻ as settlement for your invoice No. 2316 to your account at the Bank of America, Seoul, by telegraphic transfer on August 16.

Your acknowledgement of receipt in due course would be highly appreciated.

Very truly yours,

내용 AMS사가 상품수령 및 대금입금 사실을 SM사에 통보하는 내용이다.

• 주요 용어 및 표현 •

- credit : 입금시키다(＝transfer).
- to your account : 당신의 계좌에
- telegraphic transfer : 전신환(＝T/T)
- acknowledgement of receipt : 대금영수 확인, 대금영수 수령증
- in due course : 적당한 때에, 일이 순조로이 진행되면, 정식으로. 결과적으로

J4 대금지급 요청

World Trading Company
908 Park Avenue
New York, NY 10017 U.S.A.

July 10, 2021

SM Company, Inc.
511 Yeongdong-daero, Kangnam-gu
Seoul, Korea 06164

Dear Mr. Smith:

We are enclosing the statement of account showing a balance in our favor of US$ 5,000.‾ for our commission of the second quarter of this year.

We assume that you will remit the money by T/T but if you want us to draw a bill of exchange on you, please let us know.

Yours very truly,

내용 World Trading사가 SM사에 2/4분기의 수수료 지급을 청구하는 내용이다.

• 주요 용어 및 표현 •

- statement of account : 계산서(=statement)
- a balance in our favor : 우리에게 지불되어야 할 잔액
- commission : 수수료, 구전, 커미션
- second quarter : 2/4분기
- remit : 송금하다(=send).
- draw a bill of exchange on you : 당신 앞으로 어음을 발행하다.

J5 대금지급 연기 요청

AMS Trading Company

908 Park Avenue
New York, NY 10017 U.S.A.

August 20, 2021

SM Company, Inc.
4501, 45th Floor, Trade Tower
511 Yeongdong-daero, Kangnam-gu
Seoul, Korea 06164

Dear Mr. Park:

Thank you very much for your letter of August 7 reminding us that the payment for invoice No. 212 is overdue.

We have been unexpectedly faced with some difficulties collecting payments from some of our customers. As a result, we are experiencing a temporary inability to meet our payment obligations.

We would be very grateful if you would grant us a delay of one month to make the payment on your invoice. You may be certain that we will be able to settle our payment by September 20.

We hope you will excuse us for the delay and ask for your patience.

Very truly yours,

내용 AMS사가 일시적인 자금사정으로 인하여 SM사에 대금지급의 연기를 요청하는 내용이다.

• 주 요 용 어 및 표 현 •

- reminding : 생각나게 하다. 상기시키다. 일깨우다.
- is overdue : 연체된, 지불기일이 지난
- experience : 겪다. 당하다. 경험하다(＝undergo). undergo는 experience에 비해서 고통, 불쾌, 위험 등의 느낌이 포함된 단어이다.
- temporary : 일시적인, 잠정적인
- inability : 무능, ~를 할 수 없는 상태
- meet our payment obligations : 지급의무이행을 해내다.
- grant : 허용하다. 요청을 들어주다.
- you may be certain that ~ : ~를 당신은 확신해도 좋다. 확실히 ~이다.
- settle : 결제하다. 지불하다. 빚을 청산하다.
- excuse : 참아주다. 용서하다.

  excuse : 실수 등을 용서하다.

  forgive : 죄, 과실 등을 용서하다.

  pardon : 죄, 나쁜 짓에 대한 처벌을 면제하다.
- ask for your patience : 어려움을 참아주시기를 요청합니다.

  patience : 힘든 일, 고통 등을 참는 것

  endurance : 피로, 곤란, 고통 등을 참는 것

✓	어음 수표 관련용어

bill of exchange : 환어음, bill은 bill of lading, bill of rights 등에서 보듯이 어음 외에도 계산서, 청구서, 지폐, 증서, 쪽지, 목록, 소장, 법안 등의 다양한 의미로 넓게 사용된다.

bill of debt : 약속어음

promissory note : 약속어음

draft : 환어음, 수표, 지불명령서, 어음발행

check : 수표(수표는 은행에서만 발행한다는 점에 유의)

☐☐ J6 대금지급연기의 허락

SM Company, Inc.

4501, 45th Floor, Trade Tower
511 Yeongdong-daero, Kangnam-gu, Seoul, Korea 06164

August 31, 2021

AMS Trading Company
908 Park Avenue
New York, NY 10017 U.S.A.

Dear Mr. Smith:

Thank you for your letter of August 20 asking us to extend the payment date. We are pleased to inform you that we will agree to extend the clearance of the US$ 7,000.⁻ until September 20.

However, please note that if this schedule of payment is not adhered to, we shall have no choice but to refer this matter to our attorney with instructions to recover the debt.

Yours very truly,

내용 AMS사의 대금지급 연기 요청에 대하여 SM사가 이를 허락하고 연기된 기간 내에는 지급해줄 것을 부탁하는 내용이다.

• 주 요 용 어 및 표 현 •

- agree to : 동의하다.
- clearance : 대금결제, 정리
- please note that ～ : ～을 유념하십시오. ～을 주의하십시오.
- adhered to : 지켜지다. 따르다.
- have no choice but ～ : ～ 외에 다른 선택의 여지가 없다.
- refer : 회부하다. 돌리다.
- attorney : 변호사, 사무변호사
  lawyer는 변호사에 대한 일반적인 용어이고, 재판사무를 취급하는 사무변호
  사, 또는 검사를 attorney라 하고, 법정에서 재판에 참가하는 법정변호사를
  counselor라 한다. 반면 영국에서는 사무변호사를 solicitor, 법정변호사를
  barrister라 한다.
- recover : 회수하다. 되찾다.

✓	라틴계통의 비즈니스 영어단어
ad hoc	특별히(=for this special purpose)
ad valorem	종가의, 가격기준의
bona-fide	선의의(=in good faith)
circa	약, 대략(=about)
ditto	상동(=the same)
etc	등 등(=et cetra, and so on(forth))
ex	～으로부터(=ex works : 현장인도)
e.g	예를 들어(=exempli gratia, for example)
i.e.	즉(=id est, that is)
lb.	파운드(=libra, pound)
loco	현장인도의(=in the place)
No.	번호, 수(=number)
per pro	대리하여(=p.p., per procurationem)
pro-forma	견적의, 형식상의(=as a matter of from)
pro rata	～에 비례하여
re	～에 관하여(=concerning, in re)
via	～에 의하여, ～을 경유하여(=by way of)
vs.	～대, ～대응하여(=versus)

J7 대금지급독촉 1차

SM Company, Inc.

4501, 45th Floor, Trade Tower
511 Yeongdong-daero, Kangnam-gu, Seoul, Korea 06164

September 15, 2021

AMS Trading Company
908 Park Avenue
New York, NY 10017 U.S.A.

Dear Mr. Smith:

We write to inform you that we have not received payment for our invoice No. 1217 in the amount of US$ 10,000.⁻ for the DVD Players you ordered on June 23.

The payment was due on September 10. We are sure that this is an oversight on your part but we must ask you to give the matter your prompt attention.

If payment has already been made, kindly disregard this notice. Should you have any questions about your account, please do not hesitate to contact us.

Yours very truly,

내용 SM사가 AMS사에 대하여 지급기한이 지나도록 상품대금이 지급되지 않고 있음을 환기시키면서 대금지급을 요청하는 내용이다.

• 주 요 용 어 및 표 현 •

- was due on September 10 : 9월 10일이 지불일이었다. ~만기일이었다.
- we are sure that ~

  =we are certain that ~

  =we trust that ~
- oversight : 간과, 실수로 빠뜨림
- on your part : 당신측에, 귀사측에서(=at your end /≠on our part, at this end)
- give the matter your prompt attention : 빨리 이 문제에 관심을 갖다.
- disregard : 무시하다.
- account : 계산, 계산서
- contact us : 우리에게 연락하다.

✓	무역거래에서 due의 용법

① ~에 기인한 : due to the poor packing
② 예정인 : due to open May 1
③ 도착예정인 : The ship is due at 5 p.m..
④ 지급되어야 할 : commission due to agent
⑤ 만기가 된 : This bill is due on May 30.
⑥ 적당한 : in due course, after due consideration
⑦ 정, 바른 : due south
⑧ 부과금, 회비 : docks dues, club dues

J8 대금지급독촉 2차

SM Company, Inc.
4501, 45th Floor, Trade Tower
511 Yeongdong-daero, Kangnam-gu, Seoul, Korea 06164

October 12, 2021

AMS Trading Company
908 Park Avenue
New York, NY 10017 U.S.A.

Dear Mr. Smith:

May we again draw your attention to our invoice No. 1217 of July 21 for
DVD players for the amount of US$ 10,000.￣ due on September 10 which
is now one month overdue for payment?

We would like to remind you that we provided you with a deferred
payment as a special favor. We would very much appreciate it if you
would expedite a payment as soon as possible.

Yours very truly,

내용 SM사가 AMS사에게 상품대금의 조속한 지급을 재차 요청하는 내용이다.

• 주요 용어 및 표현 •

- draw attention : 주의를 환기시키다.
- due on September 10 : 9월 10일이 지불일인
- a deferred payment : 후불, 외상
- special favor : 특별한 혜택, 파격적인 대우
- expedite payment : 신속히 지급하다. 신속한 지급조치를 취하다.

J9 대금지급독촉 3차

SM Company, Inc.
4501, 45th Floor, Trade Tower
511 Yeongdong-daero, Kangnam-gu, Seoul, Korea 06164

November 5, 2021

AMS Trading Company
908 Park Avenue
New York, NY 10017 U.S.A.

Dear Mr. Smith:

We wrote you on September 15 and October 12, asking you to settle our invoice No. 1217 dated July 21 for our shipment of DVD Players.

To date we have not yet received any reply, and must again ask you to give this matter your immediate attention without further delay.

We trust this matter can be resolved amicably.

Yours very truly,

내용 SM사가 AMS사에게 상품대금의 조속한 지급을 세번째로 요청하는 내용이다.

• 주요 용어 및 표현 •

- settle : 지불하다. 청산하다. 해결하다. 처리하다.
- to date : 지금까지, 현재까지
- without further delay : 더 이상 지체 말고
- amicably : 우호적으로

J10 대금지급독촉 최후통첩

SM Company, Inc.
4501, 45th Floor, Trade Tower
511 Yeongdong-daero, Kangnam-gu, Seoul, Korea 06164

December 1, 2021

AMS Trading Company
908 Park Avenue
New York, NY 10017 U.S.A.

Dear Mr. Smith:

We regret to note that you have ignored our reminders of September 15, October 12, and November 5 concerning payment of our invoice No. 1217 dated July 21.

Accordingly, we would like to request that you settle the payment by December 20. If we do not receive your remittance in full by that time we will find it necessary to take legal procedures to protect ourselves.

Please understand that we are very reluctant to take this action, but in consideration of the circumstances, we find no alternative.

Yours very truly,

내용 SM사가 거듭된 지급요청에도 불구하고 상품대금지급을 하고 있지 않은 AMS사에게 보내는 최후 통첩이다.

• 주요 용어 및 표현 •

- reminder : 독촉장
- remittance : 송금, 송금액
- in full : 전액
- find it necessary : 불가피한, 피할 수 없는
- take legal procedures : 법적 조치를 취하다.
- reluctant to : 마음내키지 않는, 마지못해 하는
- action : 행동, 조치(＝steps)
- find no alternative : 다른 방도가 없다.(＝ － no option, － no other way)

☑ **빨 리**

무역통신에서 빨리라고 했을 때 그 시간의 길이는 얼마나 될까?

일반적인 경우에 있어서 prompt, immediate, as soon as 등으로 표현했을 때 대략 30일 정도 이내로 생각하기도 한다. 이전의 신용장통일규칙에서는 신용장에 사용된 이러한 용어에 대해서 30일 이내로 해석하는 것으로 규정된 적도 있었다.

그러나 똑같이 "빨리 갖다 달라"고 말하더라도 피자를 주문할 때와 자동차를 주문할 때에 그 기다릴 수 있는 시간이 다른 것처럼 "빨리"라고 하는 추상적인 말 속에 담겨있는 구체적인 의미는 상황에 따라 달라질 수밖에 없다. 그렇기 때문에 하나의 구체적인 수의 척도로 규정하기가 어려운 문제이다. 그래서 현행의 신용장통일규칙(2007) 제46조에서는 신용장에서 이러한 용어를 사용하지 말 것을 권하고, 만약 사용된 경우에는 문구가 없는 것과 마찬가지로 무시하도록 규정하고 있다.

상업영어에서는 가급적 구체적이고 명확하게 표현하는 것이 좋다. 애매한 표현은 당사자간의 해석차로 오해와 분쟁을 가져올 수 있기 때문에 중요한 문서에서는 특히 이를 적극 피하지 않으면 안 된다.

〈빨리, 속히의 표현〉

promptly / immediately / as soon as possible / as soon as you can / shortly / at once / right away / urgently / as promptly as possible / at one's earliest convenience / without delay / by express delivery

Useful Expressions

📄 결제방법일반

■ Our usual terms are cash with order(C.W.O.)

> *cash with order(C.W.O.)*
> *cash on delivery(C.O.D.)*
> *documents against payment(D/P)*
> *documents against acceptance(D/A)*
> *sight letter of credit(sight L/C)*
> *usance letter of credit(usance L/C)*
> *open account.*

■ We deal with our usual transactions on an L/C basis.

■ In regard to the terms of business, we make it our custom to trade on an at sight irrevocable credit.

■ To cover our shipment, we require you to open an irrevocable credit in our favor for the invoice amount with a first class bank.

■ Thank you for your letter of June 15, in which you request us to give the open account terms.

■ We have learned from your letter of June 25 that you demand payment by a draft at sight under irrevocable L/C.

■ Please note that the usance of our draft is 30 days, regardless of L/C or D/A terms.

> *the usance of*
> *the term of*

📄 환어음

■ We will draw a draft at 90 days after sight on Bank of America, New York, under an irrevocable letter of credit and ask you to honor it on presentation.

at 90 days after sight *at sight* *at 90 days from B/L date* *at 90 days after May 1*	*to honor* *to protect* *to pay or accept* *to take up*	*on presentation* *upon presentation.*

- To cover this shipment, we have drawn a <u>draft</u> <u>at sight</u> and <u>negotiated</u> it through the Korea Best Bank with your letter of credit.

To cover *Against*	*draft* *bill of exchange*	*at sight* *at 90 days after sight*	*negotiated* *sold* *discounted*

- We have negotiated our draft through the ABC Bank under irrevocable credit issued by CBA Bank, New York.

- We ask for your protection of our draft on presentation.

- We advise you that we have drawn on you against documents for the invoice value of US$ 10,000 through ABC Bank, Seoul.

계산서의 제출 및 지불청구

- We hand you our bill on your order No. 1234 amounting to US$ 10,000 which you will kindly credit to our account.

- In accordance with your request, we are enclosing a statement of your account, which we hope you will find correct.

- We will be glad to receive your check for US$ 10,000 for settlement of our commission.

- May we have your check for settlement of this invoice?

- Please favor us with your remittance for US$ 5,000.

- We would be greatly <u>obliged</u> if you <u>remit</u> a check for the goods you ordered <u>at the earliest convenience.</u>

obliged *appreciated*	*remit* *send*	*at the earliest convenience* *as soon as you can*

- Permit us to remind you that the balance of US$ 5,000 is due on June 10.

- We have the pleasure of enclosing a statement of our account showing a balance of US$ 50 in our favor, and ask for your early settlement.
- As per our statement of account, you owe us US$ 5,000 as of the end of last month; the settlement of which will be much appreciated.
- If payment has already been made, disregard this notice.

📑 수입자 또는 채무자의 대금지급 관련 통지

- We have received your letter of July 10, reminding us that payment of the amount owed on your June statement is overdue.
- We have received your letter of June 7 enclosing your Debit Note No. 31. Due to an oversight, we are very sorry not to have paid your account earlier.
- Payment will be effected through the ABC Bank on receipt of the B/L.
- For the balance of Stg. £ 5,250 in your favor, you may draw a bill of exchange on us at sight as usual.
- We have opened an Irrevocable L/C No. KU0301 through Kookmin Bank, London Branch, under which you may draw at 30 days after sight.

📑 송금통지

- We are enclosing a check, value US$ 10,000 in settlement of your account.

We are enclosing We send	in settlement of in payment of	account bill

- Enclosed, please find a check in the amount of US$ 10,000 for payment of your invoice of May 1. Please acknowledge receipt and credit our account accordingly.

- We have remitted US$ 100,000 to your bank account for the goods we purchased.

remitted sent wired

- We will send you the amount of US$ 10,000 by T/T this afternoon.

- Enclosed please find our check for US$ 500, which covers the cost of the samples and their mail charge.

- We have paid against the bill of exchange you have drawn and we have received the shipping documents

채권자의 대금영수 통지

- We have received your letter of July 5 enclosing a check for US$ 50,000 covering our Debit Note No. 15 for which we thank you.

- We acknowledge receipt of your remittance for US$ 10,000 in settlement of our invoice No. 4567.

- We received your check, value US$ 10,000 for which we enclose herewith the receipt as you requested.

- We thank you very much for your letter of June 10 enclosing a check for US$ 500 as our commission for December.

부 도

- Much to our surprise, our Bill of Exchange has <u>been dishonored</u> as <u>non-payment</u> and it has been returned by our bank.

been dishonored *been unpaid* *bounced*	*non-payment* *non-acceptance*

- The draft for US$ 5,000 drawn on the National Bank of Chicago under credit No. 1234 covering your order No. 12 has been dishonored for a reason which we cannot accept.

- As the draft was dishonored, please negotiate the matter with the drawee bank and let them protect it at once.

- We state that our draft No. 1234 for US$ 10,000 has been dishonored by non-payment.

🖺 독 촉

- We have rendered our June statement twice and regret that the amount of US$ 3,000 is still outstanding. We will be grateful for an early settlement.
- Unless the account is settled by July 31, we will refer the matter to our solicitors.
- This is to call your attention to the fact that your account of US$ 25,000 is still unpaid.
- This is to remind you that your remittance of our second quarter's commission is now more than 2 months overdue.
- We are compelled to take legal proceedings for the recovery of the amount due to us.

🖺 지급연기

- We will be much obliged if you will give us a little more time to settle your account due the 1st of May.
- We would appreciate an extension of 3 weeks for the payment of US$ 10,000. ⁻ due October 15.
- We regret that our temporary <u>financial difficulties</u> prevent us from meeting your draft <u>at maturity.</u> We will, however, make every effort to pay you either the whole or part of the amount before May 1.

financial difficulty financial pinch	at maturity upon maturity

- Since our profit is <u>marginal</u>, we cannot <u>allow</u> you a <u>postponement</u> of payment.

marginal so small	allow grant	postponement deferment

- We shall allow you a further extension of another month to help with your present difficulty.

맺는 말

- We hope you will kindly settle them at your earliest convenience.
- Should you have any questions about your account, please contact us.
- We urge you to make this settlement without delay.
- We would be grateful to receive your remittance by T/T by June 30.
- Please send us your banker's check by return mail.
- We hope that the matter will be settled to our mutual satisfaction
- We hope that you understand our present situation and ask for your patience.

Standard
Trade
English

클레임과 분쟁해결

무역업무의 주요 내용

1 클레임과 분쟁해결

상품을 선적하고 수출자는 수출대금을 받고 수입자는 운송인으로부터 상품을 인수받게 되면 무역의 전 과정은 끝나게 된다. 그러나 만약 상품에 이상이 있어 수입자가 손실을 입는 경우에는 수출자에 대하여 클레임을 제기하게 된다. 수출자도 대금회수 등의 문제로 손실이 발생한 경우에는 마찬가지로 클레임을 제기하게 된다. 클레임은 손해의 객관적인 근거제시와 이에 대한 구체적인 변상 요구이다. 이 점에서 단순한 불평(complaint), 경고(warning) 등과 구분된다.

이러한 무역분쟁에서 당사자가 스스로 해결하지 못하는 경우에는 일반적으로 중재를 통하여 해결하게 된다. 재판에 의한 사법적인 해결은 국제사법공조체제가 불완전하기 때문에 현실적으로 실효성을 갖지 못하기 때문이다.

2 무역분쟁의 해결방법

(1) **타협**(compromise) : 당사자간에 직접 합의하여 해결하는 것으로 가장 바람직한 해결방법이다.

(2) **알선**(intercession) : 당사자 일방 또는 쌍방의 의뢰에 의한 제3자나 기관 등이 개입하여 양당사자가 타협할 수 있도록 돕는 방법이다.

(3) **조정**(conciliation) : 양당사자의 합의로 제3자를 선임하고 제3자 조정안을 제시하고 이를 양당사자가 수락함으로써 해결하는 방법이다.

(4) **중재**(arbitration) : 양당사자의 중재결정에 따른다는 사전합의에 따라 중재로 결정하는 방법이다. 중재판정은 재판과 같이 양당사자를 구속한다.

(5) **소송**(litigation / law suit) : 법원의 사법적 판결로 해결하는 방법이다. 시간, 비용, 노력이 많이 들 뿐만 아니라 집행력이 보장되지 않는 단점이 있다.

1 클레임제기 서한

클레임의 제기서한의 목적은 입은 손해를 신속하게 변상받는 것이다. 따라서 자신의 손해와 불만을 상대방이 납득할 수 있도록 객관적이고 구체적인 사실에 입각하여 이성적으로 표현하여야 하며, 자신의 감정을 표출하거나 상대방을 비난하는 투가 되어서는 좋지 않다. 그리고 가능한 좋은 관계를 훼손하지 않으면서 자신에 유리한 타협점으로 상대방을 이끌어 오도록 하여야 한다. 클레임제기 서한은 대개 다음과 같은 내용으로 구성된다.

1. 상품의 주문표시 또는 선적표시
2. 문제의 내용
3. 문제의 발생원인 및 손해근거
4. 해결안의 제시 또는 제시요청
5. 빠른 해결을 위한 관심 또는 협조 요망표시

2 클레임제기에 대한 답신

클레임통지를 받으면 먼저 그 원인을 조사하여 자신에게 책임이 있는지 여부를 빨리 판단하여야 한다. 책임이 있는 경우 책임을 인정하되 지나치게 sorry를 되풀이하면 과도한 책임을 지게 되거나 비굴하게 보이게 되며, 책임이 없는 경우 책임 없음을 분명히 표현하되 나는 알 필요도 없는 일이라는 듯한 무성의한 인상을 주어서는 안 된다. 클레임제기에 대한 회신은 다음과 같은 내용으로 구성된다.

자신에게 책임이 있는 경우	1. 상대방에 대한 동정표시와 정중한 사과 2. 문제가 발생하게 된 상황 설명 3. 변상방안의 제시 4. 앞으로의 재발방지에 대한 표현
자신에게 책임이 없는 경우	1. 상대방에 동정표시 2. 자신의 잘못에 의한 것이 아님과 이에 대한 근거 3. 상대방 입장에서 해결방안의 충고

⊞ K1 품질상위에 대한 클레임 제기

AMS Trading Company

908 Park Avenue
New York, NY 10017

July 10, 2021

Asia Trading Company
212 Yoi-daero, Youngdeungpo-gu
Seoul, Korea 07325

Gentlemen:

We are writing to inform you that we have received the dress materials for our order No. 8681 shipped via S/S "Venus."

Upon unpacking the cases, we found that the quality was far inferior to the sample on which we placed the order. It is not only coarse in texture compared with the sample swatch we got before, but also has a different color than the sample. Even to an untrained eye, the difference between the sample and the shipped goods is very obvious.

We would like to make do with the delivered merchandise, but it is impossible to sell them in our market as it is not suitable for our customers needs. Therefore, we have no other choice but to ask you to replace them with the materials of the quality we ordered from the beginning. Otherwise, we will be obliged to cancel the order and ask for the return of our deposit.

We are ready to return the whole lot with the shipping cost at your expense. If you have a better way to settle this problem, please let us know immediately.

We await your prompt reply.

Very truly yours,

내용 AMS사가 수출자 Asia Trading사에게 수령한 상품이 샘플보다 열등함을 이유로 교환해줄 것을 요청하는 내용이다.

· **주요 용어 및 표현** ·

- dress materials : 의복 옷감, 정장 옷감
- upon unpacking the cases : 겉포장을 풀어보니, 포장을 풀고 상품을 꺼내보니
- far inferior to : 훨씬 못 미치는, 훨씬 낮은 질의, 훨씬 낮은 등급의
- coarse : 거친, 조잡한, 조악한, 올이 성긴, 열등한
- texture : 짜임새, 바탕, 직물, 결, 조직, 구성
- sample swatch : 샘플 천조각, 샘플
- even to an untrained eye : 일반인이 보더라도
- make do with : 그런대로 해결하다. 변통하다.
- customers needs : 고객의 수요, 고객의 취향
- have no other choice but ~ : ~할 수밖에 없다. ~ 외는 다른 도리가 없다.
- replace them with ~ : 그것들을 ~로 대체하다.
- return : 반환, 돌려받음
- deposit : 예치금, 맡긴 돈
- the whole lot : 전량, 물건전체
- at your expense : 당신의 부담으로, 당신 회사 측의 부담으로(=shouldered at your end)

✓	Claim 관련용어의 구분개념

dispute : 당사자간의 이해관계의 대립으로 발생하는 분쟁
claim : 객관적인 자료에 의한 변상요구의 주장. 넓은 의미로는 변상요구, 불평, 경고, 무역분쟁 등을 총칭하는 말로도 사용된다.
complaint : 항의나 불만의 제기
warning : 경고나 주의

K2 품질상위 클레임에 대한 답신

Asia Trading Company

212 Yoi-daero, Youngdeungpo-gu
Seoul, Korea 07325

July 20, 2021

AMS Trading Company
908 Park Avenue
New York, NY 10017 U.S.A

Gentlemen: OUR SHIPMENT OF JUNE 15

We deeply regret to learn from your letter of July 10 that you are not satisfied with the goods which we shipped on June 15 for your order No. 8681.

We are very sorry to hear that you are experiencing a problem with our dress materials. Please understand that this is a very unusual case for us, so we are very concerned about any inconvenience we may have caused you.

Upon receipt of your letter, we contacted the manufacturers to check into the matter and asked our shipping department to trace this matter thoroughly.

As the matter is under investigation now, we are not yet able to make clear our position. As soon as the result of the investigation is determined, we will contact you again and discuss how this problem can be solved. It goes without saying that we are ready to take responsibility if we are found to be at fault.

In the mean time we would like to ask you to send us by airmail a couple samples of each of the goods, at our expense, for our inspector to examine.

Thank you for your patience in this matter and we will be in touch with you soon.

Very truly yours,

내용 Asia Trading사가 수입자 AMS사의 상품품질 상위의 클레임제기에 대하여 조사에 착수했음을 알리고 조사를 위한 자료요청과 조사 후에 상의할 것을 요청하는 내용이다.

• 주 요 용 어 및 표 현 •

- are not satisfied with : 만족하지 못한
- unusual case : 드문 경우
- inconvenience : 불편(=trouble)
- upon receipt of : 받자 마자, 받고 곧
- check into the matter : 문제를 조사하다(=investigate the matter)
- trace : 알아내다. 밝혀내다. 추적하다.
- thoroughly : 철저하게
- under investigation : 조사중
- make clear our position : 우리의 입장을 명확히 밝히다.
- investigation : 조사
- it goes without saying : 말할 필요없이, 당연하게
- are ready to ~ : 기꺼이 ~하다.
- take responsibility : 책임지다.
- at fault : 잘못이 있는(=in fault)
- be responsible for : 책임이 있는
- in the meantime : 그 동안에, 그 사이에, 한편, 동시에
- at our expense : 우리의 비용부담으로
- a couple : 두세 개(=a couple of, a few)
- inspector : 조사자, 검사관
- the result of the investigation : 조사의 결과
- determined : 확정되다.
- in touch with : 연락하다. 접촉하다.

K3 품질상위에 대한 클레임 제기

AMS Trading Company

908 Park Avenue
New York, NY 10017 U.S.A.

September 30, 2021

Asia Trading Company
212 Yoi-daero, Youngdeungpo-gu
Seoul, Korea 07325

Gentlemen:

The woolen textiles we ordered on June 12 reached us September 24, but we regret to inform you that we found the entire lot to be defective as shown in the inspection report issued by CNC surveyor.

The quality of the received goods is entirely different than the sample and so the goods are useless for our purpose. For this reason, our only option is to refuse acceptance of the delivery and to return all the goods to you freight collect.

However, because of our long standing relationship and in light of the heavy loss we know this will incur to you, we feel urged to search for an alternative solution even though we both may suffer some loss. Therefore we will take your goods at a reasonable discount if you would prefer to do so.

We hope that you will take this matter into your careful consideration and give us a prompt reply by fax or e-mail.

Very truly yours,

내용 AMS사가 수출자 Asia Trading사에게 수령한 상품이 샘플보다 열등함을 이유로 가격을 깎아 줄 것을 요청하는 내용이다.

• 주요 용어 및 표현 •

- woolen textiles : 모직물
- entire lot : 전량, 전부
- defective : 결함이 있는
- inspection report : 조사보고서
- surveyor : 조사관, 검사원, 미국에서는 일반적으로 inspector라고 한다.
- entirely different than~ : ~과 완전히 다른(entirely different from~)
- for this reason : 이러한 이유로, 그렇기 때문에
- our only option : 우리가 선택할 수 있는 유일한 방법
- refuse acceptance : 인수를 거절하다.
- freight collect : 수신인 운임 부담으로, 후불 운임으로
- in light of ~ : ~의 견지에서, ~에 비추어서
- heavy loss : 큰 손실
- feel urged to search for : 찾아야 한다고 생각이 든다. 찾아야 한다고 느낀다.
- an alternative solution : 다른 해결방안, 대안의 해결
- at a reasonable reduction : 적당한 할인 가격에, 합리적인 가격삭감으로
- if you would prefer to do so : 당신이 그렇게 하기를 원한다면

✓	클레임 제기에 대한 표현
file a claim with A	enter a claim with A
lodge a claim with A	submit a claim to A
bring forward a claim with A	place a claim before A
file a claim for US$ 1,000	file a claim with A for US$ 1,000

K4 품질상위클레임에 대한 답신

Asia Trading Company
212 Yoi-daero, Youngdeungpo-gu
Seoul, Korea 07325

October 15, 2021

AMS Trading Company
908 Park Avenue
New York, NY 10017 U.S.A.

Gentlemen: OUR SHIPMENT OF AUGUST 28

In reply to your letter dated September 30, we wish to apologize for our mistake as you pointed out with our shipment of your order No. 243.

Upon checking the shipment, we found that there were some errors on our part. Our shipping department shipped the goods of pattern No. 122 instead of those of pattern No. 123 on which your order was placed. We sincerely regret that we have troubled you through this inadvertent mistake.

In order to adjust this matter, we will refund the amount you paid for invoice No. KL-3434, and reimburse you for the cost of shipping the goods in question back to us. Otherwise, if you are able to keep the goods, we are prepared to make a special allowance of 20% on them. This is a great loss to us since the price of pattern No. 122 is lower by only 5% than that of pattern No. 123.

Please accept our apology for our mistake. We will do our best not to cause you any similar inconvenience again.

Very truly yours,

내용 Asia Trading사가 수입자 AMS사의 상품품질 상위의 클레임제기에 대하여 상품선적에 착오가 있었음을 알리고 상품을 반품하거나 할인하여 인수할 것을 제의하는 내용이다.

· 주요 용어 및 표현 ·

- on our part : 우리측에(＝at this end)
- trouble : 폐를 끼치다. 수고를 끼치다. 성가시게 하다.
- inadvertent mistake : 부적당한 실수, 부주의한 잘못
- refund : 환불하다.
- reimburse : 변상하다. 상환하다. 비용을 지불하다.
- the cost of shipping the goods : 상품운송비용, 물품선적비용
- the goods in question : 문제의 상품
- keep : 보유하다. 가지다. 유지하다.
- are prepared to : ～ 준비가 되어 있다. ～할 용의가 있다.
- make a special allowance : 특별할인을 하다.
- please accept our apology for ～ : ～에 대해서 사과를 드립니다.
- do our best : 최선을 다하다.

✓	비용 및 요금
① cost : (상품 및 서비스의) 원가, 비용, 대가, 가격	
② expense : 지출, 비용, 소요경비	
③ charge : (일에 대한) 대가, 요금, 과세금	
④ surcharge : 부가요금, 추가세, 특별요금, 할증금	
⑤ fare : (기차, 전차, 버스, 배 등의) 요금, 운임	
⑥ fee : (의사, 변호사, 지도교사 등 전문 서비스에 대한) 보수, 사용료	
⑦ rate : (전기, 수도, 전화 등 일정한 요율에 따라 청구되는) 요금, 가격	
⑧ rent : 지대, 집세, 임차료	
⑨ rental : 지대수입, 집세수입, 임대료	
⑩ toll : 사용세, 도로 통행료, 항만하역료, 장거리 전화료	

K5 수량부족에 대한 클레임 제기

ANC Co., Ltd

32 Walker Street, North Sydney,
N.S.W. 2060 Australia

October 25, 2021

KSK ELECTRONICS
11 Myongdong-gil, Jung-gu
Seoul, Korea 04534

Gentlemen:

We would like to draw your attention to the cell phones shipped by the M/S "ASIANA" on September 20.

Upon checking the goods, we discovered a shortage of 3 units. More specifically, cases No. 9 and No. 10 contained only 48 and 49 units respectively, instead of the 50 each as recorded on the packing list. There was not any sign from which we can judge that they were tampered with in transit as the boxes packed were received in good condition.

The difference between the quantity received and the figures in your invoice perplexes us as to whom we should lodge our claim with, either the shipping company or the shipper. Though we are of the opinion that the shortage is due to a mistake in packing, we would like to know your explanation. If you have evidence that your figure is correct, please send it to us soon, because we need your explanation and evidence in order to process our claim with the shipping company.

In the meantime, we ask you to send 3 units immediately since our customer needs the entire quantity that we ordered.

We hope that you will correct this matter at once. We are anxiously awaiting your prompt reply.

Very truly yours,

내용 ANC사가 수출자 KSK ELECTRONICS사에게 수령한 상품의 수량부족을 알리고 이에 대한 조사와 부족수량 보충을 요청하는 내용이다.

• 주 요 용 어 및 표 현 •

- draw attention : 배려를 요청하다. 주의를 환기시키다.
- cell phones : 휴대폰(＝mobile phone, cellular phone)
- more specifically : 보다 구체적으로
- respectively : 각각
- instead of : 대신에
- was not any sign : 어떠한 징후도 없었다.
- tamper : 함부로 손대다. 만지작거리다. 개봉하다.
- in transit : 운송도중에
- perplex : 난처하게 하다. 당황케 하다.
- lodge : 제기하다. 항의를 제출하다(＝file).
- the shipper : 선적인, 송화인(＝consignor)
- are of the opinion that ~ : ~라고 생각하다. ~라는 의견이다.
- is due to ~ : ~에 원인이 있는 것으로, ~에 기인하는 것으로
- evidence : 증거, 증거물건
- process claim with : 보상금을 청구하다(＝submit claim to).
- in the meantime : 그 동안에, 한편, 동시에
- entire quantity : 전량(＝whole quantity)
- at once : 곧, 즉시

✓	**물품운송 관계자**

① carrier : 운송인(＝shipping company)
② forwarder : 운송주선업자, 운송인과 송화인간에 운송절차를 돕는 사람
③ shipper : 송화인, 하주, 수출자, 선적인(＝consignor)
④ consignee : 수화인, 화물인수자, 수입자, 수탁자

K6 수량부족 클레임에 대한 답신

KSK ELECTRONICS

11 Myongdong-gil, Jung-gu
Seoul, Korea 04534

November 2, 2021

ANC Co., Ltd
32 Walker Street, North Sydney
N.S.W. 2060 Australia

Gentlemen: OUR SHIPMENT OF SEPTEMBER 20

We received your fax of October 25 informing us of the shortages of our last shipment and thank you for the opportunity you have given us to promptly rectify our error.

We sent you by UPS Express today the 3 units of cellular phones that you requested to compensate for the deficit. The shipment should reach you by the end of next week.

We really don't know exactly how this could have happened. There may have been an error during the packing of goods by our shipping department.

We trust that the matter is now settled to your satisfaction and we will do our best to make sure that this sort of mistake will not occur again.

We sincerely apologize for the inconvenience this may have caused you.

Sincerely yours,

내용 KSK ELECTRONICS사가 수입자 ANC사의 상품수량부족의 클레임제기에 대하여 상품부족분을 즉시 발송하고 다음부터 같은 일이 재발하지 않도록 하겠다는 약속과 사과를 보내는 내용이다.

• 주요 용어 및 표현 •

- rectify : 바로 잡다. 교정하다. 고치다.
- by UPS express : UPS사 편으로. UPS는 DHL처럼 소형화물 급송배달회사. 우편의 경우 속달 소포는 express parcel post라 한다.
- to compensate for : ~을 메우다. 보충하다. 보정하다.
  =as compensation for ~
- deficit : 부족분, 결손
- there may have been an error : 실수가 있었던 것 같다.
- during the packing : 포장과정에서(=in the course of packing)
- shipping department : 선적부
- do our best : 최선을 다하다.
- make sure that ~ : 꼭 ~하다. ~하도록 확실히 하다. ~하도록 대책을 세우다.
- inconvenience : 불편, 폐

✓	~에 관하여
For ~ As for ~ In regard to ~ Regarding ~ Concerning ~	About ~ As to ~ With regard to ~ As regards ~

✓	요청, 지시 등에 따라
As requested, ~ At your request, ~ In accordance with your request, ~ Pursuant to your request, ~	As instructed, ~ In compliance with your request, ~ According to your request, ~

K7 물품파손에 대한 클레임 제기

HK Trading Inc.

12/Floor, St. John's Building
33 Garden Road, Central, Hong Kong

August 25, 2021

SM Company, Inc.
4501, 45th Floor, Trade Tower
511 Yeongdong-daero, Kangnam-gu
Seoul, Korea 06164

Gentlemen:

We thank you for having shipped your Sales Contract No. 1991 for electronic toys via the M/V "Mariana", however, we regret to inform you that 4 cases were found to be crushed and their contents badly damaged.

We found that the cases were too fragile and the packing was not sufficient for ocean transportation and so the contents of the crushed cases were broken and are now in an unsaleable condition. We enclose the authorized surveyors report showing the damage to be the result of poor packing.

We ask you, therefore, either to send us your replacement right away by air freight at your expense or to reimburse us US$ 320.⁻ to cover the price of the damaged goods and our losses accrued for the import duty and charges of the inspector.

We are awaiting your prompt decision on this matter.

Very truly yours,

내용 HK사가 수출자 SM사에게 수령한 상품이 포장잘못으로 파손되었음을 알리고 이에 대해 교환을 해주거나 대금상환을 해줄 것을 요청하는 내용이다.

• 주요 용어 및 표현 •

- electronic toy : 전자 장난감, 전자 완구
- to be crushed : 부서지다. 눌려 부서지다. 구겨지다.
- contents : 내용물
- badly damaged : 몹시 손상되다. 심각한 손상을 입다.
- we found that ~ : =we discovered that ~
- fragile : 약한, 깨지기 쉬운, 허약한
- was not sufficient for ~ : ~에 불충분한
- ocean transportation : 해상운송, 대양운송
- unsaleable : 팔 수 없는, 팔리지 않는(=unmarketable)
- authorized surveyors report : 공인 검사보고서. 미국에서는 일반적으로 surveyor보다 inspector라고 한다.
- damage : 손상, 손해, 피해
- the result of ~ : ~ 결과로
- poor packing : 불충분한 포장, 잘못된 포장
- replacement : 교환품, 대체품, 교환
- right away : 즉시
- by air freight : 항공화물운송편으로
- at your expense : 당신의 비용부담으로
- reimburse : 변제하다. 상환하다.
- loss : 손실, 손해액수, 감손, 상실
- accrued : 발생한
- import duty : 수입관세
- charges of the inspector : 조사관 수수료, 조사비용

K8 물품파손 클레임에 대한 답신

SM Company, Inc.

4501, 45th Floor, Trade Tower
511 Yeongdong-daero, Kangnam-gu, Seoul, Korea 06164

September 7, 2021

HK Trading Inc.
12/Floor, St. John's Building
33 Garden Road, Central, Hong Kong

Gentlemen:

Thank you very much for your fax of yesterday informing us that the goods supplied to you were damaged upon delivery. Because you may think that we should be responsible for the damage of this shipment, we must clarify our position as follows:

First, the goods in question were inspected thoroughly by us before packing and loaded onto the ship in perfect condition. The clean on board Bill of Lading shows that everything was in order at the time the goods were loaded onto the ship.

Secondly, the packaging was in full compliance with the standards of packing for international ocean transportation and the specifications of the packaging were agreed upon by you in the contract.

Thirdly, since this transaction is based on FOB, we are free from any liabilities for the shipment upon loading onto your designated vessel.

Fourth, we are of the opinion that the damage done to the goods was caused by rough handling during the voyage or during unloading at your port.

Under these circumstances, we would suggest that you file a claim with the insurance company or shipping company. You may trust that we will cooperate with you in expediting the process of your claim of loss.

If you need any further assistance, we will be more than happy to assist you in any way we can.

Very truly yours,

내용 SM사가 수입자 HK사의 상품파손에 대한 클레임제기에 대하여 자사의 책임이 없음을 설명하고 선박회사나 보험회사에 보상요청을 할 것을 제의하는 내용이다.

• 주요 용어 및 표현 •

- upon delivery : 도착시에
- be responsible for ~ : ~에 대하여 책임이 있는
- clarify our position : 우리의 입장을 명확히 하다.
- as follows : 다음과 같이
- loaded onto the ship : 선박에 선적하다.
- the goods in question : 문제의 상품, 해당 상품
- in perfect condition : 완전한 상태로
- clean on board Bill of Lading : 무사고 선적 선하증권
- in order : 제대로, 무사히, 정상의
- packaging : 포장(=packing)
- in full compliance with ~ : ~ 완전히 ~에 따라
- the standards of packing : 포장규격, 포장표준
- specifications : 명세, 명세서
- agree upon : 합의를 한(=agree on)
- based on FOB : FOB(본선인도) 조건으로
- are free from any liabilities : 어떤 책임도 없다.
- upon loading ~ vessel : 당신이 지정한 선박에 선적함으로써
- rough handling : 거친 취급, 난폭하게 다룸
- voyage : 항해
- unloading : 하역, 양륙
- at your port : 그쪽 항, 목적항
- under these circumstances : 이러한 상황에서
- file a claim : 클레임을 제기하다(=lodge a claim).
- expedite : 신속히 처리하다. 촉진시키다.
- claim of loss : 손실에 대한 보상청구

K9 물품지연도착에 대한 클레임 제기

ABBA Co., Inc.

1156 5th Avenue
New York, NY 10017 U.S.A.

December 12, 2021

Asia Trading Company
212 Yoi-daero, Youngdeungpo-gu
Seoul, Korea 07325

Gentlemen:

This letter is in reference to our order of September 2 for women's sweaters which arrived on December 10.

We regret to inform you that we cannot accept them because they arrived nearly one month past the agreed upon delivery date. We had already pressed you for these goods in two previous letters dated October 30 and November 16 in which we strongly advised that the goods should arrive here by the end of November in order for us to sell them during the winter season.

The failure to receive the goods on time has caused us serious problems. This resulted in many scheduling problems and damage to our business reputation.

We are enclosing a financial statement of our losses caused by this delay, and ask you to arrange compensation without delay. In the mean time we are holding the goods at your disposal awaiting your reply.

Your immediate attention to this matter is highly appreciated.

Very truly yours,

내용 ABBA사가 수출자 Asia Trading사에게 지연되어 도착한 상품에 대해서 수령거부와 함께 이로 인한 손해배상을 청구하는 내용이다.

· 주 요 용 어 및 표 현 ·

- in reference to ~ : ~와 관련하여
- the agreed upon delivery date : 합의된 인도일
- pressed : 재촉하다. 간청하다. 최고하다.
- the failure to receive goods : 상품을 받지 못한 것
- on time : 제 때에, 정시에
- cause us serious problem : 우리에게 심각한 문제를 가져다주다.
- evade : 피하다. 모면하다.
- confusion : 혼란, 혼동
- business schedule : 사업계획
- credit : 신용, 평판, 명예(=good reputation)
- business associates : 사업 거래처, 사업거래선
- financial statement : 금전 계산서, 계산서
- arrange compensation : 변상하다. 변상 처리하다.
- without delay : 지체 없이, 곧
- in the mean time : 그 동안, 그 사이에(=in the meantime, in the meanwhile)
- at your disposal : 당신이 임의로 처분할 수 있도록, 당신의 책임하에

✓	당신의 편지, 요청 등에 대한 답신으로
In reference to ~	In response to ~
In answer to ~	In reply to ~
Replying to ~	In compliance with ~

K10 물품지연도착 클레임에 대한 답신

Asia Trading Company

212 Yoi-daero, Youngdeungpo-gu
Seoul, Korea 07325

December 23, 2021

ABBA Co., Inc.
1156 5th Avenue
New York, NY 10017 U.S.A.

Gentlemen:

Thank you very much for your letter of December 12 regarding the late delivery of the goods you ordered on September 2. Please accept our sincere apologies for this matter.

Please allow us to explain. Last month, there was a series of nationwide labor strikes here in Korea which lasted for 20 days. Therefore, we experienced a shortage of materials needed for the production of our goods.

Despite our best efforts, we were not able to secure some key materials in time to meet our planned production schedule. Even though we sped up production after obtaining the materials, it was impossible for us to ship on time.

To date, we have enjoyed a reputation of punctuality, but this time, we regret that we could not avoid a delay of delivery despite our best efforts.

Even though the delay was mostly attributable to a cause beyond our control, we offer our sincerest apologies for it. As a result, we are ready to compensate your loss caused by the late delivery and will be grateful if you accept the goods with a 20% reduction of price.

We are expecting that this will be a satisfactory solution and we assure you that this sort of incident will not occur again.

Very truly yours,

내용 Asia Trading사가 수입자 ABBA사의 상품인도지연의 클레임제기에 대하여 지연의 원인을 설명하고, 불가항력이기 때문에 자사가 책임을 져야하는 것은 아니지만 원만한 해결을 위해서 가격할인을 해주겠다는 내용이다.

• 주요 용어 및 표현 •

- apology : 사과, 사죄. 실질적인 잘못이 있는 경우에만 사용되는 표현이다. 이에 비해서 excuse는 작은 실수나 결례 등에 사용된다.
- a series of nationwide labor strikes : 일련의 전국적인 노동파업
- lasted for 20 days : 20일간 지속되다.
- despite our best efforts : 우리가 최선을 다했음에도 불구하고
- key materials : 핵심부품
- in time : 제 때에, 꼭 맞는 때에, 기간 내에
- sped up : 속도를 더하다. 박차를 가하다(=accelerated).
- on time : 정시에
- to date : 지금까지(=until now)
- punctuality : 시간엄수, 꼼꼼함
- attributable to ~ : ~의 탓, ~에 기인하는
- cause beyond our control : 우리가 통제할 수 없는 원인, 즉 불가항력
- offer sincerest apologies : 매우 깊은 사과를 드리다.
- as a result : 그 결과
- a 20% reduction of price : 20% 가격할인
- a satisfactory solution : 만족스러운 해결방안

✓	사고, 사건, 행사
	incident : 사고, 일어난 일, 부수 사건
	incident : 중대사건으로 발전할 위험이 있는 부수적인 사건
	accident : 사고, 재난, 뜻하지 않게 일어난 사고
	event : 사건, 일어난 일, 행사

Useful Expressions

① 클레임 제기

📋 품질문제

1. Sample과 상위

- We are writing to notify you that the goods sent in execution of our order No. 345 do not agree with your sample.
- We have to draw your attention to the fact that the goods don't correspond to the sample which you sent us at the time of contract.
- You have delivered goods which are below the standard we expected from the samples.
- When comparing the goods received with the sample, we found that the color is different.
- Unpacking the goods, we found that the goods differed from the original sample you sent.

Unpacking *Upon unpacking* *While unpacking* *When checking* *On inspection of* *After careful examination of*	*found* *discovered*	*differed from* *didn't correspond to* *were not same as* *were not in accordance with*

- We have received the goods you shipped and found to our regret that the goods didn't correspond to the sample.

2. 품질 나쁨

- We very much regret to inform you that the goods you shipped are much inferior in quality.
- We were very surprised to receive such poor quality merchandise.

> *surprised*
> *disappointed*
> *dismayed*

■ Our laboratory reports that the crackers supplied by you contain at least 4.5% fat. Such a high percentage will not be accepted in this market.

■ The goods invoiced on June 2 are so poor in quality that we were unable to deliver them to our customer.

■ Please compare the cuttings enclosed and you will readily admit the reasonableness of our claim.

3. 품종 및 규격 상위

■ We cannot accept the goods as they are not of the shape we ordered.

■ You have evidently supplied us the wrong merchandise on our order No. 123. This error is causing us much trouble with our customers.

■ As to the car stereos you sent us the wrong type. Please ship immediately a replacement of this article, exactly as ordered by us.

수량부족

■ When checking the goods received, we found that some items on your invoice had not been packed.

■ Fifteen service articles are entered on the invoice, but there were only twelve in the case.

■ To our regret, the case contains only 10 bottles instead of 12 as entered on the invoice.

■ You have not sent us all the goods we ordered; the following are missing:

■ To cover this shortage of supply, we ask you to make up the difference immediately.

■ We thank you for your prompt delivery of order No. 123, but have noticed that there is a shortage of Model No. 789. We ordered 200 dozen, but only

50 were delivered. We hope you will arrange delivery of the remaining 150 dozen as soon as you possibly can.

- To prove the shortage, we are enclosing a certificate of a <u>sworn measurer.</u>

| *sworn measurer* |
| *tallyman* |

상품의 파손 및 포장불량

- This is to inform you that we have received 20 cartons of car radios shipped by the s.s. "Silver Star V–5," but have found cartons No. 18 and 19 badly <u>damaged.</u>

| *damaged* |
| *cracked* |

- We have cleared your shipment by the s.s. "Silver Star V–5" today. An <u>examination</u> has <u>shown</u> that <u>damage</u> <u>occurred</u> in transit.

| *examination* *analysis* *test* | *shown* *proved* | *damage* *loss* *breakage* | *occurred* *happened* |

- The goods we ordered on July 18, 2021 have arrived in damaged condition.
- The goods we ordered from you on May 10 covering our order No. 123 by the s.s. "Moon Star V–7" reached us in an unsatisfactory condition.
- These damages are obviously due to defective packing of the goods. They were packed without any padding.
- We found to our regret that several cases were partially damaged by poor packing.
- Upon unpacking the cases we found the goods soaked by seawater.
- Upon unpacking order No. 123, we found that the case was damaged and the contents unusable.

- The stuffing inside the case was so loose that some cups and plates were broken.
- All things considered, we concluded that the damage was caused by poor packing.
- We believe that the case was too fragile and that the packing was not sufficient for export shipment.

📑 지 연

- The goods we ordered from you on July 9 have not yet been delivered.

> *have not yet been delivered.*
> *should have reached us a week ago.*

- Our order No. 123 of May 5 for DVD players is considerably overdue.

> *is considerably overdue*
> *is now urgently required*
> *is now a matter of urgency*

- You promised before we place the an order that the goods would be shipped by November 15.
- This terrible delay has caused us a great loss of business.
- It is most essential that the delivery should be punctual, otherwise our summer sale cannot be carried out.
- The delivery time was clearly mentioned in our letter and was duly acknowledged by you.
- If the goods have not yet been shipped, we must ask you to send them by air.

📑 대책의 요청

- We expect your explanation to be quite acceptable to us.
- Please check this matter at your end once more.

check look into investigate	at your end on your part	once more thoroughly

- Please let us know without delay how you propose to remedy this.
- Kindly tell us what steps you are going to take in the way of compensation for the damage.
- Please investigate the matter and forward to us the replacement of the damaged cartons by airfreight.

🗐 보상요구 조건제시

- We, therefore, leave it to your option whether you will grant a 20% allowance or take back the goods, and ask you to e-mail your decision to us.
- Regarding this matter on your shipment, we must claim <u>an allowance of</u> at least 30 percent.

an allowance of a deduction of a reduction of a discount of

- Please let us know if you want to take the goods back or let us sell them at a discount of 25 percent.
- We are compelled to claim a compensation of US$ 20,000.
- In these circumstances, we have to claim compensation of US$ 5,000 from you for the damage.

🗐 계약 취소 및 반품

- Unless the goods can be shipped by the 30th of June, we will have to cancel the order.
- As the goods were specially ordered for the Christmas season, we must ask you to cancel our order.

- As our order No. 123 is now long overdue, we have to cancel it. As you know punctual delivery is essential for our order.
- We would like to return the goods to you for replacement.

맺는 말

- Please look into the matter and let us know your instruction by July 31.
- Please investigate this matter and resolve it without delay.
- We hope that you will immediately take this matter into your careful consideration and furnish us with a prompt solution by e-mail.
- Your early settlement will be appreciated.
- Please give this matter your prompt attention.
- Please look into the matter and let us know your decision immediately.
- We shall be glad to learn that you are prepared to make some allowance for the damage we have reported.
- We ask that you replace the damaged goods at once.
- Would you please make sure that this kind of problem doesn't happen in the future?

2 클레임제기에 대한 답신

서 두

- We are <u>sorry</u> to learn from your letter that <u>you are not satisfied</u> with our shipment of silk jackets.

sorry / very sorry *extremely sorry* *exceedingly sorry*	*you are not satisfied* *you had trouble*

- Thank you very much for your letter about the goods you have recently purchased.

- Thank you for <u>the opportunity you've given us to rectify</u> our error.

the opportunity you've given us to rectify calling attention to notifying us of	rectify put right straighten out adjust

- We are extremely <u>sorry</u> to <u>hear</u> of your complaint regarding the last shipment.

sorry shocked	hear learn

- We very much regret having given you cause for complaint.
- Thank you for calling our attention to our shipment of silk jackets.
- We hasten to reply to your letter of June 10 and we apologize for the unfortunate mistake you pointed out.

 **조　사**

- <u>As soon as we received</u> your letter, we got in touch with the shipping agents to <u>check into</u> the matter and asked our shipping department to trace this matter thoroughly.

As soon as we received Immediately upon receipt of	check into investigate

- We are checking the cause of the damage you mentioned with the packers.
- We have already taken up the matter with the railway authority and we will phone you as soon as we have any information.
- Please send us the wrong goods by return mail, and we will examine them carefully to see what can be done about the matter.
- Upon receipt of your letter, we checked the matter ourselves and report to you the findings as follows:
- We found that the packers misread the number, and have instructed them to send you the right goods immediately.

- We feel your claim is somewhat unreasonable and we have asked international surveyors to examine this matter.

📑 사 과

- We have received your letter of complaint and offer our deepest apologies for sending you goods of inferior quality.
- Please accept our sincere apology for the mistake we made on the last shipment.
- We are very sorry for our mistaken numbering, which resulted in your receiving the wrong goods.
- We offer our sincere apologies for the error in our shipment, and are sending you our correct shipment immediately.
- We are very sorry for the delay in the execution of your order No. 123.
- We very much regret the delayed delivery and the inconvenience it has caused you.

📑 경위설명

- The defect may be due to a fault in a machine, therefore we are now checking all machines.
- Upon checking the above shipment, we found that our shipping department shipped the goods of pattern No. 122 instead of those of pattern No. 123 on which your order was placed.
- The fungus damage seems to be due to humidity exposure caused by broken cases during landing.
- The packers maintain that the cartons must have been handled roughly.
- The delayed shipment is entirely attributable to the recent strike.

> *strike*
> *typhoon*
> *shortage of raw materials*

- The flood of orders for this model made it impossible to supply it on time.
- We have enjoyed a reputation for being punctual in meeting the delivery time stipulated, and never have we failed to deliver our customers' orders on time.
- We are sorry for the delay, even though it was attributable to a cause beyond our control.
- We had already shipped the goods. Your letter must have crossed with ours informing you of the shipment of your order.

📋 해결방안의 제시

1. 가격할인

- In order to adjust the matter, we are willing to grant you a 15% discount off the invoice amount.
- In view of our longstanding business relationship, we will meet you halfway by offering a discount of 5%.
- In order to adjust this matter, we suggest you to accept the goods at a reduction of 20% though it is a great loss to us since the price of pattern No. 122 is only 10% lower than that of pattern No. 123.
- If you are able to <u>keep</u> the leather gloves received, we are prepared to make a special <u>allowance on them</u> of 10%.

keep retain hold	allowance on them allowance for them

- May we ask you to keep the goods to save the return freight provided we make you an extra allowance of 20%?
- While we find no reason to accept your claim, we will, however, permit a 10% allowance for your continued patronage.

2. 금전보상

- We shall <u>make every effort</u> to alleviate your financial loss.

> *make every effort*
> *do everything in our power*

- Upon completion of our investigation, we shall make a satisfactory compensation for the loss you suffered.

- Considering our long-standing relationship, we agree to pay 5 percent of the total invoice amount in compensation for your loss.

- In order to adjust this matter, we will refund the amount you paid for invoice No.123, and ask you to return the goods with freight collect.

3. 상품회수 및 교환

- We will be obliged if you will keep the goods until our agent call on you for replacement.

- We are sending you today patterns of goods in stock, and would like to ask you to select the patterns you need. We can promise to ship the replacement by the next direct vessel.

- We would appreciate your returning the goods to us as soon as possible at our expense.

- Of course, we are ready to replace the damaged goods with new ones and will be grateful if you will send the damaged ones back to us.

- If you want to replace the article, we will send you another one immediately.

- We would ship a replacement to you right away. In the mean time, would you please return the product in question to us?

4. 지연의 경우 발송조치

- The goods were forwarded today by air and will definitely be there within a couple of days.

- We surely will be able to send the goods by the very next vessel sailing on July 12, 2021, and we rely upon your leniency in the matter of recent delay.
- The goods are already on their way and the documents were given to the bank.

🗐 해결안 제시의 요청

- Please let us know what settlement you consider fair under these circumstances.
- We were extremely busy, but that is no excuse. Will you please state what compensation would be most acceptable to you?
- As we have full confidence in your fairness, we would rather leave it to you to propose a method of settlement.

🗐 책임

- As the matter is under investigation now, we will advise you of the results as soon as they appear and will give our suggestions if we are responsible for the damage.
- We are ready to take responsibility if we are found to be at fault.
- We can't assume full responsibility for it
- You can't put all the blame on us but need to share some of them. What do you say if we meet you half way?

🗐 책임 없음

- We have confirmed with our shipping company that the goods were put on board the ship in perfect condition.
- The signature on the loading documents shows that everything was in order at the time the goods were loaded onto the ship.

- We can only assume that the shipment suffered the damage while it was being unloaded or while it was being trucked to your warehouse.

- We have enclosed copies of documents which will prove that the goods left the port in good condition.

- The clean B/L fully proves that the goods in question were loaded in good order.

- Upon investigation, we have found that there wasn't any mistake on our part.

- The goods passed double inspection by the Korea Inspection Center for Textiles as certified in the shipping documents. You can also see the label of "Export Packing" on each case, which was given to us by the authorized inspectors.

📄 선박회사 및 보험회사에 알아볼 것을 권유

- We feel that we are not at fault and suggest that you file a claim with the shipping company or the landing agents.

- After careful investigation we could find no error on our part. We suggest that you place a claim with the insurance company.

- We feel that the steamship is responsible for the shortage and we suggest that you take up the matter with the shipping company rather than with us, as we have obtained a clean B/L.

> *take up the matter with*
> *file / lodge your claim with*

- As the shipment was insured, I assume that you are covered for the damage.

- As this is beyond our control due to force majeure, we suggest that you file your claim with the insurance company.

- Although we will make inquiries from our end, I suggest you that you contact the trucking company that handled the delivery of goods.

📄 상대방 요구의 거절

- We are unable to consider your demand for a discount.

- Under such a circumstance, we hope you will understand why we cannot accept your claim.

- It is difficult for us to accept your demand since your claim is quite unreasonable.

- Upon looking into the matter, we find that we sent you goods exactly according to the sample; we therefore are unable to consider your demand for a discount.

📄 중재위에 회부

- We would like to suggest that this claim be settled in accordance with the arbitration rules of the Korean Commercial Arbitration Board.

- Should you insist on a discount of 20% for the damaged goods, we have no choice but to put the matter before the Korean Commercial Arbitration Board.

- As you consider our proposals unsatisfactory, we suggest that the matter be submitted to arbitration.

- We wish to settle this dispute in a friendly way, and we therefore suggest that we submit it to arbitration and abide by the arbitrator's decision.

a friendly way an amicable manner	submit refer

📄 맺는 말

- We trust that the matter is now settled to your satisfaction and assure you that this sort of mistake will not occur again in the future.

- You may be sure that we will make every effort to see that such a mistake does not happen again.

make every effort to see make sure	a mistake an error

- Again let us apologize for the delay and let us assure you that <u>measures</u> have been taken so that a similar situation will not <u>arise</u>.

measures	arise
steps	occur

- We hope this will now settle the matter to your complete satisfaction.
- We trust that the matter is thus <u>settled</u> to our mutual satisfaction.

settled
in order

- We are glad that we could come to such an amicable agreement. We hope that through this occasion we can strengthen our friendship.
- We hope that this small incident will not deter our good relationship which we have enjoyed thus far.
- Please accept our sincere apologies for the delay and the inconvenience it has caused you.
- We thank you for the opportunity to correct our error.
- We apologize for any trouble our mistake may have caused you.
- We sincerely hope that you will <u>be satisfied with</u> our explanation and will not misunderstand our position.

be satisfied with
accept

- If you need anything else, we will be more than happy to assist you in any way we can.

✓	편지 쓰기에 도움되는 접속어
설　　명	Namely(즉, 다시 말해) In other words(바꾸어 말하면) For example, For instance(예를 들면) That is to say(즉 다시 말해) In fact, As a matter of fact(사실은, 실제로는)
순서나열	First(첫째로, 최초로) Secondly(둘째로) Thirdly(셋째로) Finally, Lastly(마지막으로) Originally(처음에는, 원래, 처음부터) First of all(첫째로, 우선) To begin with(우선, 첫째로)
부　　연	Additionally(따라서, 그러므로) Also(또한, 마찬가지로) Besides(그 밖에, 게다가) Fortunately(다행스럽게도) Incidentally(부수적으로) Likewise(게다가, 마찬가지로) Moreover(게다가, 더욱더) At the same time(동시에) Furthermore, In addition(게다가, 더구나, 그 위에)
전　　환	Anyway, Anyhow(여하튼, 어차피, 좌우간) In any case(하여튼, 어쨌든)
강　　조	Naturally(당연히, 물론) Especially, Particularly(특히, 각별히)
반　　대	However(그러나) Otherwise(그렇지 않으면) Still(그럼에도 불구하고, 그래도) On the contrary(이에 반하여, 도리어, 그렇기는 커녕) On the other hand(반면에, 이에 반해서) Nevertheless, Notwithstanding(그럼에도 불구하고)
결　　과	Accordingly(따라서, 그러므로) Consequently(따라서, 그 결과로서) Therefore(그러므로, 그런 이유로, 그 결과) Then(게다가, 그렇다면) As a result(그 결과) In conclusion(최후로, 결론적으로) For this reason, Because of this(이러한 이유로)

Standard
Trade
English

1. 취업관련 영문서면
2. 업무연관 편지(Social Correspondence in Business)
3. 무역편지작성에 유용한 기초표현
4. 주요 무역용어

1 취업관련 영문서면

취업지원통신문은 취업을 희망하는 지원자가 자신의 취업희망의사를 전달하는 통신문이다. 구직자가 자신의 적성, 능력, 성격 등을 채용자에 잘 알림으로써 원하는 직장을 구할 수 있을 뿐만 아니라 채용자측에서도 기업에 필요한 인재를 찾는 데 도움을 주게 된다.

구직자가 자신이 원하는 직장에 채용되기를 원한다면 채용자로 하여금 자신이 그 직장에서 필요로 하는 적격한 인물임을 납득시키고 자신을 채용함으로써 회사에 이득이 된다는 확신을 주어야 한다.

1) 취업지원서

취직지원서는 대개 다음과 같은 사항을 포함하게 된다.

1. 지원하게 된 동기 및 배경
2. 자신이 갖고 있는 장점과 능력
3. 자신이 해당기업에서 기여할 수 있는 사항
4. 해당기업에서 일하고자 하는 자신의 열의와 성실성
5. 경력자인 경우에는 자신의 경험이 해당기업에 기여할 수 있는 사항
6. 경력증명서, 이력서, 추천서 등에 대한 사항 언급
7. 면접의 희망 및 자신의 연락처 전화번호 및 시간 등에 대한 사항

2) 취업지원서류 작성요령

1. 자신의 능력과 장점을 빠짐 없이 알린다.
2. 적극적, 진취적인 느낌이 오도록 한다. 따라서 용어에 있어서도 develop, promote, complete, initiate 등과 같은 긍정적인 단어를 사용한다.
3. 간결하고 일관성 있게 작성한다. 보는 사람을 생각해서 가능한 한 1 page 이내로 작성하며, 경력을 현재부터 과거로 기술하는 것도 한 방법이다.
4. 깔끔하고 정돈된 느낌을 주도록 한다. 여러 이력서 중에서 눈길을 끌 수 있도록 종이, 글씨, 문단배열 등에 신경써야 하며, 오자나 문장상의 실수가 없도록 한다.

1. 지원서(Letter of Application)

Dear Sirs,

I am applying to be an employee in the export division of your company as I feel I am qualified for the position.

I was born and brought up in the town of Jeju, Jeju-Do, Korea until graduation from high school. In March, 2015, I entered ABC University, one of the most authoritative institutions in the field of business administration in Korea, majoring in international trade. I am scheduled to graduate from the university in February next year. My GPA at the university is 3.5/4.5 currently.

I have taken every available credit course in international trade and business at university. I am sure that I have acquired quite a good knowledge of international business to the degree of being able to carry out the work of export and import myself.

In addition to the study of international business at the university, I have experienced several kinds of part time jobs in companies for my business training in the field during my college years. Especially, the internship experience at the international division of SS Co., Ltd. for three months last summer gave me a chance to get valuable knowledge related to international business transactions.

I would like to work for a well organized trading company like yours, and I believe my enthusiasm and knowledge of international business will be of interest to you. If I can work for your company I will do my best to contribute to developing your company.

Please contact me for more information at +82-10-911-9119 between 2:00 PM and 7:00 PM from Monday to Friday.

I am looking forward to hearing your favorable reply soon.

Sincerely yours,

2. 이력서(Personal history)

PERSONAL HISTORY

Photo

Name in Full   : Min-Jae Kim
Address   : 202, Sungbuk-gil, Sungbug-gu, Seoul
Telephone   : 02) 911-9119
Date of Birth   : October 17, 1997
Sex   : Male
Family Relation : First son of Sooil Kim
Personal Data   : Height 177 Cm. Weight 66 Kg.
Marital Status : Single
Education   :
  March 2012-Feb. 2015 ABC High School, Seoul
  March 2015-Feb. 2021 ABC University, Business Administration College
Military Service :
  Feb. 2018-Feb. 2020 Drafted to the army and discharged as sergeant.
Experience   :
  June-Aug. 2021 Worked for SS Co., Ltd. as an intern.
Reference   :
  Prof. Jinho Lee, ABC University, Business Administration College.
Qualifications   :
  Second Grade Certificate of Business English(Korea Chamber of Commerce and Industry)

I hereby declare upon my honor that the above statement is true and correct in every detail.

November 25, 2021

Min-Jae Kim
Min-Jae Kim

※ 이력서는 personal history 외에 resume, curriculum vitae라고도 한다.

3. 추천서(Letter of Recommendation)

Letter of Recommendation

November 9, 2021

To Whom It May Concern:

I am please to recommend Mr. Min-Jae Kim as an employee of your company. Since he entered our school in 2015, I have been closely associated with him as an academic advisor in international trade and business.

Mr. Kim was one of the brightest students in his class and has been active in many extracurricular activities. I taught him in my International Trade English class, where he fully demonstrated his academic excellence and sincerity and obtained the highest possible grade.

As for his personal character, he got along well with his classmates and teachers, and we used to praise him for his leadership abilities. He was also progressive in his approach to life, as well as being positive and cooperative with others.

I believe that Mr. Kim will work with a sense of responsibility and adjust well to your company. I would be very pleased if you would pay him your favorable consideration.

Sincerely yours,

ABC University

Hyunjun Joh

Hyunjun Joh
Professor of Business Administration

2 업무연관 편지(Social Correspondence in Business)

1. 초대장(Invitation to Opening of a Branch)

The president and officers of the Korea Trading Company
request the pleasure of the company
of Mr. and Mrs. Harold Baker
at the formal opening of their New York branch
on Saturday, the First of June
from four to six o'clock P.M.

R.S.V.P.
02) 501-2114

※ R.S.V.P.(Repondez sil vous plait) : reply, if you please, 응답해 주시면 감사하겠습니다.

2. 초대의 승낙 편지(Acceptance of Invitation)

Mr. and Mrs. Harold Baker
accept with pleasure the kind invitation
to the formal opening of your New York branch
on Saturday, the First of June
from four to six o'clock P.M.

3. 초대의 거절 편지(Decline of Invitation)

Mr. and Mrs. Harold Baker
regret that they are unable to accept the very kind invitation
to the formal opening of your New York branch
on Saturday, the First of June.

4. 통보 편지(Announcement)

> DONG YANG TRADING CORPORATION ANNOUNCES THE
> ELECTION OF MR. SUNMYUNG KANG TO ITS BOARD OF
> DIRECTORS
>
> Dong Yang Corporation announces the election of Sunmyung Kang to the company's Board of Directors effective immediately. Mr. Kang recently retired from Apex Motors after a distinguished career which began in 1994.
>
> Mr. Kang is one of the industry's most knowledgeable and successful executives. We are honored to welcome him to our team.

5. 축하 편지(Congratulations for an Election)

> Congratulations on your recent election as President of the Korea Trading Company.
>
> You certainly deserve recognition for your many years of loyal service and excellent achievements for the company.
>
> Best wishes for your continued success in your new office.

6. 소개 편지(Letter of Introduction)

SM Company, Inc.

4501, 45th Floor, Trade Tower
511 Yeongdong-daero, Kangnam-gu, Seoul, Korea 06164

April 12, 2021

General Materials Corporation
1180 State Street
Chicago, IL 60602
U.S.A.

Attn : Mr. George Black, Manager

Dear Sir,

We take pleasure in introducing Mr. Min-Jae Kim, our import manager. Mr. Kim will leave for the United States towards the end of this month for an important purchasing mission. As he does not know all the suppliers of electrical appliances, we believe your assistance and advice would be of great help to him.

Any cooperation and assistance you may render him during his stay in your area will be much appreciated.

Sincerely yours,

SM Company, Inc.

Sung-Kwang Yang

Executive Director

7. 감사 편지(Letter of Thanks for Courtesy on a Visit)

SM Company, Inc.

4501, 45th Floor, Trade Tower
511 Yeongdong-daero, Kangnam-gu, Seoul, Korea 06164

May 10, 2021

General Materials Corporation
1180 State Street
Chicago, IL 60602
U.S.A.

Dear Mr. George Black,

Now that I am back in Seoul, I felt that I must write to thank you most warmly for all the kindness and hospitality shown to me in Chicago. I appreciated your showing me around many historical and scenic places during my visit.

It was a great pleasure to have the opportunity of meeting the directors of American Airlines and talking things over personally. I was extremely interested in the various new processes you were good enough to show me, and I would appreciate it very much if you would convey my thanks to Mr. Smith for the trouble he took in his technical explanations.

I hope that before long we shall be receiving you in Seoul on a visit to our new offices.

Let me thank you once again.

Sincerely yours,

SM Company, Inc.

Min-Jae Kim
Import Manager

8. 신년인사 편지(Holiday Greetings)

We wish you all the best and a very Happy New Year. May this year bring health, prosperity, and peace to us all.

9. 사과 편지(Apologies)

I would like to apologize for the last-minute cancellation of our meeting scheduled for September 4. I had to fly to New York suddenly on unexpected business. I am sorry for any inconvenience this has caused you and sincerely hope that we can reschedule the meeting at your earliest convenience.

10. 조의 편지(Sympathy upon Death)

I was deeply saddened to hear of the death of your wife. Though I did not have the honor of knowing her personally, I know that she was admired and respected by many. You must miss her very much. Please accept my sincere sympathy and that of my entire organization.

3 무역편지작성에 유용한 기초표현

1. ~와 거래관계를 갖고자 합니다.

We wish to establish business relations with ~.

We desire to do business with ~.

We would like to open an account with ~.

2. A를 통하여 귀사를 알게 되었습니다.

We have learned(heard, come to know) your name from(through) A.

Your name has been recommended(introduced, supplied, given) to us by A.

We have seen your advertisement in A.

A has introduced you to me.

3. A를 통하여 귀사가 ~라는 사실을 알게 되었다.

Through A we learned your name as ~.

We have come to know from A that you are ~.

4. A가 ~에 관하여 귀사에 알아보라고 하였다.

A suggested that we write to you about ~.

A has informed us to get in touch with you concerning ~.

5. XX일자의 귀사의 편지(조회, 오퍼, 주문, 샘플) 잘 받았습니다.

Thank you for your letter of XX.

We have received with thanks your letter of XX.

We acknowledge with thanks your letter of XX.

We are pleased to have your letter of XX.

Your letter of April 16 has been received.

6. ~에 관한 XX일자의 귀사의 편지(조회, 오퍼, 주문, 샘플) 잘 받았습니다.

Thank you for your letter of XX concerning ~.

Thank you for your letter of XX which ~.

Thank you for your letter of XX informing us that ~.

7. ~ 용건으로 서신을 드립니다.

We are writing to you in the hope of ~ing.

We write to you with a desire to ~.

We are writing this letter to ~

We have the honor of writing to you ~.

We are approaching you with a desire to ~.

Permit us to write a request to you ~.

Permit us to trouble you to request that ~.

Allow us to write a request to you ~.

8. ~에 대하여 감사드립니다.

Thank you for ~.

Many thanks for ~.

We appreciate ~.

We are grateful for ~.

We express our gratitude for ~.

It was very thoughtful of you to ~.

9. ~을 알려 드립니다.

We inform you that / of ~.

We are pleased to let you know that / of ~.

We inform you as follows.

We inform you of the following matters ~.

We wish to advise you that / of ~.

We would like to inform you that / of ~.

We have to notify you that ~.

We have the pleasure of informing you that / of ~.

We take great pleasure in informing you ~.

It is with great pleasure that we inform you that / of ~.

10. ~을 알려 주십시오.

Please inform us that / of ~.

Please let us know about ~.

Please tell me that / of ~.

Will you please let us know about ~?

Will you please advise us that / of ~?

We wish to have your information on ~.

11. ~하여 주십시오. ~를 해주시면 감사하겠습니다.

We would appreciate it if you would ~.

We would appreciate your ~ing ~.

It would be appreciated if you could ~.

We would be pleased(glad, happy) if ~.

May we ask you to ~?

We have to ask you to ~.

We wish you to ~.

We hope to / that ~.

We expect to ~.

We expect your ~ing ~.

We would like you to ~.

We would require your ~.

We would welcome ~.

May we ask a favor of you by ~?

Kindly ~.

Please ~.

Will you please ~?

12. 기꺼이 ~하겠습니다.

We are pleased to ~.

We will feel happy to ~.

It gives us much pleasure to ~.

We have the pleasure of ~ing ~.

We will gladly ~.

13. 우리는 ~은 할 수 없습니다.

We are not in a position to ~.

We have to decline ~ing ~.

We have to refrain from ~ing ~.

We could not possibly do ~.

We have much difficulty in ~ing ~.

We may not be able to accept ~.

We are compelled to decline ~.

We are unable to accept ~.

We regret we must decline ~.

We regret our inability to accept ~.

We have no choice but to decline ~.

It has come to be impossible for us that ~.

It is almost impossible for us to ~.

It is too ~ to accept ~.

It is not acceptable for us to ~.

The matter has made it impossible to ~.

14. 우리는 ~을 확신합니다. 틀림없이 ~ 하겠습니다.

We are certain that ~.

We trust that ~.

We are convinced that ~.

We assure you that ~.

We are sure that ~.

You may rest assured ~.

You may be assured that ~.

15. ~을 권합니다.

We (would) advise you to ~.

We (would) suggest that ~.

We (would) recommend that ~.

We would like to recommend ~.

We believe it recommendable for you to ~.

It will be beneficial for you to ~.

16. ~을 동봉합니다. ~을 보내드립니다.

We enclose ~.

We are enclosing ~.

We are attaching ~.

We enclose herewith ~.

We are sending you ~.

We are pleased to enclose ~.

Enclosed, please find ~.

Enclosed are ~.

17. ~을 보내주십시오.

We would appreciate it if you would send us ~.

We will be pleased if you send us ~.

We ask you to submit ~.

We wish to have ~.

We hope you will ~.

We would like you to send ~.

We request that you will send us ~.

We are looking forward to receiving ~.

Be good enough to send us ~.

Please send us ~.

Please let us have ~.

Please ship / dispatch ∼.

Please forward ∼.

18. ∼하게 되어 기쁘게 생각합니다.

We are pleased to / that ∼.

We have the pleasure to / of / that ∼.

It is with great pleasure that we inform you that / of ∼.

We are glad to / that ∼.

We are glad to hear that / of ∼.

We are happy to / that ∼.

19. ∼하게 되어 유감으로 생각합니다.

We are sorry that / to ∼.

We feel sorry for being unable to ∼.

We regret that / to ∼.

We are regretful that ∼.

We express our regret at ∼ing ∼.

It is regrettable that ∼.

It is our deep regret to inform you that ∼.

To our regret, we inform you that ∼.

20. ∼을 사과 드립니다. 용서를 빕니다.

We are really sorry for ∼.

We deeply apologize for ∼.

We apologize to you for ∼.

We hope you will pardon us for ∼.

We hope you will forgive me for ∼.

Please excuse us for ∼.

Please accept our deep apologies for ∼.

Please excuse us for our mistakes in ∼.

21. ~을 축하드립니다.

Please accept our sincere congratulations.

We are writing to offer our sincere congratulations ~.

Allow us to congratulate you on ~.

May we congratulate you on ~!

Hearty congratulations to you on ~!

22. 답신을 부탁합니다.

We look forward to your reply.

We hope to hear from you.

We would appreciate your information very soon.

We are looking forward to your report with interest.

We await your answer immediately.

We are waiting for your prompt reply.

We wish to receive your answer as soon as possible.

May we remind you that we are still awaiting your early reply?

May we request the favor of your early reply?

May we expect your reply soon?

Your reply would be highly appreciated.

Your prompt reply is eagerly awaited.

Please reply immediately.

Please let us have your reply upon receipt of this letter.

Please favor us with your reply as early as possible.

We await good news with patience.

We await your instructions in this matter.

23. 끝맺음 인사말(답신요청 제외)

We assure you of our best services at all times.

We look forward to your utmost consideration.

We look forward to your continued patronage.

We hope you will give this your utmost consideration.

We hope that you will be able to assist us in this matter.

We wish to assure you of our appreciation of your courtesy in this matter.

We trust our request will meet your prompt attention.

We will be pleased to be of service to you at all times.

We solicit a continuance of your confidence and support.

We request you to favor us with a continuance of your kind support.

Your best attention to this will be much appreciated.

Your continued cooperation and assistance will be highly appreciated.

Please accept our thanks in advance for your usual kind attention.

4 주요 무역용어

용 어	약 어	의 미
A		
abandonment		위부
acceptance		인수, 수락
account	a/c	계정, 회계
account current	A/C	당좌계정
account sales	A/S	매상계정서
accreditee		신용장수령인, 수익자
act of God		천재
actual total loss	ATL	현실전손
ad hoc arbitration		임시기관중재
ad valorem	A/V	종가, 가격기준
ad valorem duty		종가세
ad valorem freight		종가운임
advance payment		선지급
advance payment bond	AP bond	선수금 환급보증
advising bank		신용장의 통지은행
agency		대리권, 대리점
agency agreement		대리점 계약
agency commission		대리점 수수료
agent		대리인, 대행자
agreement		계약(=contract)
agreement on general terms and con-ditions		일반거래조건협정
air freight		항공화물 air cargo
airfreight forwarder		항공운송주선인
airway bill	AWB	항공화물운송장(=air waybill)
all risks	A/R	전위험담보
allowance		공제, 할인(=deduction)
America Land Bridge	ALB	미대륙 횡단 운송경로
amount	amt.	금액
applicant		신용장개설 의뢰인
arbitration		중재

용 어	약 어	의 미
arbitrator		중재인
arrival notice	A/N	화물도착통지서
assign		양도하다(=transfer).
as soon as possible	ASAP	가능한 빨리
assortment		혼합포장
assured		피보험자(=insured)
assurer		보험자(=insurer)
at	@	단가
at sight	a/s	일람불, 일람출급
attention	Attn.	참조, 주의
attorney	atty.	대리인, 변호사
authority to pay	A/P	어음지급수권서
authority to purchase	A/P	어음매입수권서
automatic approval	A.A.	자동승인
avenue	ave.	가, 큰 거리
average		해손
award		중재의 판정
B		
back to back L/C		동시발행 신용장
bailee		수탁자
balance		잔고, 잔액
balance sheet	B/S	대차대조표
bale		곤포 짐짝, 포대
bank credit		은행신용
Bank for International Settlements	BIS	국제결제은행
bank note	B/N	은행권
bank reference		은행신용조회처
banker's credit		은행신용장
bankruptcy		파산
bareboat charter		나용선계약
barratry		선원(장)의 불법행위
barrel(s)	bbl	배럴(42 gals)
bearer		소지인

용 어	약 어	의 미
beneficiary		수익자
beneficial duty		편익관세
berth terms		적화양화 선주부담조건
bid		입찰
bid bond	B-Bond	입찰보증
bill bought		매입어음
bill for collection	B/C	추심어음
bill of exchange	B/E	환어음
bill of lading	B/L	선하증권
bill of lading date		선하증권 발행일
bill payable	B/P	지급어음
blank endorsement		백지배서, 무기명배서
bona-fide holder		선의의 소지인
bonded area		보세구역
bonded factory		보세공장
bonded transportation		보세운송
bonded warehouse		보세창고(=bonded shed)
bonded warehouse transaction	BWT	보세창고인도조건 거래
both to blame collision		쌍방과실충돌
bottom		선복, 바닥
boulevard	blvd.	큰거리
brand		상표
breakage		파손
brought forward	b/f	전기이월
bulk cargo		살화물, 거대대량화물(=bulky cargo)
bull market		강세시장(≠ bearish market)
bunker adjustment factor	BAF	유가할증료
bunker surcharge		유가할증료
bushel(s)	bu.	부셸(36 liters, 8 gallons)
business standing		영업상태
buying agent		매입대리점, 수입대리점

용 어	약 어	의 미
C		
cable		전보
carbon copy	c.c.	사본
care mark		주의표시
care of	c/o	~의 방
cargo insurance		적화보험
carriage		운송, 운임
carriage and insurance paid to	CIP	운송비·보험료 지급 조건
carriage paid to	CPT	운송비지급인도조건
carrier		운송인
carton	C/T	종이포장상자
cash against documents	CAD	서류상환지급
cash on delivery	COD	현금상환인도
cash with order	C.W.O.	주문불, 선불
catalog	cat.	상품목록
cent	¢	센트
centum weight	cwt.	중량단위
certificate of inspection		검사증명서
certificate of insurance	C/I	보험증명서
certificate of origin	C/O	원산지증명서
certificate of weight		중량증명서
Chamber of Commerce	CC	상업회의소
charter		용선하다.
charterer		용선자
charter party	C/P	용선계약, 용선계약서
check		수표
chief mate		일등항해사
circular letter		권유장, 안내장
claim		클레임, 손해배상청구
claimant		클레임 제기자
claimee		클레임 피제기자
clean B/L		무사고선하증권
clean bill of exchange		무화환어음
clean credit		무담보신용장, 무화환신용장

용 어	약 어	의 미
clearing house		어음교환소
clear out		출항하다.
closed conference		폐쇄식 해운동맹
code book		전신암호서
coinsurance		공동보험
collect on delivery	COD	현금상환인도
collecting bank		추심은행
combined transport document	CTD	복합운송서류
combined transport operator	CTO	복합운송인
commercial credit agency		상업흥신소(=mercantile agency)
commercial invoice	C/I	상업송장
commercial L/C		상업신용장
commission	Comm.	수수료
company	Co.	회사
compensation trade		구상무역
complimentary close		인사결문, 결미인사
compromise		타협, 화해
compulsory arbitration		강제적 중재
concern		회사
conciliation		조정
confer	cf.	(L) 참조하다. 비교하다.
conference		해운동맹
conference liner		해운동맹선
confirmation of cable		전보확인
confirmed credit		확인신용장
confirming bank		확인은행
consideration		상호대가, 약인
consignee		수탁인, 수하인
consignor		위탁자, 송하인
consignment		위탁판매
constructive total loss	CTL	추정전손
construe		해석하다.
consular invoice		영사송장
container		컨테이너, 용기
container freight station	CFS	컨테이너 화물집하소

용 어	약 어	의 미
container load cargo		컨테이너 화물
container terminal	C/T	컨테이너 터미널
container yard	CY	컨테이너 야적장
contingency insurance		미필이익보험
continued		계속, 미완성
contract		계약(=agreement)
contract note		매매계약서
contract of sale		매도계약
contract rate system		계약운임제
contract with oil &/or other cargo	COOC	유류 및 타물과의 접촉
cooperative	co-op., coop.	협동조합
corporation	Corp.	회사
correspondent bank		환취결은행, 환거래은행
cost and freight	CFR	운임 포함가격
cost, insurance and freight	CIF, c.i.f.	운임, 보험료 포함가격
cost, insurance, freight and commission	CIF & C	운임, 보험료 및 수수료 포함가격
cost, insurance, freight and exchange	CIF & E	운임, 보험료 및 환비용 포함가격
cost, insurance, freight and interest	CIF & I	운임, 보험료 및 이자 포함가격
counter offer		반대청약
counter purchase	CP	대응구매
counter sample		반대견본
counter trade		연계무역
countervailing duty		상계관세
courier		특사, 서류배달 서비스
cover note		보험부보각서
craft clause		부선약관
credit	L/C	신용장
credit inquiry		신용조회
credit note	C/N, c/n	대변표
credit standing		신용상태
creditor		채권자
cubic foot(feet)	cft.	입방피트
cubic meter	cbm	입방미터
currency adjustment factor	CAF	통화할증료
customary quick dispatch	CQD	관습적 조속하역

용 어	약 어	의 미
customs broker		통관업자
customs clearance		통관
Customs Cooperation Council	CCC	관세협력 이사회
customs duty		관세
customs house		세관
customs invoice		세관송장
D		
dead freight		부적운임
dead weight tonnage	DWT	재화중량톤수
debit note	D/N	차변표
debt		부채, 채무
default		채무불이행
deferred payment		연지급
deferred rebate system		운임연불제
definite policy		확정보험증권
del credere agent		지급보증대리점
del credere commission		지급보증수수료
delayed shipment		선적지연
delivered at frontier	DAF	국경인도조건
delivered at place	DAP	도착지인도조건
delivered at place unloaded	DPU	도착지양하인도조건
delivered duty paid	DDP	관세지급인도
delivered duty unpaid	DDU	관세미지급인도
delivered ex quay	DEQ	부두인도
delivered ex ship	DES	착선인도
delivery		인도
delivery order	D/O	화물인도지시서
demand draft	D/D	요구불어음
demise charter		선박임대차(=bareboat charter)
demurrage		체선료
description		명세
despatch money		조출료
destination		목적지
detour		우회하다.
devaluation		평가절하

용 어	약 어	의 미
deviation		이로 항로변경
direct steamer		직항선
dirty B/L		사고부 선하증권, 고장선하증권
disclosure		고지
discount		할인
discrepancy		불일치
dishonored bill		부도어음
distributor		판매점
distributorship agreement	do.	판매점 계약
ditto		상동, 위와 같음
dividend	D/R	배당
dock receipt	D/A	부두수령증
documentary against acceptance	D/P	인수도조건
documentary against payment		지급도조건
documentary bill of exchange		화환어음
documentary L/C	doc.	화환신용장
documents	$	서류
dollar		달러
domestic L/C		내국신용장
draft		환어음(=bill of exchange)
draft at sight		일람출급환어음
draw back		관세환급
drawee		어음의 지급인
drawer		어음의 발행인
due date		만기일
duplicate		부본
duty		관세
duty free		면세
E		
electronic data interchange	EDI	전자문서교환
embargo		수출금지, 출항금지
enclosure	enc., encl.	동봉물(=inclosure(inc., incl.))
endorsement		배서, 보증

용 어	약 어	의 미
endorser		배서인, 이서인
enquiry		조회, 문의(=inquiry)
en route		도중에(=on the way)
escrow L/C		기탁신용장
estimated time of arrival	ETA	도착예정일(=expected ~)
estimated time of departure	ETD	출항예정일(=expected ~)
ex factory		공장인도(=ex mill)
ex quay	DEQ	부두인도(=ex dock, ex wharf)
ex warehouse		창고인도
ex works	EXW	공장인도, 현장인도
ex, Ex		~에서, ~으로부터
excess		소손해 면책
exchange market		외환시장
exclusive agency agreement		독점대리점 계약
exclusive agent		독점대리점
exclusive contract		독점계약
exclusive distributor		독점판매점
expiry date	E/D	만기일, 유효기일
export declaration	E/D	수출신고, 수출신고서
export insurance		수출보험
export license	E/L	수출승인, 수출승인서
export permit	E/P	수출허가, 수출허가서
F		
fair average quality	FAQ	평균중등품질
feeler sample		시험견본(=test sample)
financial standing		재정상태
firm offer		확정청약
first class	Al	일등, 최상, 제1급
fixture memo		선복확약서
floating policy		선명미정보험
force marjeure		불가항력
foreign exchange	FX	외국환
foreign exchange bank		외국환은행

용 어	약 어	의 미
foreign exchange rate		환율
forwarding agent		운송대리인
foul B/L		사고부 선하증권
franchise		소손해 면책, 독점판매권
franco		반입인도
free alongside ship	FAS	선측인도
free carrier	FCA	운송인인도
free from particular average	FPA	분손부담보, 단독해손부담보
free in	FI	양화비용 화주부담 조건
free in and out	FIO	적화양화비용 화주부담 조건
free offer		불확정청약
free on board	FOB	본선인도
free on rail	FOR	철도인도
free on truck	FOT	화차인도
free out	FO	적화비용 화주부담 조건
freight		운송, 운임
freight collect		후지급 운임, 운임 후지급
freight conference		운임해운동맹
freight forwarder		운송주선인
freight prepaid		운임선지급, 선지급운임
freight rate		운임률
freight space		선복
frustration		계약이행불능
G		
general average	G/A	공동해손
general cargo		일반화물
general L/C		보통신용장(＝open L/C)
general terms and conditions of business		일반거래조건
generalized system of preferences	GSP	일반특혜관세제도
good merchantable quality	GMQ	판매적격품질
governing law		준거법
grace period		은혜기간, 유예기간
great gross		728개(12×12×12)

용 어	약 어	의 미
gross	gr.	그로스, 144개(12×12)
gross profit		총이익
gross ton		총톤
gross weight	gr. wt.	총중량
GSP certificate of origin	GSPCO	일반특혜관세원산지 증명서
gurantee		보증
H		
hatch cargo		선창화물
heat damage		열손해, 열파손
heavy cargo		중량화물
honor		어음의 인수 또는 지급
Honorable	Hon.	각하
hull insurance		선박보험
I		
id est	i.e.	(L) 즉, 환언하면(=that is)
imaginary profit		희망이익
import declaration	ID	수입신고서
import duties		수입관세
import license	I/L	수입승인
import permit	I/P	수입허가, 수입허가서
import quota	I/Q	수입할당
improvement trade		가공무역
incorporated	inc.	법인조직의, 주식회사
indemnity		보상
indent		매입신청, 주문, 구매위탁
industrial property		산업재산권, 공업소유권
inferior quality		열등품질
infringement		위배, 권리침해
inherent vice or nature		고유의 하자 또는 성질
initial order		첫 주문
inland container depot	ICD	내륙 컨테이너 운송기지
inland transit extension	ITE	내륙운송확장담보조건
inquiry		조회, 문의(=enquiry)
insolvency		지급불능, 파산

용 어	약 어	의 미
inspection certificate	I/C	검사증명서
installment shipment		할부선적
instant	inst.	(L) 이번 달(=of this month)
institute cargo clause	ICC	협회적하약관
institute clause		협회약관
insurable interest		피보험이익
insurable value		보험가액
insurance certificate		보험증명서
insurance policy	I/P	보험증권
insurance premium		보험료
insured		피보험자
insured amount		보험금액
insurer		보험자(=underwriter)
insurrection		반란, 폭동
inter alia		특히, 그 중에서도
Int'l Air Transport Association	IATA	국제항공운송협회
Int'l Federation of Forwarding Agent Association	FIATA	운송주선인협회국제연맹
Int'l Rules for the Interpretation of Trade Terms	Incoterms	무역조건의 해석에 관한 국제규칙
International Chamber of Commerce	ICC	국제상업회의소
International Maritime Committee	CMI	국제해사위원회
inventory		재고, 재고품
invoice	inv.	송장, 청구서, 명세서
invoice amount		송장 금액
IOU		차용증(=I Owe You)
irrevocable L/C		취소 불능신용장
issuing bank		신용장 개설은행
J		
Japan External Trade Organization	JETRO	일본무역진흥회
Japan Industrial Standard	JIS	일본공업규격
jettison		투하
joint venture		합자기업, 합병기업
jurisdiction		재판관할권

용 어	약 어	의 미
K		
Korea Chamber of Commerce and Industry	KCCI	대한상공회의소
Korea International Trade Association	KITA	한국무역협회
Korea Trade-Investment Promotion Agency	KOTRA	대한무역투자진흥공사
Korean Standards	KS	한국공업규격
L		
large order		대량주문(=substantial order)
landed quality terms		양륙품질조건
landed quantity terms		양륙수량조건
landed weght terms		양륙중량조건
layday		정박일, 정박기간
leakage		누손
lengthy cargo		장척화물
less than container load	LCL	컨테이너단위미달화물
letter of attorney		위임장
letter of credit	L/C	신용장
letter of guarantee	L/G	보증서
let ter of guarantee	L/G	수입화물선취보증장
letter of indemnity	L/I	파손화물보상장
letter of indication	L/I	서명감
letter telegram	LT	서신전보
libra (=pound sterling)	£	(L) 영국통화, 파운드
libra(=pound in weight)	lb.	(L) 파운드(중량단위)
licensing agreement		라이선스 협정
lien		유치권
lighter		부선
lighterage		부선료
limited	Ltd.	유한책임의, 주식회사
limited partnership		합자회사
liner		정기선
liner terms		적화 양화 선주부담(=berth terms)
litigation		소송(=law suit)

용 어	약 어	의 미
Lloyd's Underwriters' Association		로이즈보험자협회
local L/C		내국신용장
loco		현장인도
long ton	L/T	영국톤(2240 lbs, 1016.1 kgs)
lump sum charter		총괄운임용선계약
M		
Madame, Mesdames	Mme., Mmes.	부인
maintenance bond		하자보증
manager	mgr.	부장, 지점장
manifest	M/F	적화목록
manufacturing	mfg	제조, 제조업
manuscript	MS	원고, 사본
margin of profit		이윤마진
marine insurance		해상보험
marine insurance policy	MIP	해상보험증권
marine insurance premium		해상보험료
marine risk		해상위험
mark		화인
market research		시장조사
master contract		포괄계약, 장기계약
mate's receipt	M/R	본선수취증
maximum	max	최대한도
measurement ton	M/T	용적톤
mediation		조정(=conciliation)
medium	med.	중간
memorandum	memo	각서, 메모
memorandum clause		면책률약관
merchandise	mdse.	상품
Messieurs	Messrs.	남성의 복수형
meter	m	미터
metric ton	M/T	미터 톤(2,204 lbs, 1,000 kgs)
minimum quantity		최소주문수량, 최소인수수량
Mister	Mr.	님, 씨, 귀하
Mistress	mrs.	부인, 여주인
moderate		약간, 10 중에서 3~4

용 어	약 어	의 미
more or less clause		과부족용인조항
motor ship	m.s., M/S	기선(=motor vessel(M/V, S/S))
multimodal transport		복합운송
multimodal transport operator	MTO	복합운송인
N		
negotiable B/L		유통선화증권
negotiable instrument		유통증권
negotiating bank		신용장 매입은행
negotiation		환어음매입
net weight		순중량
non-delivery		불착
non-negotiable B/L		비유통선화증권
nota bene	n.b., NB	(L)유의하라(=note well).
notify party		착화통지처
notifying bank		신용장 통지은행
number	No., #	번호
null and void		무효의
O		
ocean B/L		해양선하증권
offer		매도신청, 청약
offer on approval		점검승인부 청약
offer on sale or return		반품허용조건부 청약
offer subject to being unsold		재고잔유조건 청약
offer subject to confirmation		확인조건부 청약
offer subject to prior sale		선착순판매조건 청약
on board B/L		본선적재선하증권
on deck cargo		갑판적화물
open cover		예정보험, 포괄보험
open L/C		보통신용장, 자유매입신용장
open policy		포괄예정보험(=floating policy)
opening bank		신용장 개설은행
optional cargo		양륙지선택화물
order B/L		지시식선하증권
ordinary leakage		통상의 누손

용 어	약 어	의 미
order sheet		주문서
original		정본
original equipment manufacturing	OEM	주문자상표 부착생산
original sample		원견본
ounce	oz	(L) 온스
overdue		기간이 경과한

P		
package	pkg	포장꾸러미
packing list		포장명세서
parcel post	p.p.	소포우편
partial loss		분손
partial payment		분할지급
partial shipment		분할선적
particular average	P/A	단독해손
payee		피지급인, 수취인
payment on credit		후지급, 외상급
payment terms		지급조건
penny		펜스
per annum	p.a.	(L) 연간(=by the year)
per cent	%	퍼센트
per procuration	P.P., p.p.	대리로
performance bond	P-Bond	계약이행보증
peril		위험, 사고가 날 수 있는 상황
perils of the sea		해상고유의 위험
piece	pc.	한 개, 한 필
pilferage		발화, 좀도둑
please turn over.	P.T.O.	뒷면을 보시오.
port charge		항비
port of call		기항지
port of discharge		양륙항
port of shipment		선적항
post office box	p.o.box	우편사서함
postal order	p.o.	우편환
postscript	p.s.	(L) 추신

용 어	약 어	의 미
power of attorney		위임장
pre-advice		사전통지
premium		보험료
price list		가격표
price terms		가격조건
prime rate		우대대출금리
principal		본인
printed matter		인쇄물
profit and loss statement		손익계산서
proforma invoice		견적송장
progressive payment		누진지급, 누진불
promissory note	P/N	약속어음
provisional policy		예정보험
proximo	prox.	(L) 다음 달(=of next month)
public weigher		공인검량인
purchase note	P/N	주문서, 매약서
Q		
quality product		좋은 품질제품
quality terms		품질조건
quantity discount		수량할인
quantity order		대량주문
quantity terms		수량조건
quotation		가격, 가격산정
R		
rain & fresh water damage	RFWD	우, 담수 손해
re		(L) ~관하여, ~의 건(=relating to)
reasonable time		상당한 시간, 합리적인 기간
re-insurance		재보험
rebate		리베이트, 환불
receipt		영수증
received B/L		수취선하증권
recourse		상환청구
red clause L/C		전대 신용장
redemption		상환, 회수

용 어	약 어	의 미
reference	ref.	조회, 조회처
reimbursement		상환
remarks		적요, 비고
remittance		송금
replacement		대체품
repondez s'il vous plait	RSVP	(F) 회답바랍니다(=reply if you please)
representation		대리, 대표, 고지의무
reputable		평판이 좋은
restricted L/C		특정신용장(=special L/C)
retailer		소매상
revaluate		재평가하다. 평가절상하다.
Revised American Foreign Trade Def-initions		개정미국무역정의
revocable L/C		취소가능신용장
revolving L/C		회전신용장
rock-bottom price		최저가격
running laydays		연속정박기간
running number		일련번호
rush of order		주문의 쇄도
rust		녹손해
rye terms	R/T	양륙품질조건
S		
safeguard		긴급수입제한조치
sailing schedule		배선표
sale on consignment		위탁판매
sales agent		판매대리점
sales contract		판매계약
sales note		매약서
Sales of Goods Act	SGA	영국물품매매법
salutation		인사호칭, 서두인사
sample		견본
sanitary certificate		위생증명서
sea waybill		해상화물운송장
sea damaged	S/D	해수손해 매도인책임의 선적품질조건

용 어	약 어	의 미
seaworthiness		내항성, 감항성
selling agent		판매대리점
settling bank		결제은행
ship's space		선복
shipment sample		선적견본
shipped B/L		선적선하증권
shipped quality terms		선적품질조건
shipped quantity terms		선적수량조건
shipped weight terms		선적중량조건
shipper		송화인
shipping advice	S/A	선적통지(=shipping notice)
shipping agent		선적대리점
shipping date	S/D	선적일
shipping documents		선적서류
shipping instructions		선적지시서
shipping marks		화인
shipping order	S/O	선적지시서
shipping request	S/R	선복신청서
short ton	S/T	미국톤(2,000 lbs, 907.2 kgs)
Siberia Land Bridge	SLB	시베리아 횡단 운송경로
sight bill		일람출급환어음(=sight draft)
sight L/C		일람출급신용장
skyrocket		급등하다.
sluggish		활발하지 못한
Society for Worldwide Interbank Financial Telecommunication	SWIFT	세계은행간 금융통신망
sole agent		독점대리점
sole distributor		독점판매점
solvency		변상능력, 지불능력
space charter		선박대차
special delivery		속달
special instruction		특별지시사항
special L/C		특정신용장
specific duty		종량세
specification		명세서

용　어	약　어	의　미
spot price		현물가격, 즉시지급가격
square foot(feet)	sp. ft.	평방피트
stale B/L		기한경과 선하증권
stand-by L/C		보증신용장
standard	std.	표준
steamship	s.s., S/S	기선
sterling pound	stg.	영국파운드, 영국화폐
stevedorage		하역적재요금
stevedore		하역인부, 하역노동자
storage		보관료, 창고료
stowage		선내화물적재, 적재물, 적하료
straight B/L		기명식선하증권
street	st.	가
strikes, riots, civil commotions	SR&CC	동맹파업, 폭동, 소요 위험
subrogation		대위
substitute		대체하다. 대체품
sue and labor charge		손해방지비용
sunday holidays excepted	SHEX	일요일, 공휴일 제외 하역조건
sundries		잡화
surcharge		할증료
surrender		명도하다. 인도하다. 양도하다.
survey report		감정보고서
surveyor		감정인
sweat damage		땀, 물방울 손해
T		
tale quale	TQ	선적품질조건
tally		검수하다. 부합하다.
tally sheet		검수서
tallyman		검수인
tare		포장
tariff		관세
tariff quota		관세할당
telegram		전보
telegraphic transfer	T/T	전신환

용 어	약 어	의 미
telegraphic transfer buying rate	TTB rate	전신환매입률
telegraphic transfer selling rate	TTS rate	전신환매도율
tempest		폭풍우
tender		입찰, 신청, 입찰하다.
tenor		어음만기
term bill		기한부 환어음(= time bill)
terms and conditions		거래조건
terms of payment		지급조건
theft, pilferage and non-delivery	TPND	도난, 발하 및 불착위험
through B/L		통선하증권
time bill		기한부 환어음
time charter		정기용선
to the order of shipper		송화인 지시식
total loss		전손
total loss only	TLO	전손담보
trade mark		상표
trade reference		동업자조회
trade terms		거래조건
tramp		부정기선(=tramper)
transaction		거래
transferable L/C		양도가능신용장
transit trade		통과무역
transshipment		환적
trial order		시험주문
triplicate		3통
trust reccipt	T/R	수입화물대도
turn-key		일괄수주방식
U		
ultimo	Ult.	(L) 지난 달(=of last month)
unconfirmed L/C		미확인신용장
underwriter		보험자, 보험회사
Uniform Commercial Code	UCC	미국통일상법전
Uniform Customs and Practice for Documentary Credits	UCP	화환신용장통일규칙 및 관례
Uniform Rules for Collection	URC	추심에 관한 통일규칙

용 어	약 어	의 미
United Nations Commission on Int'l Trade Law	UNCITRAL	유엔국제무역법위원회
unvalued policy		금액미정보험
urgent telegram		지급전보
usance bill of exchange		기한부환어음
usance L/C		기한부신용장
V		
valid		유효한
vendor		매도인, 행상인
versus	vs.	(L) 대
vessel		선박, 본선
videlicet	viz.	(L)즉, 바꿔 말하면(＝namely)
voyage charter		항해용선(＝trip charter)
W		
waiver		포기, 국적선불취항증명서
war risks	WR	전쟁위험
war/strikes, riots and civil commotions	W/SRCC	전쟁, 동맹파업, 폭동, 소요 위험
warehouse to warehouse clause	W/W Clause	창고간약관
warrant		창고증권
warranty		담보, 보증
washing over board	WOB	갑판유실
weather working days	WWD	호천하역일 기산조건
weight	wt.	중량
wharfage		부두사용료
wholesaler		도매상
with average	W.A.	단독해손담보
withholding tax		원천과세
with particular average	WPA	단독해손담보
with recourse L/C		상환청구가능 신용장
without recourse L/C		상환청구불능 신용장
Y		
yard(s)	yd(s).	야드(＝3 ft)
yen	￥	일본통화, 엔
York-Antwerp Rules	Y.A.R.	요크-앤트워프 규칙

참 고 문 헌

강원진, 「무역영어」, 박영사, 1997

강호경, 「최신 무역영어」, 두남, 1997

김복문, 「최신 무역영어」, 법경사, 1998

김행권, 「현대 무역영어강의」, 법문사, 1986

남풍우, 「무역영어」, 두남, 2001

박대위, 「무역영어」, 법문사, 1987

손태빈, 「신 무역영어」, 두남, 2000

송용섭·유병주, 「신 무역영어」, 무역경영사, 1983

시사영어사, 「A Hand Book of Business English」, 시사영어사, 1994

이신규, 「무역상담영어」, 두남, 1999

이찬승, 절차별무역상담영어, 능률영어사, 1989

장치순, 「현대 무역영어」, 형설출판사, 1999

전창원, 「신고 무역영어통신」, 법문사, 1987

조영정, 「무역영어」 제2판, 법문사, 2008

조영정, 「무역학개론」 제4판, 박영사, 2019

한주섭, 「현대 무역영어」 제4판, 동성사, 1989

허재창, 「인터넷시대의 무역영어」, 법문사, 1998

Junji Miyano, Emiko Iizumi, 「영문계약서 A에서 Z까지」, 인터원, 2000

Poe, Roy W., *Great Business Writing*, 산지출판사, 2005

Ryan, Kevin and Koji Nagatsuna, 비즈니스 영문 E-mail, 조은문화사, 1997

Miyoko Ikezaki, *Business letter Handbook*, 시사영어사, 2001

藤田榮一, *Seminar on International Trade*, 創元社, 1997

民俗泰敏, 「貿易英語文例集」, 日本實業出版社, 1996

Baugh, L. Sue, *How to Write First-Class Letters*, McGraw-Hill, 1993

Brittney, Lynn, *E-Mail and Business Letter Writing*, Foulsham & Co., Ltd., 2001

Buchman, Dian Dincin and Seli Groves, *Guide to Manuscript Formats*, Writer's
        Digest Books, 1987

Clark, Lyn R., et al., *Business English and Communication*, McGraw-Hill Book
        Company, 1988

Dignen, Bob, *Communicating In Business English*, Compass Publishing, Inc., 2003

Doris Lillian and Besse May Miller, *Complete Secretary's Handbook*, Englewood Cliffs, 1980

Enelow, Wendy S., *201 Winning Cover Letters For $ 100,000 And Jobs*, Impact Publication, 1998

Frailey, L. E., *Handbook of Business Letters*, Prentice Hall, 1989

Gartside, L., *Model business letters*, Macdonald and Evans, 1982

Geffner, Andrea B., *Business English*, Barron's Educational Series, Inc., 1993

Guffey, Mary Ellen, *Essential of Business Communication*, South-Western College Publishing, 2001

Jones, J. Hamilton, *Business Letters That Get Results*, Bob Adams, Inc., 1991

Jones, Leo and Richard Alexander, *International Business English*, Cambridge University Press, 1989

Kay, Andrea, *Resumes That Will Get You The Job You Want*, Betterway Book, 1997

Lindsell-Roberts, Sheryl, *Business Letter Writing*, Macmillan, 1995

Longheed, L., *Business Correspondence*, Addison-Wesley Pub. Co., 1993

Naterop, Bertha J., et al., *Business letters for All*, Oxford University Press, 1977

Sandler, Corey and Janice Keefe, *1001 Letters for All Occations*, Adams Media, 2004

Taylor, Shirley, *Gartside's Model Business Letters*, Prentice Hall, 1998

Thill, John V. and Courtland L. Bovee, *Excellence In Business Communication, 6th ed.*, Prentice Hall, 2005

국 문 색 인

영 문 색 인

저자 소개

조 영 정

고려대학교 경영대학 무역학과(학사)
고려대학교 대학원 무역학과(석사)
고려대학교 대학원 무역학과(박사)
미국 Harvard University Executive과정(국제무역)

고려대학교 경영대학 및 대학원 강사
국제대학교 무역학과 교수
서경대학교 국제통상학과 교수
KOTRA 아카데미 강사
무역영어 자격시험, 국가고시 출제위원
대한상사중재원 중재인
지방행정연수원 국제관계 주임교수
미국 UCLA 객원교수
미국 U.C. Berkeley 객원교수

<저서 및 논문>

「국제경영」(공저), 학현사, 1996.
「국제통상학」, 학현사, 1999.
「국제통상법의 이해」, 무역경영사, 2000.
「무역영어」, 법문사, 2002.
「국제통상론」, 법문사, 2003.
「무역정책론」, 무역경영사, 2009.
「무역학개론」, 박영사, 2010.
「표준 무역영어」, 박영사, 2011.
「국인주의 이론」, 박영사, 2015.
「무역정책」, 박영사, 2016.
「미국의 내셔널리즘」, 사회사상연구원, 2018.
「일본의 내셔널리즘」, 사회사상연구원, 2019.
「중국의 내셔널리즘」, 사회사상연구원, 2020.

"수입자유화의 한국수입구조에 대한 영향분석," 「무역학회지」외 수십여 편.

E-mail: joyzz@daum.net

감수자 소개

Robert Jalali

University of Cambridge Judge Business School Lecturer
University of Pennsylvania Wharton School Lecturer
World Bank Consultant
15 Years Experience in Trade

제3판
표준무역영어

초판발행	2011년 8월 30일
제2판발행	2014년 3월 20일
제3판발행	2020년 2월 28일
지은이	조영정
펴낸이	안종만·안상준
편 집	전채린
기획/마케팅	오치웅
표지디자인	박현정
제 작	우인도·고철민

펴낸곳	(주) **박영사**
	서울특별시 종로구 새문안로3길 36, 1601
	등록 1959. 3. 11. 제300-1959-1호(倫)
전 화	02)733-6771
f a x	02)736-4818
e-mail	pys@pybook.co.kr
homepage	www.pybook.co.kr
ISBN	979-11-303-0943-9 93320

정 가   29,000원